CORPORATE FRICTION

Corporate law in the United States requires directors to manage firms in the interests of shareholders, which means never sacrificing profits in service of other stakeholders or interests. In this timely, groundbreaking book, David Yosifon argues that this rule of "shareholder primacy" is logically, ethically, and practically unsound and should be replaced by a new standard that compels directors of our largest corporations to manage firms in a socially responsible way. In addition to summarizing existing debates on the issue – and giving special attention to the Supreme Court's decision in *Citizens United* – Yosifon explores the problem of corporate patriotism and develops a novel approach to the relationship between corporate law and consumer culture. The book's technical acumen will appeal to experts, while its engaging prose will satisfy anyone interested in what our corporate law does and what it should do better.

David Yosifon is a professor at Santa Clara University School of Law in Santa Clara, California. He teaches business law and legal ethics. He is on the faculty of Santa Clara University's Markkula Center for Applied Ethics and is also a member of the Markkula Center's Business Ethics Partnership. Yosifon's scholarship on corporate governance and corporate social responsibility has appeared in numerous law journals, including the *North Carolina Law Review*, the *Berkeley Business Law Journal*, and the *Delaware Journal of Corporate Law*. His opinion pieces have appeared in the *New York Times*, the *San Francisco Chronicle*, and the *San Jose Mercury News*.

Corporate Friction

HOW CORPORATE LAW IMPEDES AMERICAN PROGRESS AND WHAT TO DO ABOUT IT

David Yosifon

Santa Clara University School of Law

CAMBRIDGE
UNIVERSITY PRESS

University Printing House, Cambridge CB2 8BS, United Kingdom

One Liberty Plaza, 20th Floor, New York, NY 10006, USA

477 Williamstown Road, Port Melbourne, VIC 3207, Australia

314–321, 3rd Floor, Plot 3, Splendor Forum, Jasola District Centre, New Delhi – 110025, India

79 Anson Road, #06–04/06, Singapore 079906

Cambridge University Press is part of the University of Cambridge.

It furthers the University's mission by disseminating knowledge in the pursuit of education, learning, and research at the highest international levels of excellence.

www.cambridge.org
Information on this title: www.cambridge.org/9781107186408
DOI: 10.1017/9781316890578

© David Yosifon 2018

First published 2018

Printed in the United Kingdom by Clays, St Ives plc

A catalogue record for this publication is available from the British Library.

Library of Congress Cataloging-in-Publication Data
Names: Yosifon, David G., 1973– author.
Title: Corporate friction : how corporate law impedes American progress and what to do about it / David Yosifon, Santa Clara Law School.
Description: Cambridge, United Kingdom ; New York, NY, USA : Cambridge University Press, 2018. | Includes bibliographical references and index.
Identifiers: LCCN 2017057521| ISBN 9781107186408 (Hardback) | ISBN 9781316637173 (Paperback)
Subjects: LCSH: Corporation law–Political aspects–United States. | Corporation law–Economic aspects–United States. | Corporation law–Moral and ethical aspects–United States.
Classification: LCC KF1414 .Y67 2018 | DDC 346.73/066–dc23
LC record available at https://lccn.loc.gov/2017057521

ISBN 978-1-107-18640-8 Hardback
ISBN 978-1-316-63717-3 Paperback

for Janice

CONTENTS

CONTENTS

ACKNOWLEDGEMENTS

I want to thank my wife, Janice Kim Yosifon, and our children, Corianna Kim Yosifon and Joshua Kim Yosifon, for their love and inspiration. I want to thank my loving parents, Michael and Viola Yosifon. When we were growing up, your famous line was, "I will always buy you books." This one is on me. I want to thank my brothers, Michael Yosifon, Jr., and Stephen Yosifon. I also want to thank Jong and Jungsuh Kim, and Eunice and Jim Kim, my wonderful family by marriage. And Evan, Oliver, and Eleanor, my nephews and niece. I am blessed to have you all behind this book.

I want to give special thanks to my great mentor and friend, Professor Jon Hanson of Harvard Law School. The ideas, techniques, and ethics he taught me are reflected on every page of this book. His generosity I am still striving to replicate.

This book reports an intellectual journey that has been aided by countless friends and strangers. Many of the strangers (and some of the friends) are in the footnotes. Among the friends, I especially want to thank Don Polden, Lisa Kloppenberg, the Honorable Patti B. Saris, Brad Joondeph, Pratheepan Gulasekaram, Gary Neustadter, Margaret Russell, Tseming Yang, Eric Wright, Kandis Scott, Nancy Wright, Gerald Uelman, Adrianna Duffy-Horling, Dorothy Glancy, Stephanie Wildman, Marina Hsieh, Allen Hammond, Ken Manaster, Colleen Chien, Alan Scheflin, Kirk Hanson, June Carbone, David Sloss, David Friedman, Kerry Macintosh, Stephen Diamond, David Ball, Cookie Ridolfi, Ellen Kreitzberg, Patty Rauch-Neustadter, William Woodward, Tyler Ochoa, Michelle Oberman, Kyle Graham, Anna Han, Father Paul Goda, S.J., Gary Spitko, the Rutgers crew, Robert Shanklin, the late James Balassone, all my great teachers from the public schools of Vernon, New Jersey, Lyman Johnson, David Millon, Kent

Greenfield, Faith Stevelman, David Westbrook, Stephen Bainbridge, Stefan Padfield, Yawu Miller, Melvin Miller, Joseph Mueller, James Livingston, John Gillis, Lloyd Gardner, Joseph Singer, Lani Guinier, Christine Desan, Scott Sandage, Peter Stearns, Joshua Idjadi, Janie Yoo, Heaven Chee, Alex Frischer, Sarah Vickers, and Corey Wallace. I am grateful to Mary Sexton and Ellen Platt for their skillful assistance in obtaining research materials.

All errors are mine alone.

INTRODUCTION

Our ascent from the muck, our way out of the Garden, has been eased by the power of the corporate organizational form. From railroads to smartphones, basic needs and delights alike have been served by corporate operations. But the corporation has also catalyzed menace, orchestrating exploitation of some people on behalf of others, polluting nature and culture, and subverting our democratic politics. The achievements and disgraces of corporate conduct can both be attributed, in part, to its legal design. This book is an interrogation of that design and an exploration of reforms that could improve upon it. To thrive as a species, to prosper as a nation, to flourish as individuals, we must have what is good in corporate law. And we must be rid of what is corrupting in it.

In the United States, the fundamental law of corporate governance is that firms must be managed in the best interests of their shareholders. Corporate directors may not sacrifice shareholder value in order to advance the competing interests of their workers, consumers, the environment, local communities, or anything else. Proponents of this rule, which I will refer to as "shareholder primacy,"[1] have

---

[1] Corporate theory is burdened with a semantic logjam regarding the term "shareholder primacy." The phrase is sometimes used to specify *what* corporations should be doing (i.e., pursuing shareholder interests), and is sometimes used to denote *who* should control the corporation (i.e., shareholders should have significant influence in corporate decision-making). Some scholars support "shareholder primacy" in both senses. *See e.g.*, Lucian Arye Bebchuk, *The Case for Increasing Shareholder Power*, 118 HARV. L. REV. 133 (2005). But other scholars support only one of these views. Stephen Bainbridge, for example, supports shareholder primacy in the first sense (purpose) but not the second (means) because he believes corporate directors and not shareholders should dominate decision-making. *See* Stephen M. Bainbridge, *Director Primacy and Shareholder Disempowerment*, 119 HARV. L. REV. 1735 (2006). We should stop using the term "shareholder primacy" to refer to both purpose and means. It inhibits clear expression and exchange of ideas.

sophisticated, sincere arguments for why they think it is the best possible corporate law design, one which makes everybody better off, not just shareholders. (Some scholars insist that shareholder primacy is *not* the law of corporate governance, but they are wrong. I show that they are wrong in Chapter 4). My view is that shareholder primacy is responsible for unnecessary suffering, cultural confusion, and political dysfunction in the United States. The justifications that shareholder primacy's supporters offer on its behalf do not cohere. My reformative focus is on the theoretical and practical imperative of changing the law to make the directors of our largest corporations responsible for considering the interests of all corporate stakeholders, and not just shareholders, in corporate decision-making.

The law of corporate purpose should be regarded as a basic fulcrum of social policy, but it hides in plain sight in contemporary social and political discourse in the United States. Politicians blame powerful corporate interests for blocking this or that regulatory change, but the reproach always takes the form of moralistic shaming of corporations for being mean or greedy, as if corporations are doing anything other than what the law of shareholder primacy compels them to do. They *could* do other than what they are doing, if we altered the law of corporate governance. But beyond castigation, the familiar scripts of ordinary American politics do not critically engage our corporate governance law. It is bigger than healthcare yet escapes routine scrutiny in public life. It is easier to alter than the structure of the Electoral College, or the Supreme Court's decision in the *Citizens United* case, yet receives less attention in general policy debates. This book aims to provide a set of ideas and arguments that can inform a broader, deeper conversation about what corporate law is doing in our society, and what it might do differently.

In *The Road to Wigan Pier*, his study of working-class life in northern England in the 1930s, George Orwell wrote, "before you can be sure whether you are genuinely in favour of socialism, you have got to decide whether things at present are tolerable or not

---

"Shareholder primacy" should signify an idea of corporate purpose, and "shareholder power" or "shareholder control" should be used for the idea of shareholders having influence in corporate governance. That is the way I use these terms in this book.

tolerable."[2] Orwell reports working and living conditions in the mining towns he visited that were rife with danger, penury, and gloom. Best known as an anti-fascist and anti-communist, Orwell never wavered from his conclusion that the capitalist situation was intolerable and that he was a socialist. In a sense, the same question might guide our thinking about how corporations operate in our society today. To know whether you support the prevailing corporate system, you must decide whether things affected by it – economic output, labor conditions, consumer satisfaction, the culture, the national standing – are tolerable or not tolerable. What our policy does in the world should guide our assessment of whether the policy is sound or unsound, whether it should remain steady or must change.

Yet, in another sense, Orwell's point of departure is glib. The situation may *seem* intolerable, in the sense that it is terrible, and yet it may be an improvement over an even deeper misery that preceded it, or that awaits if one goes messing with the system. In *God and Man at Yale* (1951), William F. Buckley, Jr., denounced his economics professors for emphasizing the ruthlessness of American corporations. For Buckley, this was "special pleading" such as would "condemn Lincoln as 'that man who put his feet up on the desk and told coarse stories.'"[3] Buckley would instead emphasize the liberating power, the great increase in the general standard of living, the massive expansion of the nation's capital stock, the taming of the wilderness, that American corporations have achieved.

Then again, things may seem tolerable, but only because of lethargy in our imagination of alternatives. A fetishization of existing institutional arrangements, Roberto Unger urges us to see, stunts the working-out of alternative designs that would make the present situation seem intolerable.[4] Aren't we capable of more? More prosperity. More fairness? People tolerate both too little and too much. In this sense, it is our *approach* to assessing the situation that is crucial to our determination of whether it is tolerable or not tolerable.

---

[2] GEORGE ORWELL, THE ROAD TO WIGAN PIER 153 (1937, 1958).

[3] WILLIAM F. BUCKLEY, JR., GOD AND MAN AT YALE 48 (1951, 1986).

[4] *See* ROBERTO MANGABEIRA UNGER, WHAT SHOULD LEGAL ANALYSIS BECOME? (Verso, 1996).

My approach to the corporation is law and legal theory. This book is not an accounting or audit. My conclusion that something is seriously wrong with our corporate system, and that it can be fixed, is reached not by netting out utility and harm, but by critically engaging core *arguments* about what corporate law is, what it does, and what it might do. I make use of economics, history, psychology, literature, and cultural analysis, but all for the purpose of advancing our understanding of how corporate *law* works and how it shapes corporate operations. From my point of view, it is corporate law that makes the corporate soul, and a change to corporate law can remake it in a different image.

I title this book *Corporate Friction* because my emphasis is on the ways in which our corporate law forces a grinding, rough relationship between corporations and the society they are meant to serve. Social welfare is burned off in this friction, wastefully, as with the friction in any badly set machine. And the friction of the shareholder primacy norm produces not just heat but smoke. It creates confusion, obfuscation, and disintegrity in the way we think and talk about corporate operations. The work of this book is to clear the smoke and offer a better calibration of corporate law, so that it might produce more light with less fire.

In choosing this title, I also mean to draw on the closeness of the word friction to the word "fiction," which is often heard in corporate law conversation to highlight the artificial nature of corporate existence. By turning corporate fiction to friction, I am emphasizing that what is at stake in corporate theory and corporate law is no fiction at all. Corporate law has made the word of shareholder primacy theory flesh. It lives in our world, moves in it, and stymies movement in it.

Finally, I like *Friction* for this study of corporate law because it has an erotic quality. The Nobel Laureate Bob Dylan sang, "You're gonna need my help sweetheart / you can't make love all by yourself."[5] There is no provocation in the world of ideas without sensitive engagement, there is no beauty in argument unless the tensions are set-upon joyfully. I find – and hope to present – corporate theory to be charming even where it is wrong, engrossing even where it is confused. Only the

---

[5] Bob Dylan, "Lonesome Day Blues," on LOVE AND THEFT (Columbia Records, 2001).

friction of thesis and anti-thesis can spawn new ideas for the next generation of corporate operations. So read it after the kids are in bed.

My aim has been to make this book appealing to both newcomers and experts in the field. Novices will, I think, find in it a fair synthesis of a lot of material that will place them squarely within an important conversation about what corporate law should be. Veterans, I hope, will find here both new critiques of familiar claims, and original thematic contributions with which they might tangle. A lot of work in the critical corporate law tradition has focused on the prevailing regime as it relates especially to the interests of workers. I use that material here. I also contribute a fresh perspective and new set of insights regarding the consumer interest in corporate law, a vantage that has generally been under-theorized in corporate law scholarship. Additionally, I squarely address the problem of corporate patriotism, a crucial social policy concern that has been long latent in corporate theory but rarely explicitly addressed.

Each chapter contributes to an overarching claim that we should fundamentally reform our corporate governance law. Chapter 1 provides an overview of the theoretical case in favor of the prevailing system. It is so fairly presented, the reader may be convinced. But then comes Chapter 2, in which I introduce a general critique of shareholder primacy, arguing that it is theoretically flawed and makes for bad social policy. Chapter 3 delves more deeply into the problems introduced into corporate social responsibility concerns by the Supreme Court's *Citizens United* decision on corporate political speech rights. Chapter 4 pauses the theoretical work to provide a nuanced (but entertaining) doctrinal exegesis showing that shareholder primacy is, in fact, and contrary to what some scholars and activists claim, the prevailing corporate governance law in the United States. This positive assessment highlights the urgency of the book's normative claims. Chapters 5 and 6 return to the theoretical examination, with Chapter 5 taking up the problem of corporate patriotism and Chapter 6 examining the relationship between corporate law and the meaning of consumer culture. The final chapters engage the prospect for reform. Chapter 7 takes a look at alternative models of corporate governance, beyond shareholder primacy, which are in place in other wealthy democracies around the world, and which might usefully inform changes to the corporate system in the United States. Chapter 8 explicates a socially responsible governance standard for American corporations that I argue should replace the shareholder primacy regime we have. There is a brief conclusion addressing the feasibility of the reforms I have suggested in the context of our current political environment.

1 APOLOGIES FOR OUR SYSTEM

A CREATURE OF LAW

Corporations are not found in nature. They cannot be captured in the wild nor dug out of the ground. They cannot be spliced together in a laboratory nor coded on a computer. Corporations are *legal* entities, created only by specific, affirmative state action: the issuing of a corporate charter. Once created, a corporation has a distinct legal existence, separate from that of the natural people who invest their money in it, work for it, or consume its products. A corporate legal entity owns property and enters into contracts in its own name. It is the only one responsible for its debts. It has perpetual existence (it does not die of old age). The reason that governments create corporations is because it is in the public interest to do so. Or, rather, governments can only *legitimately* grant corporate charters if doing so is in the public interest.[1]

Corporations have been used by human societies for a very long time. Versions of them were deployed in ancient Egypt and in ancient Rome. Historically, however, governments have created corporations – or allowed their creation – only sparingly, fearing they would compete with other established interests and institutions, especially the

---

[1] A lot of ink has been spilled in corporate theory arguing about whether the corporate form should be thought of as "concession" from the state or as a species of private contracting, i.e., a "nexus of contracts." While I think there is good reason to consider corporate law a distinct body of law, distinguishable from contract law, that debate really has no bearing on whether or not shareholder primacy should be the rule of corporate governance. As Hansmann and Kraakman put it, "corporations – whether 'concessions' or contracts – should be regulated when it is in the public interest to do so." Henry Hansmann & Reinier Kraakman, *The End of History for Corporate Law*, 89 GEO. L. J. 439, 441 n. 5 (2001). We are addressing when it is in the public interest to do so.

government itself. In the early days of the American republic, corporate charters were granted only by specific legislative acts to facilitate particular undertakings, such as the building of a road or the digging of a canal. After the Civil War, in part to finance war debts, in part to spur socially useful industrial activity, in part to democratize access to business entities, states began selling corporate charters with abandon, essentially to anyone willing to pay for them. Today, corporations are ubiquitous in American life.[2]

The bedrock rule of American corporate governance law is that corporate directors must manage their firms solely in the interests of the shareholders.[3] They may not sacrifice shareholder profit in service of any other stakeholders, such as workers, consumers, the environment, or the nation. This rule may seem at first hard to square with the idea that governments should only grant corporate charters if doing so serves the public interest. But defenders of our corporate governance system insist that there is no contradiction because shareholder primacy *is* the rule that advances the interests of all corporate stakeholders, and society generally, better than could any alternative system. Let us review the justifications for that claim.

OWNERSHIP IS NOT EXPLANATORY

To see clearly our subject, we must push past the common sense idea that corporations should be run for shareholders because they *own* the corporation. That kind of assertion ends the inquiry where it must instead begin. How do we know that it is *shareholders* who own the corporation, rather than somebody else, or nobody in particular? What is ownership, anyway? Ownership is the name we give to a set of legal rights. Among the traditional rights of ownership are the right to

---

[2] Excellent histories of the corporate form can be found in JOHN MICKLETHWAIT & ADRIAN WOOLDRIDGE, THE COMPANY: A SHORT HISTORY OF A REVOLUTIONARY IDEA (2003); Martin J. Sklar, THE CORPORATE RECONSTRUCTION OF AMERICAN CAPITALISM, 1890–1916: THE MARKET, THE LAW, AND POLITICS (1988); Edwin Merrick Dodd, AMERICAN BUSINESS CORPORATIONS UNTIL 1860 (1954); and S. Samuel Arsht, *A History of Delaware Corporation Law*, 1 DEL. J. CORP. L. 1 (1976).

[3] *See* Chapter 4 (demonstrating that this is the law of corporate purpose in the United States).

occupy, the right to exclude, the right to control, and the right to alienate. I get to occupy my house and use my iPhone, and I get to keep others from doing the same. I own them. The state will enforce my right to do these things, with violence, if necessary. But if I am a stockholder in Apple, Inc., and I go to corporate headquarters demanding entry, I will not be admitted. Indeed, the state will forcibly exclude me from entering, if necessary. If I tried to exclude others – say, a member of Apple's board of directors or the janitor – from occupying Apple, I would be arrested. If I tell Apple that as a shareholder, I insist they not use sweatshop labor or reduce their prices, I am ignored. Yes, I (or the person I bought the stock from) invested money in the firm, but workers give their labor to the firm, and consumers give their cash to it, and the state gives it a corporate charter. Why does the shareholder's investment entitle her to be the *sole* focus of corporate governance?[4]

WE ARE (NOT) ALL SHAREHOLDERS NOW

Sometimes one hears that "shareholder primacy" in firm governance is good social policy because, essentially, we are all shareholders now. As a result of equity holdings in retirement plans, investments in mutual funds, etc., almost everyone's interests are served by the shareholder primacy rule.[5] This argument has a long pedigree in corporate law discourse, going back at least to the 1930s, when it was run up the flagpole in a famous debate about corporate purpose in the *Harvard Law Review*.[6] But it was not really true then, and it is not really true

---

[4] *See generally* Joseph William Singer, *The Reliance Interest in Property*, 40 STAN. L. REV. 611 (1987). The "ownership" view of shareholder rights is more often heard today in nonacademic conversation than in corporate law scholarship, where the idea has largely been rejected as unhelpful, for the reasons described here. One does see the trope in influential places, however. It motivates Milton Friedman's argument in his famous *New York Times Magazine* essay, *The Social Responsibility of Business Is to Increase Its Profits*, THE NEW YORK TIMES MAGAZINE (Sep 13, 1970). I discuss that essay further in Chapter 8.

[5] *See*, e.g., Hansmann & Kraakman, *The End of History for Corporate Law*, *supra* note 1, at 451–53 (making this argument).

[6] *See* Adolf A. Berle, Jr., *For Whom Corporate Managers Are Trustees: A Note*, 45 HARV. L. REV. 1365, 1367–68 (1932) (stating that "not less than half the population of the country" had a direct equity interest in publicly traded corporations).

now. Around half of all Americans have some investment in stocks, mostly through retirement savings.[7] That is not all of us. Even among those who have an interest in stocks, some are more interested than others. The wealthiest 20 percent of Americans own 90 percent of stocks.[8] Nearly 70 percent of American stock ownership is in the hands of 5 percent of the population. It is therefore inaccurate to think that most Americans are *directly* served when corporate governance is focused only on shareholders. Even if many workers and consumers have some equity interest in firms through retirement savings, their more crucial connections to corporations are as workers, consumers, and citizens, not as shareholders.

So how does shareholder primacy in corporate governance make everyone better off?

INCENTIVE TO INVEST

The canonical view is that shareholders must have exclusive attention in corporate governance in order to give them the incentive to invest in corporate enterprise. Other stakeholders can get what they want out of corporate operations without protections in the boardroom. Workers, individually or through unions, can bargain with the firm for wages and working conditions, and they can threaten to leave and work elsewhere if the firm comes up short for them. Consumers can monitor their own interests at the cash register, deciding whether to give their money over for corporate goods on offer or walk away. Shareholders, on the other hand, are powerless to compel the firm to treat them fairly. They need the law to do it for them. Unlike workers and consumers, shareholders are dispersed and distant from corporate operations. More importantly, unlike workers and consumers, shareholders have no threat of exit. In exchange for turning her capital over to the firm, the shareholder receives stock entitling her to a pro rata share of future profits. She cannot, after investing, demand that the corporation buy back her shares. She cannot force dissolution of the company and claim her pro rata share of assets after liabilities. Once she invests, she is locked in.

---

[7] *See generally* Kent Greenfield, The Failure of Corporate Law 175–78 (2007).   [8] *Id.*

Her only hope is either that the firm pays dividends or that she can find someone else willing to buy her shares.[9] And the firm can only pay her dividends *after* goods have been delivered to consumers, wages have been paid to workers, and taxes have been paid to the government. So, while we call it "shareholder primacy," shareholders actually come *last*. By telling directors to steer the corporate ship always towards the horizon where there is gain for shareholders, the law ensures that directors end up satisfying all other corporate stakeholders along the way. That is how shareholder primacy makes everybody better off.[10]

Because proponents of shareholder primacy consider their system to be objectively desirable, they also regard it as the system that all corporate stakeholders would *choose* if they went into a conference room to actually negotiate the terms of how corporations should be run. Non-shareholders are not getting stuck with the short end of the corporate law stick in these hypothetical, or mythical, negotiations. Workers and consumers *prefer* to be excluded from directors' duties, as this makes it easier for the firm to attract capital, which makes it possible to employ more workers and produce more goods for sale. In the canonical account, shareholder primacy is thus draped in both sacred vestments: efficiency and volunteerism. These themes are mutually reinforcing. Because shareholder primacy is efficient, all

---

[9] The corporate shareholder's "lock-in" predicament contrasts with that of a sole proprietor, who can sell her business assets for cash at any time. Common law partners and even LLC members also have a default right to be disassociated from their investment by being paid a fair market rate for their ownership stake whenever they choose. Capital "lock-in" was one of the features that made the corporate form such a stable, powerful mechanism to organize business in the capital-intense industries of the late nineteenth century. The lock-in term assures investors in corporate enterprise that *fellow* shareholders will not be able to drain the enterprise of capital or force its dissolution before it reaps profits. Lock-in provides stability, but it exacerbates the shareholder agency problem, making exclusive attention to shareholders in the boardroom all the more important. *See* Margaret M. Blair, *Locking in Capital: What Corporate Law Achieved for Business Organizers in the Nineteenth Century*, 51 UCLA L. REV. 387 (2003). *But see* Larry E. Ribstein, *Should History Lock in Lock-In?*, 41 TULSA L. REV. 523 (2006) (critiquing Blair's account and doubting the centrality of capital lock-in to facilitating large-scale business enterprise).

[10] There are numerous canonical defenses of shareholder primacy in the academic literature. Among my favorites are: STEPHEN M. BAINBRIDGE, THE NEW CORPORATE GOVERNANCE IN THEORY AND PRACTICE 127–29 (2008); Michael C. Jensen, *Value Maximization, Stakeholder Theory, and the Corporate Objective Function*, 7 EUR. FIN. MGMT. 297 (2001); and FRANK H. EASTERBROOK & DANIEL R. FISCHEL, THE ECONOMIC STRUCTURE OF CORPORATE LAW (1996).

corporate stakeholders would voluntarily choose it; since it is what the parties would voluntarily choose, it is efficient to supply it to them. Of course, shareholders, workers, consumers, and other stakeholders do not *actually* sit down to negotiate the shareholder primacy rule. That would not be practically feasible. Instead, the law supplies the corporate governance rule that all of the stakeholders *would have chosen*. The law honors the will of the parties and doubles down on the honor by relieving them of the burden of exercising it.

(Implicit in this origin story is that participants in the mythical conference room would receive a solid homily from a persuasive corporate law scholar before they started negotiating. If you polled workers or consumers before such a lecture, they might very well say they did not favor shareholder primacy in corporate governance and would prefer a rule that required directors also to serve their interests.)

Many corporate law rules simply establish defaults that the parties involved in corporate operations can alter if they so desire. Sometimes, capital investors insist on changes to default rules relating to *how* their interests will be served (e.g., how frequently directors will stand for election). But the insurmountable practical impediments to getting all corporate stakeholders together to negotiate a default rule of corporate purpose also make it impossible for such groups to *alter* the default rule of corporate purpose.[11] Further, the government's provision of the shareholder primacy rule affects the way shareholders and others value corporate governance norms. While corporate theorists justify shareholder primacy purely on instrumental grounds, it settles in psychologically as a shareholder entitlement – an endowment, which, once established, people are reluctant to give up.[12] Non-shareholding stakeholders are stuck with shareholder primacy in firm governance unless corporate law prescribes some other default. The stakes in corporate theory and corporate law, therefore, are high.

---

[11] *See generally* David G. Yosifon, *Opting Out of Shareholder Primacy: Is the Public Benefit Corporate Trivial?*, 41 Del. J. Corp. L. 461 (2017) (discussing mutability of the law of corporate purpose).

[12] *See* Jon Hanson & David Yosifon, *The Situation: An Introduction to Critical Realism, the Situational Character, Power Economics, and Deep Capture*, 152 U. Pa. L. Rev. 129 (2003) (reviewing psychological studies on the endowment effect and status quo bias).

DELAWARE DOMINANCE IN CORPORATE LAW

There is not just one single body of corporate law in the United States. Corporate charters are offered for sale by every state government. But American courts enforce what is known as the "internal affairs" doctrine, which holds that the corporate governance law that applies to any corporation is the law of its state of incorporation, not the state where it is headquartered or where it operates. Because of this rule, corporate promoters can choose to incorporate under whatever state offers the corporate governance law they desire. Corporate promoters want shareholder primacy, and the surest provider of that law is the state of Delaware. Consequently, most large corporations in the United States are chartered in Delaware, and Delaware law dominates the economic landscape in the United States. As of 2010, 63 percent of Fortune 500 companies were Delaware firms, and 76 percent of initial public offerings in the United States were Delaware firms.[13] When I refer to corporate law in this book, I am generally describing Delaware law, although the fundamental governance requirements of other important chartering states, like California, are similar on the issues of relevance here.[14]

Some states, for example, Connecticut, have a corporate law that does not clearly reflect the shareholder primacy standard. But such law is not crucial to our inquiry because powerful firms almost never use it. In the final chapter, I suggest getting rid of state-based incorporation and replacing it with federal chartering as a way of moving from shareholder primacy to multi-stakeholder governance in our largest firms.

THE PROBLEM AS THE CANONICAL ACCOUNT SEES IT

Having worked out that shareholder primacy *should* reign in the boardroom, the principal problem for the prevailing system becomes figuring

---

[13] *See* John Armour, et al., *Delaware's Balancing Act*, 87 IND. L. J. 1345 (2012) (reviewing explanations for Delaware's dominance).

[14] *See* Yosifon, *Opting Out of Shareholder Primacy*, *supra* note 11 at 471 n. 39 (discussing California law). As noted in the introduction, some scholars think that shareholder primacy is not the law in Delaware; I address their claims in Chapter 4.

out how to get directors to abide by that instruction. How do you compel corporate directors to operate faithfully on behalf of shareholders, rather than in their own self-interest (through outright stealing, diverting corporate assets to pet projects, or general malingering)? The problem as it is still understood today was squarely framed by Adam Smith in 1776, when he wrote in *The Wealth of Nations*:

> The trade of a joint stock company is always managed by a court [board] of directors. This court . . . [is] subject, in many respects, to the control of a general court of proprietors [shareholders]. But the greater part of those proprietors seldom pretend to understand anything of the business of the company . . . The directors of such companies . . . being the managers rather of other people's money than of their own, it cannot well be expected that they should watch over it with the same anxious vigilance with which the partners in a private copartnery frequently watch over their own . . . Negligence and profusion, therefore, must always prevail, more or less, in the management of the affairs of such a company.[15]

This shareholder "agency problem" has continually commanded the attention of corporate law scholars. Its modern statement is pinned to Adolf Berle and Gardiner Means's totemic *The Modern Corporation and Private Property*, published in 1932, and its "formalization" credited to Michael Jensen and William Meckling's *Theory of the Firm* article in 1976.[16] Every year, still, the law reviews are filled with studies and arguments treating the problem with ever greater nuance.

Adam Smith thought that the agency problems attendant to the separation of ownership and control were so great as to preclude the viability of widely held corporations in competitive environments. His passage above concludes: "[i]t is upon this account that joint stock

---

[15] ADAM SMITH, THE WEALTH OF NATIONS 849 (1776, 1904). Smith's analysis could be seen as prescient, as he was describing a social problem that would not become widespread until several generations after he lived. But really, Smith is describing a problem that has been with humankind in all epochs, whenever some have purported to work on behalf of others. *See* MICKLETHWAIT & WOOLDRIDGE, THE COMPANY, *supra* note 2 (tracing agency problems in business operations back to the ancient world).

[16] *See* Adolf A. Berle & Gardiner C. Means, THE MODERN CORPORATION AND PRIVATE PROPERTY (Harcourt, Brace & World, Inc., 1932); Michael C. Jensen & William H. Meckling, *Theory of the Firm: Managerial Behavior, Agency Costs and Ownership Structure*, 3 J. FIN. ECON. 305 (1976).

companies for foreign trade have seldom been able to maintain the competition against private adventurers."[17] The generations of intellectual and practical labors since Smith, however, have yielded powerful solutions to the shareholder agency problem, such that corporations now dominate economic activity all over the world.

Solutions to the problem of "negligence and profusion" in the management of corporate enterprise are based in law, economics, and culture. First, and from the perspective of this book, most importantly, the law binds corporate directors with the yoke of *fiduciary* obligation to the shareholders. Directors are legally required to work with care and loyalty on behalf of shareholders, and nobody else. They may be enjoined, and they may have to pay money damages, if they breach these duties.[18] Around these fiduciary duties have also developed a strong culture and ethic of directorial fidelity to the shareholder interest.[19] Second, directors traditionally hold their seats subject to the vote of the stockholders. Those who shirk, steal, or sacrifice profits in favor of workers, consumers, or the environment may find themselves ousted and replaced by a new management team. As Smith noted, individual, diversified shareholders have little incentive to actively engage in corporate democracy. But institutional investors and activist investors can and do exert pressure on boards through corporate elections.[20] Third, director compensation can be structured with a heavy dose of stock options to better align director and shareholder interest. Fourth, wealthy individuals or other corporations can

---

[17] ADAM SMITH, THE WEALTH OF NATIONS, *supra* note 15.

[18] As corporate law has developed, courts rigorously inspect transactions involving directors' conflicts of interest but give wide discretion to boards for ordinary business judgments made in good faith. *See* BAINBRIDGE, THE NEW CORPORATE GOVERNANCE, *supra* note 10 at 127–29 (explaining and justifying this "business judgment rule" for disinterested transactions).

[19] *See* Mark J. Roe, *The Shareholder Wealth Maximization Norm and Industrial Organization*, 149 U. PA. L. REV. 2063 (2001).

[20] *See* Ronald J. Gilson & Jeffrey N. Gordon, *The Agency Costs of Agency Capitalism: Activist Investors and the Revaluation of Governance Rights*, 113 COLUM. L. REV. 863, 865 (2013) (reporting that 70 percent of the stock of S&P 1000 corporations is owned by institutional investors). Some large contemporary corporations have gone public with stock that has no voting rights. This development puts all the more pressure on the bedrock fiduciary duties of directors as the primary solution to the shareholder agency problem. I discuss the implications of non-voting stock in Chapter 8, when exploring alternatives to the shareholder primacy norm.

scour the market for underperforming firms, purchase a controlling block of undervalued shares, and unleash the pent-up value of the firm for themselves. The very threat of this "market for control" haunts incumbent management. Directors know that if they do not continuously maximize profits for shareholders, they will become a target for a takeover.[21]

These solutions to the shareholder agency problem, the only corporate design problem that mainstream corporate theory sees, are thought to work well. There is always lingering concern that corporate governance is coming up short for shareholders. But the overall outlook among apologists for shareholder primacy in corporate governance is one of satisfaction with a system that is well justified and well functioning. Acolytes profess the "Genius"[22] of the regime, and declare that the American shareholder primacy system represents "The End of History"[23] in humanity's search for effective corporate governance design.

---

[21] Henry G. Manne, *Mergers and the Market for Corporate Control*, 73 J. POL. ECON. 110 (1965). The efficacy of the market for control is limited because courts give incumbent corporate directors considerable latitude to establish defenses to hostile threats if they are pursuing, in good faith, their long-term vision for the firm's profitability. In the end, it is fiduciary obligation, not the economics of the market for control, that is the law's core answer to the shareholder agency problem. *See, e.g.,* Paramount Comm., Inc. v. Time Inc., 571 A.2d 1140, 1142 (Del. 1989).

[22] *See* ROBERTA ROMANO, THE GENIUS OF AMERICAN CORPORATE LAW (The American Enterprise Institute Press, 1993).

[23] *See* Hansmann & Kraakman, *The End of History for Corporate Law, supra* note 1 at 441.

2   CRITIQUE OF SHAREHOLDER PRIMACY

"The expedition of my violent love
Outran the pauser, reason. Here lay Duncan."
                                    - William Shakespeare, *Macbeth*[1]

THE SOLUTION IS THE PROBLEM

Canonical shareholder primacy theory is seductive. Its seeming logic gives it an impression of elegance, even beauty. Examined in a critical light, however, blemishes become evident. Studied to their deeper consequence, these faults are seen to be cancerous. But they can be treated.

Corporate law makes the pursuit of shareholder interests the sole task of corporate governance. This is a solution to the shareholder agency problem, but it creates a problem for non-shareholders. There is a direct connection between the way corporate law commands firms treat shareholders, and the way they end up dealing with others. The duty to do everything profitable *for* shareholders implies an obligation to do anything profitable *to* non-shareholders. Told to serve only the shareholders, and to do it with a fiduciary verve, corporations are oriented to overreach in their dealings with workers, consumers, and other stakeholders, in order to increase profits, when they can get away with it. This might mean shutting down factories and moving jobs to other countries with cheaper labor, wrecking communities that have built up over generations around corporate operations in a particular region. It might mean manipulating consumer risk perceptions

---

[1] WILLIAM SHAKESPEARE, MACBETH, Act II, Scene III (1606).

regarding the health consequences of using a corporate product. It could involve expelling pollutants into the air or seas to save on production costs. It might mean dealing with a foreign government whose interests are hostile to the United States or its values. These things serve shareholders but undermine the social utility of corporate enterprise.[2]

THE PARETO FALLACY OF CORPORATE PROFITABILITY

Serious inquiry into the legitimacy of our corporate operations must be ever on guard against the common rhetorical move I call the "Pareto fallacy of corporate profitability."[3] It might less pedantically be called "the responsible tide lifts all boats" fallacy. This trope insists that, in the end, the best way for corporate directors to maximize profits is to treat all of the firm's stakeholders well, and therefore, there is no tension between corporate profitability and corporate responsibility.

Of course, the law does not *require* that firms behave rapaciously. *Sometimes* the best way to make profits will be to pay workers well, give consumers quality products, and steward the environment in a sustainable fashion. Such conduct can attract fine workers and loyal customers, and can ease relations with the local community and government. As was said in a nineteenth-century British case: "the law does not say

---

[2] In a remarkable article, Professor Donald Langevoort once argued that whether a "half-truth" should give rise to a shareholder cause of action for securities fraud depends on to whom the "half-truth" was directed. Donald C. Langevoort, *Half-Truths: Protecting Mistaken Inferences by Investors and Others*, 52 STAN. L. REV. 87, 124 (1999). If a firm tells a "half-truth" about the quality of its products but directs the statement to consumers rather than shareholders, shareholders should not have a cause of action. The reason for this, according to Langevoort, is that shareholders stand to gain from such statements. "Half-truths" are part of the solution for shareholders, and that solution is part of the problem for everyone else. *Id.* at 122 ("[e]xpressions of optimism should not be actionable in those settings where hype is most commonplace: the kinds of statements made with customer and employee audiences largely in mind").

[3] Vilfredo Pareto (1848–1923) was an Italian economist. His name is commonly used as shorthand to describe a transaction or policy that makes everyone better off and nobody worse off. This was an idea Pareto worked on. It is an important concept that could probably use a better name. *See* RICHARD POSNER, ECONOMIC ANALYSIS OF LAW 14–15 (5th ed. 2007).

that there are to be no cakes and ale, but there are to be no cakes and ale except such as are required for the benefit of the company."[4] This is well and good. But it is also true that *sometimes* profits are to be found by dealing sharply with non-shareholders. Corporations charged solely with pursuing shareholder profits will have the incentive to pursue both courses. Some will focus on one or the other, some will do both. Which they will do depends not on ethics, but only on the business exigencies of the firm. A compass always points north, but it would be moral error to regard the compass as principled when it happens to point to the high road. Shareholder primacy always points to profits, but the fact that profits can sometimes be found in socially desirable conduct should not give us confidence that the rule is an instrument of justice.

The Pareto fallacy of corporate profitability debilitates honest discussion about the consequences of shareholder primacy in corporate governance. The urtext of this fallacy is the Johnson & Johnson Corporation's response to the cyanide-in-the-Tylenol tragedy of 1982. A still unknown malefactor laced several bottles of Tylenol in the Chicago area with cyanide, and seven people were killed.[5] The company's response was quick and transparent. They fully briefed the public and voluntarily pulled all their products off the market. I was nine years old at the time and remember vividly the images of rows of Tylenol products being swept off store shelves into garbage cans. Such forthright, upstanding conduct was widely credited with helping Johnson & Johnson quickly regain its market share when the company came back to market a month later with substantially improved safety mechanisms on their pill bottles.[6] Johnson & Johnson had made good on its ballyhooed "credo" of putting the health of its customers first *and* it worked out great for the company's shareholders.[7] One does not attend many conferences on corporate social responsibility without hearing the Tylenol story, especially if representatives from industry are present.

---

[4] Hutton v. West Cork Railway, 23 CH. D. 645, 673 (1883).

[5] *See* Harvey L. Pitt & Karl A. Groskaufmanis, *When Bad Things Happen to Good Companies*, 15 CARDOZO L. REV. 951 (1994).

[6] *Id.* at 951.

[7] Corporate "credos" such as Johnson & Johnson's have no legal standing as a matter of corporate governance. They do not suffice to alter the law's command that directors put shareholder interests before those of other stakeholders. *See* Chapter 4.

But seven people were killed. The company came back to market in just *one* month with a much safer, tamper-resistant product. Is it possible that shareholder primacy had something to do with the fact that the tamper-resistant packaging was not already being used? Is it possible that a different corporate governance system would have put the safer packaging in place before the disaster? I am not concerned with this particular episode but about the conceit. Salient examples of profitable corporate responsibility should not distract us from recognizing the logic and fact that shortcuts and manipulation will be an important part of the overall pursuit of profits for shareholder primacy firms in many industries. Indeed, it has been part of the profit formula for Johnson & Johnson. In 2013, to give just one example, Johnson & Johnson agreed to pay $2 *billion* in civil and criminal fines to the federal government after acknowledging that it had promoted a drug, which was approved by the FDA only to treat schizophrenia, as also being useful for the routine treatment of symptoms such as anxiety and depression in elderly people.[8] That kind of overreach is predicted by proper assessment of the shareholder primacy norm, and that kind of misconduct is widely observed. Just because the crisp twenty-dollar bill lying on the high ground is gathered up does not mean that the filthy ten lying underground in the dark valley will be left unexploited.

Among the most visible acolytes of the Pareto fallacy of corporate profitability is John Mackey, the founder of Whole Foods Markets, Inc. In his book *Conscious Capitalism,* Mackey insists that there is no need to alter the shareholder primacy norm in order to achieve corporate social responsibility because business is most profitable when it "consciously" cares for non-shareholders. He writes: "In addition to creating social, cultural, intellectual, physical, ecological, emotional, and spiritual value for all stakeholders, conscious businesses also excel at delivering exceptional financial performance over the long term."[9] Mackey even predicts that because rapacious firms are less profitable, "[e]ventually, the marketplace will weed out businesses that aren't

---

[8] *See* Press Release, Department of Justice, Johnson and Johnson to Pay More than $2 Billion to Resolve Criminal and Civil Investigations (Nov 4, 2013), www.justice.gov/opa/pr/john son-johnson-pay-more-22-billion-resolve-criminal-and-civil-investigations.

[9] JOHN MACKEY & RAJ SISODIA, CONSCIOUS CAPITALISM: LIBERATING THE HEROIC SPIRIT OF BUSINESS 35 (Harvard Business School Publishing Corporation, 2013).

sufficiently conscious."[10] But this is plainly wrong. If weeds are profitable, then they are likely to persist. As the economist Armen Alchian explained 50 years ago, firms do not need to maximize profits in order to survive; they just need to make *some* profits.[11] If there is profit to be made in exploitative conduct, and shareholder primacy reigns, then loyal directors will find it.

The promise which Mackey and other genitors of the Pareto fallacy of corporate profitability make, that things will work out for all stakeholders in the "long term," is a mystical trope. We are never told what kind of time-horizon is in mind for the "long term." Is it a decade? A century? Millennia? As John Maynard Keynes said: "[i]n the long run we are all dead."[12] Something shorter than "eventually" may be all some people, values, or ecosystems have left. In the shorter-term, individual suffering, family disintegration, community collapse, and cultural decay may beckon. Bookish people are perhaps especially prone to giving the dubious "long-term" escape hatch a pass. In the world of ideas, the past, present, and future are all connected, and transcended. That is part of the charm of the place, for as Emerson said, among the pleasures of reading great thinkers is "the abstraction of all time from their verses."[13] Timelessness in ideas is indeed sublime, but in social policy, "the vice of fetishism is abdication."[14] Corporate social responsibility discourse must snap out of its slumbers over the long term. "Economists," Keynes wrote, "set themselves too easy, too useless a task if in

---

[10] *Id.* at 276–77, 289.

[11] *See* Armen A. Alchian, *Uncertainty, Evolution, and Economic Theory*, 58 J. POL. ECON. 211, 213 (1950) ("Realized positive profits, not *maximum* profits, are the mark of success and viability... The fact of its accomplishment is sufficient. This is the criterion by which the economic system selects survivors: those who realize *positive profits* are the survivors; those who suffer losses disappear.") (emphasis in original); *see also* Bernard S. Black, *Is Corporate Law Trivial?: A Political and Economic Analysis*, 84 NW. U. L. REV. 542, 579–80 (1990) (summarizing reasons why markets cannot force the reform of underperforming firms, including, perhaps most importantly, the inefficacy of markets for control, "given the ability of target managers to impose substantial costs and risks on unwanted bidders").

[12] JOHN MAYNARD KEYNES, A TRACT ON MONETARY REFORM 80 (1923) (emphasis omitted).

[13] RALPH WALDO EMERSON, *The American Scholar*, in COMPLETE WORKS: ESSAYS 92 (1841, 1929) (emphasis omitted).

[14] MICHAEL STOKES PAULSEN, *The Most Dangerous Branch: Executive Power to Say What the Law Is*, 83 GEO. L. J. 217, 344 (1994).

tempestuous seasons they can only tell us that when the storm is long past the ocean is flat again."[15]

(There will be no long term for Whole Foods Markets, Inc. During the drafting of this book, Mackey and the rest of the Whole Foods board voted to sell their company to Amazon, Inc., for $13.4 billion).[16]

RATIONAL ACTORS AND COMMON SENSE

Clear-eyed assessment of shareholder primacy theory must predict that firms operating under such a standard will endeavor to take profits at the expense of other stakeholders, if they can. The canonical account takes the position that non-shareholders are well positioned to protect themselves from such conduct. Workers, of course, will try to look out for themselves. But asbestos in the production materials, or repetitive stress injuries lurking in production routines, are hard to see. Consumers, too, are on guard, but they cannot easily see or understand the risks associated with many products: ammonia in the cigarettes, trans fats in the fries, weird math in the sub-prime mortgage instruments, or habit-forming user-interfaces in the social media. The problem is not just that these things are hard to see, but that shareholder primacy incentivizes firms to keep them from being seen. Corporations can distort stakeholder perceptions through workplace and product design, advertising, and other marketing efforts. Technology intersects with shareholder primacy to ever improve upon corporate efficiency in these pursuits. When it came to putting addiction-intensifying ingredients in cigarettes, individuals at tobacco companies actually had to work out how to do it and what effect it would have on consumers and profits.[17] But in the

---

[15] KEYNES, A TRACT ON MONETARY REFORM, *supra* note 12 at 80. *See also* Lynn A. Stout, *Killing Conscience: The Unintended Behavioral Consequences of "Pay for Performance,"* 39 J. CORP. L. 525 (2014) (tying executive compensation to stock price causes managers to focus on short-term gains, which do not necessarily require developing responsible relationships with stakeholders).

[16] *See* Nick Wingfield & Michael J. de la Merced, *Amazon to Buy Whole Foods for $13.4 Billion,* NEW YORK TIMES, Jun 16, 2017 at A1 ("The $13.4 billion deal . . . could lead to job losses at Whole Foods stores.").

[17] *See* Jon Hanson & Douglas Kysar, *Taking Behavioralism Seriously: Some Evidence of Market Manipulation,* 112 HARV. L. REV. 1420, 1477 (1999).

digital era, the shareholder primacy norm is being built into automated systems. The compulsive attributes of social media platforms are built by data-crunching computers that have the command of shareholder primacy as the first postulate of their algorithms.[18]

Proponents of shareholder primacy know their system incentivizes firms to try to overreach in dealing with non-shareholders, but they do not think firms often succeed in actually doing so. Adam Smith again set the tone long ago:

> The prejudices of some political writers against shopkeepers and tradesmen are altogether without foundation ... Some of them, perhaps, may sometimes decoy a weak customer to buy what he has no occasion for. This evil, however, is of too little importance to deserve the public attention ... It is not the multitude of alehouses, to give the most suspicious example, that occasions a general disposition to drunkenness among the common people; but that disposition, arising from other causes, necessarily gives employment to a multitude of alehouses.[19]

Smith was confident that corporations generate profits by discerning and serving consumer "disposition[s]," not by "decoy[ing]" them. This is the position taken by Smith's modern heirs in corporate law scholarship. Corporate stakeholders are construed as pursuing their privately ordered preferences by rationally evaluating options available to them in the market. With such a framework in place, employment or consumption decisions are easily seen as "revealed preferences," and corporate exploitation or manipulation is rarely identified.[20] This

---

[18] Tristan Harris, the former chief design ethicist at Google, Inc., explains the role of machine learning in designing choice architecture in social media such as Facebook and Twitter, in Tristan Harris, *How Technology Hijacks People's Minds – From a Magician and Google's Design Ethicist*, May 19, 2016, www.tristanharris.com/essays/. *See also* Sam Harris, Interview with Tristan Harris (no relation) on THE WAKING UP PODCAST, Episode #71, "*What is Technology Doing to Us?*," Apr 14, 2017, available on iTunes.

[19] ADAM SMITH, THE WEALTH OF NATIONS 407 (1904, 1776). Here we see already in Smith a prejudice that continues to haunt corporate law discourse. Analysts who deal with shareholder exploitation get the neutral title "economist," while those who address the problem of consumer exploitation are maligned as "political writers."

[20] Easterbrook and Fischel, echoing Smith, write that worries about consumers miscalculating the "costs and benefits" of doing business with a corporation are unwarranted: "The more likely hypothesis ... is that the people who are backing their beliefs with cash are correct; they have every reason to avoid mistakes, while critics (be they academics or

picture is alluring because it patronizes common-sense intuitions about human behavior.

But intuitions can be misleading, and, importantly, they can be misled. Research in social psychology, and other social sciences, has developed a picture of human decision-making that shows that we humans are in many ways less "rational" than we think we are. Our thinking is subject to systematic and predictable biases stemming from cognitive shortcuts (heuristics) that our brains use to process information, and visceral drives, such as self-affirmation, hunger, and sex instincts, which distort our reasoning.[21] We are not consciously aware that our decision-making is subject to these influences. Instead, we mistakenly regard ourselves as, for the most part, soberly, deliberately, rationally gathering information that helps us come to decisions that further our authentic, autonomously formed desires and preferences. We may regard other people as being subject to biased and motivated reasoning, but we usually think we are immune to it. It turns out that we are right about others, and wrong about ourselves.[22]

Cass Sunstein and Richard Thaler made something of a mainstream splash with this "behavioral economics" material in their 2008 book *Nudge*, which argued that policymakers could use insights from the decision sciences to improve people's well-being without unduly limiting their autonomy.[23] A well-known illustration of their

---

regulators) are rewarded for novel rather than accurate beliefs." FRANK H. EASTERBROOK & DANIEL R. FISCHEL, THE ECONOMIC STRUCTURE OF CORPORATE LAW 31 (1996).

[21] The importance of this literature was signaled in 2010 when one of its leading figures, Daniel Khaneman, was awarded the Nobel Prize in Economics. Shortly after receiving the honor, Khaneman published a massive synthesis of work in his field, titled *Thinking: Fast and Slow* (2011), which gained popular prominence.

[22] It is possible that some people are more subject to cognitive biases and motivated reasoning than others, because of differences in intelligence, education, or the way we are raised. *See* Colin Camerer, *Regulation for Conservatives: Behavioral Economics and the Case for "Asymmetric Paternalism,"* 15 U. PA. L. REV. 1211 (2003). If that is true, then a corporate law, like shareholder primacy, which presumes that people are not easily "decoyed," may serve the interests of some kinds of people at the expense of others, who are left more vulnerable because of it.

[23] CASS SUNSTEIN & RICHARD THALER, NUDGE: IMPROVING DECISIONS ABOUT HEALTH, WEALTH, AND HAPPINESS (2008). The book was an extension of Sunstein and Thaler's influential article, *Libertarian Paternalism Is Not an Oxymoron,* 70 U. CHI. L. REV. 1159 (2003). I critique the idea of "libertarian paternalism" (and "nudging") in David G. Yosifon, *Legal Theoretic Inadequacy and Obesity Epidemic Analysis,* 15 GEO. MASON L. REV. 681 (2008).

point is automatic enrollment of employees in 401(k) retirement savings plans as part of their compensation package, with an opt-out for those who prefer all-cash compensation. By operation of the "endowment effect"[24] and "status quo bias"[25] most people will stick with that default compensation arrangement, which experts consider prudent, even though people would take more cash and less savings if the default were that you had to affirmatively enroll in the savings plan.

It is a nice insight that benevolent designers of choice architecture can guide people into decisions that make them better off. But as Jon Hanson and his co-authors (I am one of them) have argued, the more pressing, troubling implication of the "behavioral economics" litera-ture is that our corporate law compels powerful firms to "nudge" behavior not in a way meant to serve the person being nudged, but in a way directed at advancing the interests of a different party altogether, namely shareholders.[26] Corporations have the incentive and ability to discern and exploit the same cognitive biases, and other unseen mech-anics of decision-making, that social psychologists have tracked, but which ordinary people tend not to see. The pressures of market com-petition will push corporations to engage in such conduct. Firms that even accidentally stumble into such kinds of practice, as if guided by an invisible hand, will thrive as against firms that fail to do so.[27] With a

---

[24] People tend to value something they already have, or regard themselves as already having a right to, more than they would value that same thing if they did not already have it, or thought they did not already have a right to it. Jon Hanson & David Yosifon, *The Situational Character: A Critical Realist Perspective on the Human Animal*, 93 GEO. L. J. 1, 41 (2004) (reviewing studies).

[25] People tend to stick with default arrangements even when given an option to alter them. *Id.*

[26] *See, e.g.,* Jon Hanson & David Yosifon, *The Situation: An Introduction to Critical Realism, the Situational Character, Power Economics, and Deep Capture,* 152 U. PA. L. REV. 129 (2003); Hanson & Yosifon, *The Situational Character, supra* note 24; Jon D. Hanson & Douglas A. Kysar, *Taking Behavioralism Seriously: The Problem of Market Manipulation,* 74 N.Y.U. L. REV. 630 (1999) (analyzing the problem of market manipulation); Jon D. Hanson & Douglas A. Kysar, *Taking Behavioralism Seriously: Some Evidence of Market Manipulation, supra* note 26 at 1467–1553 (describing industry efforts to manipulate consumer risk perception regarding smoking, with specific reference to manipulation of science); Ronald Chen & Jon Hanson, *The Illusion of Law: The Legitimating Schemas of Modern Policy and Corporate Law,* 103 MICH. L. REV. 1, 83–84 (2004); Adam Beforado & Jon Hanson, *Naïve Cynicism: Maintaining False Perceptions in Policy Debates,* 57 EMORY L. J. 499 (2008).

[27] Hanson and Kysar made the intriguing conjecture that a most effective way to do psychological research would be to study the behavior of successful firms in competitive markets, in order to see the truths about human thinking that markets reveal: "Consumer

framework in place that anticipates this kind of conduct, evidence of such efforts is easily seen in many markets. It was there in the ways the tobacco industry worked to exploit cognitive and motivational biases to manipulate consumer perceptions about the health effects of smoking.[28] It is seen in similar efforts made by fast food companies to manipulate consumer perceptions of the health risks associated with routinely eating their products.[29] It is happening now in the way machines exploit any advantage they can find in the way the human mind processes information in order to increase use of social media. This kind of corporate conduct is obvious everywhere but in mainstream corporate theory.

STAKEHOLDER VULNERABILITY TO CORPORATE LOCK-IN

The standard defense of shareholder primacy rests much of its confidence that workers and consumers do not need fiduciary attention in corporate governance on the assumption that these stakeholders can always walk away from dealing with a corporation if they are being treated unfairly. This constant threat of exit keeps sharp dealing in check. The fact that shareholders, in contrast, have no viable threat of exit, is a core reason that the standard account insists that the law must privilege shareholder interests in the boardroom. But the problem of "lock-in" is not unique to the shareholders. Workers and consumers also get locked into relationships with corporations in ways that make them vulnerable to exploitation.

When a worker commits scarce cognitive and physical resources to becoming expert in the particular skills associated with a specific job, her mind and body become less valuable to other potential employers who need other kinds of skills and work habits. Sometimes people can

---

product markets may represent the ultimate laboratory for behavioral researchers." Hanson & Kysar, *Taking Behavioralism: Some Evidence of Market Manipulation, supra* note 26 at 1467 n. 254 (1999).

[28] *See id.*

[29] *See* Adam Benforado, Jon Hanson, & David Yosifon, *Broken Scales: Obesity and Justice in America,* 53 Emory L. J. 1645 (2004).

retrain, but not always, and only ever at a cost of time and money. Once made, firm-specific investment of human capital diminishes a worker's ability to threaten exit. With a diminished threat of exit, directors can deal more sharply with workers. It becomes easier to require them to work longer hours, expose them to more danger, or provide less pay and fewer benefits. With their human capital invested in a particular firm, workers come to have unfixed, long-term interests in a corporation.[30] Above all, they need the corporation to stay in business. Workers therefore want firms to be managed in a conservative, risk-averse way. Diversified shareholders, on the other hand, are risk preferring as to the future of any one firm. They want all of the firms in their portfolio to be managed aggressively, even if that means some of them fail, leaving workers stranded. (Shareholders lose only their investment in firms that go bankrupt, but enjoy unlimited upside from highly profitable firms.) The canonical story, that workers do not need fiduciary attention in corporate governance because their continuous threat of exit keeps firms from dealing sharply with them, is fallacious.[31]

Consumers are also subject to lock-in problems that leave them vulnerable to corporate machinations on behalf of shareholders.[32] In the standard account, the consumer is construed as having an "arm's-length" relationship to the firm. Consumption is seen as involving serial, "sharp in by clear agreement, sharp out by clear performance"[33] exchanges of money for discrete goods or services. Consumers might repeat transactions, but each transaction is fully contained. This depiction undergirds the idea that consumers do not need fiduciary attention in corporate governance. Consumers who are left unsatisfied can always choose to not come back, and that

---

[30] *See* KENT GREENFIELD, THE FAILURE OF CORPORATE LAW 175–78 (2007).

[31] *See* Margaret M. Blair & Lynn A. Stout, *A Team Production Theory of the Firm*, 85 VA. L. REV. 247 (1999) (reviewing literature on worker lock-in). The reverse of this is also possible. Corporations must invest time and money in specific employees in order to build up their capacity to do the particular work of the firm. After the firm has invested those resources, the employees can threaten to leave and hold up the firm for extra wages.

[32] *See generally*, David G. Yosifon, *Consumer Lock-In and the Theory of the Firm*, 35 SEATTLE U. L. REV. 1429 (2012), and David G. Yosifon, *Towards a Firm-Based Theory of Consumption*, 46 WAKE FOREST L. REV. 447 (2011).

[33] Ian R. Macneil, *The Many Futures of Contract*, 47 S. CAL L. REV. 691, 738 (1974).

threat keeps firms from treating them poorly. But consumer dealings with corporations are far more relational and indeterminate than is captured by this characterization. Modern consumers routinely make explicit and implicit commitments to ongoing engagements with particular firms. Such commitments create vulnerabilities. And vulnerabilities, for firms charged with maximizing returns to shareholders, are opportunities.

Like workers, consumers commit their minds and bodies to learning how to use and habituate to particular goods. This is true of food, cosmetics, clothing, cars, entertainment, credit cards, technology, and all sorts of things.[34] Committing cognitive resources and developing behavioral patterns in relation to a product creates a "switching cost" that looms over any decision to change consumption patterns.[35] This dynamic process happens in the formation of wholly new markets, for example, with new technologies, and it happens generationally as new consumers enter into established markets, like when banks offer "gifts" (the proverbial toaster) to college students who open bank accounts that later will begin to charge fees. Economists used to assume consumer lock-in was rare when switching costs were low in absolute terms, but behavior in digital landscapes, where search costs are objectively low, have shown that assumption to be without merit.[36] Consumers are invested in the firms they patronize. Switching costs diminish consumers' threat of exit. Without that threat, corporations

---

[34] See Joseph Farrell & Paul Klemperer, *Coordination and Lock-In: Competition with Switching Costs and Network Effects, in* 3 HANDBOOK OF INDUSTRIAL ORGANIZATIONS 1967, at 1980–81 (Mark Armstrong & Robert H. Porter eds., 2007). *See also* Lawrence M. Ausubel, *The Failure of Competition in the Credit Card Market,* 81 AM. ECON. REV. 50, 65–66 (1991) (arguing that switching costs is the only factor that explains the premium banks pay to other banks in the sale of credit card accounts).

[35] A principal cause of this switching-cost lock-in is that, psychologically, we weigh our present interests more heavily than our future ones. This may be an authentic value choice at some level, but it is also raw, unseen cognitive bias, as "switching costs dominate these later decisions in ways that consumers do not anticipate when making the initial decision." Gal Zauberman, *The Intertemporal Dynamics of Consumer Lock-In,* 30 J. CONSUMER RES. 405, 406 (2003). *See also* Kyle B. Murray & Gerald Haubl, *Explaining Cognitive Lock-In: The Role of Skill-Based Habits of Use in Consumer Choice,* 34 J. CONSUMER RES. 77, 78 (2007) ("Unlike traditional notions of loyalty, cognitive lock-in does not require a positive attitude towards the product, trust in the product, or objectively superior product functionality.").

[36] Zauberman, *supra* note 35, at 406.

may respond by increasing prices or decreasing quality, in pursuit of increased profits for shareholders.[37]

Other kinds of consumer lock-in are more blatant. An example is consumer loyalty programs. By patronizing a particular firm, consumers generate "points" or "miles" that can later be redeemed for prizes or discounts on future purchases. Participants in loyalty programs have a long-term stake in the firm's continued operation. But the consumer's long-term interest may be in tension with that of the shareholders. For example, firms might increase profits by closing retail shops, curbing customer service, or shutting down flight paths. This benefits shareholders but leaves locked-in consumers with "points" or "miles" that are worth less than when they were earned. Similar problems are seen when consumers "invest" in durable goods, such as appliances, automobiles, or technology, which are meant to yield benefits many years after purchase.[38] If the firm decides to maximize profits by closing service outlets, or stalling software upgrades, the consumer's loss is the shareholder's gain. Some consumer durables are like equity investments in that their value is unfixed, with upside potential. Personal computers can become *more* useful over time as new applications are developed for existing machines. But the interests of consumers and shareholders in this kind of investment are not always aligned. When Texas Instruments abruptly exited the home computer market in the 1980s, it left more than a million customers with computers for which no new software programs would be developed.[39] The shareholders benefited from the customers getting left behind, as Texas Instruments' stock price shot up after the firm made its

---

[37] Theoretically, it is possible that switching costs can increase consumer-friendly competition. Where there are significant switching costs, the argument goes, sellers must dramatically slash prices to "unlock" consumers from competitors. But researchers conclude that "things do not usually work so well." *See* Farrell & Klemperer, *supra* note 34 at 1972. To unlock the consumer, a seller might need to offer prices below the seller's costs.

[38] *See* MARTHA L. OLNEY, BUY NOW, PAY LATER: ADVERTISING, CREDIT, AND CONSUMER DURABLES IN THE 1920S 47–48 (1991).

[39] *See* ANDREW POLLACK, *Texas Instruments' Pullout*, NEW YORK TIMES, Oct 31, 1983, at D4. A large portion of those stuck holding Texas Instruments computers were public schools, which had invested heavily in such computers for early technology instruction programs. *Id.*

move.[40] This consumer predicament is not anticipated or justified by prevailing corporate governance theory.

Analytic attention to vulnerabilities associated with firm-specific investment by non-shareholders has given rise to a distinct "theory of the firm" known as "team production theory."[41] (As the name suggests, this theory was developed with a focus on workers, but the arguments I have made here about consumer lock-in fit the mold, or expand it). In this approach, pioneered by Margaret Blair and Lynn Stout, the corporate board of directors is construed not as the agent of the shareholders, but as a "mediating hierarch" responsible for managing the firm in such a way as will encourage all stakeholders – including shareholders, creditors, and labor – to contribute to the corporate team. Because the "mediating hierarch" is responsible for orchestrating the various firm inputs, the vulnerabilities and hold-up problems attendant to firm-specific investment are ameliorated. This is a fine prescriptive position, and it is a foundation for the reformative agenda I describe in the last chapter, but it fails as a descriptive account. The law in the United States is that boards serve the shareholders, not that boards mediate among different stakeholders.[42] Exploitation attendant to firm-specific "lock-in" is, therefore, a real and continuing problem for non-shareholders that needs to be critically assessed and dealt with in a reformative program.

EXTERNAL REGULATION

Shareholder primacy advocates know that their preferred corporate governance norm incentivizes firms to "externalize" costs to other stakeholders, even if they do not expect manipulation and exploitation to be widespread. They nevertheless insist that it would be destructive to give up the clarity and efficiency of shareholder primacy in corporate governance to stop this problem. Instead, they argue that

---

[40] A more recent example is seen in Hewlett-Packard's abrupt decision in 2011 to discontinue support of the operating system used for its ill-fated TouchPad tablet line. Brian X. Chen, *In Flop of H.P. Touchpad, an Object Lesson for the Tech Sector*, NEW YORK TIMES, Jan 2, 2012, at B1.

[41] *Id.*   [42] *See* Chapter 4.

non-shareholders should be protected from corporate exploitation through *external* government regulation, such as employment law and consumer protection statutes. External regulation is also the solution shareholder primacy theory offers to the harms corporations, in their quest for shareholder gain, cause to the environment, nonhuman animals, future generations, and others not in any contractual relationship with the firm. Government regulation, the canonical account promises, can force shareholder primacy firms to pursue profits in a socially responsible way. With such regulation in place, profit maximization can remain the bedrock rule of corporate governance, incentivizing investment and efficient productive enterprise.[43]

But "ought" implies "can."[44] Before we say that regulation, rather than corporate governance, should protect non-shareholders from corporate overreach, we must be sure that regulation can do it. If not, then corporate theory ought to be rethought. In fact, external regulation is no reliable salve to the predictable problem of corporate malfeasance under shareholder primacy. Competent directors will recognize the importance of stunting the development of such a regulatory system. Loyal directors will work hard not just in the marketplace, but also in the halls of government, to protect their shareholders from regulation that would aid non-shareholders at the expense of corporate profits. Established, wealthy firms may also go to government seeking *artificially* onerous regulation of their industry. Big firms can weather a costly, pointless regulatory atmosphere, but smaller firms and new entrants cannot. This reduces competition that would otherwise benefit workers and consumers, but not shareholders. Firms have no ideological preference for unregulated or heavily regulated markets; they will pursue whatever government policies are profitable.[45]

---

[43] *See, e.g.*, Henry Hansmann & Reinier Kraakman, *The End of History for Corporate Law*, 89 GEO. L. J. 439, 442 (2001).

[44] *See* Dan Kahan, *The Cognitively Illiberal State*, 60 STAN. L. REV. 116 (2007) (discussing Immanuel Kant).

[45] *See* John C. Coates IV, *Corporate Politics, Governance, and Value Before and After Citizens United*, 9 J. EMPIRICAL LEGAL STUD. 657 (2012) (reporting widespread political activity among S&P 500 firms).

Of course, corporations are not alone in working to influence government regulation. But "public choice" theory explains that small groups with narrow, committed interests can more effectively engage in collective action than can larger, more widely dispersed groups with diverse interests.[46] Corporations, by virtue of their smaller numbers, singular interest, and access to persuasive agents (like lawyers and lobbyists) are better positioned to succeed in the competition for regulatory favor than are non-shareholders, who are scattered, have multiple interests, and cannot pool their resources and energies effectively to pursue regulatory intervention. While some workers may enjoy union representation, most do not.[47] It is illogical to expect that "regulation" will be able to contain the excesses of shareholder primacy.[48]

Corporations influence regulatory law in many ways. Bribery is not technically available but finer methods of influence abound. There are tight restrictions on corporate campaign *contributions* to particular political candidates, but firms can independently spend as much of their own money as they wish to promote their preferred candidates, or undermine candidates who stand in the way of their profit maximization charge.[49] Involvement in political campaigns is the starkest form of corporate political activity, but it is not necessarily the most important. Probably the most influential (and the most pernicious) kind of corporate political speech takes place privately

---

[46] MANCUR OLSON, THE LOGIC OF COLLECTIVE ACTION (1965).

[47] Where labor is especially successful in influencing government, other corporate stakeholders, such as consumers, may find themselves no better off, or even worse off, than when corporations prevail in the quest for regulatory capture.

[48] There is an extensive literature on regulatory capture within economics generally, but its implications for shareholder primacy theory have largely been ignored by corporate law scholars. *See, e.g.,* OWEN M. FISS, LIBERALISM DIVIDED 42–46 (1996); CHARLES E. LINDBLOM, POLITICS AND MARKETS 170–200 (1977); George Stigler, *The Theory of Economic Regulation,* 3 BELL J. ECON. & MGMT. SCI. 3, 3–4 (1971). Some commentators focus on the extent to which the logic of collective action benefits firm managers at the expense of shareholders. This is true, but it is a separate issue. Just because directors take from shareholder for themselves does not mean they do not also take for shareholders from everyone else. Shareholders, with corporations and their directors as their servants, have a collective action advantage over workers and consumers.

[49] Many corporations find it cost-effective to give money to political action committees with expertise in political activity, rather than engaging in politics directly. *Cf.* Ronald Coase, *The Nature of the Firm,* 4 ECONOMICA 386 (1937).

and face-to-face in offices and meeting rooms, through direct lobbying by corporate agents.[50]

The public choice problem I am describing here is not fundamentally about smoke-filled-room corruption. Efforts to draw attention to
the problem of corporate influence in government lose credibility when
discussed in such terms. The black-heart idiom especially lacks credibility among politicians and businesspeople who see themselves as
ethically upstanding and see that corruption is deplorable to everyone
they know, just as it is among academics or activists.[51] Like all human
beings, politicians are motivated to view themselves in affirming ways,
as hard working, competent, and principled.[52] Effectuating pro-
corporate policies merely to maintain the salaries and trappings of
office would be unsatisfying to most politicians. They must also sincerely believe the policies they support are sound. In the sardonic tones
of Stephen Bainbridge: "Any sensible theory of the relationship
between politics and corporate governance thus must consider not
only naked self-interest, but also the possibility that ideology matters,
even in the halls of Congress."[53] A crucial arena in which the competition for regulation takes place, then, is inside the mind of the policy-
maker. An important piece of the work of regulatory capture is done by
funding think tanks and other kinds of knowledge production, which
cultivate shareholder-friendly arguments that can be deployed by
lobbyists with persuasive skills to make the corporate case to politicians
who are already motivated to be receptive to deep-pocketed corporate

---

[50] At some level, we must rely on corporations to inform policymaking. Regulators can only
know a bit about the conditions affecting particular industries. Government needs information and perspective from industry in order to develop sound policy. As one corporate
lobbyist put it to the journalist Stephen Brill: "If you banned all lobbying tomorrow, the
legislative process would grind to a halt. . . . [T]he ones who are especially interested are the
ones who can explain the consequences of writing a bill this way or that way." *See, e.g.*,
Steven Brill, *On Sale: Your Government. Why Lobbying Is Washington's Best Bargain*,
TIME, Jul 12, 2010, at 28 (quoting Dave Wenhold, President of the American League
of Lobbyists). The problem is not that corporations speak. The problem is the exclusive
shareholder-centric motive behind their speech.

[51] *Id.*

[52] *See* Hanson & Yosifon, *The Situational Character, supra* note 24, at 90–106 (discussing
self, group, and system affirmation motives in human psychology).

[53] Stephen M. Bainbridge, *The Politics of Corporate Governance*, 18 HARV. J.L. & PUB. POL´Y
671, 689 (1995).

constituencies, with all parties operating in good faith every step of the way. Call this "deep capture."[54]

Without the organizational advantage of the firm, other stakeholders – and consumers in particular – cannot convene the kinds of elaborate, systematic efforts that firms deploy on behalf of their shareholders. Of course, there are ebbs and flows to corporate political influence, and corporations do not always win. Especially in hot political moments, such as during presidential elections or in times of acute social crises, dispersed groups can come together for a time and overcome the collective action disadvantages they suffer in the ordinary course. But broad public pronouncements and high-profile regulatory interventions made in hot political times are reliably followed by porous enforcement and the development of numerous loopholes when the ordinary course is resumed.[55]

The public choice problem that I have been describing is bad for society, but it is catastrophic to shareholder primacy theory, which relies on the availability of a robust regulatory system that is capable of containing the corporate excesses that shareholder primacy itself spurs. Shareholder primacy theory *might* be coherent if corporations could be restrained from influencing the political process. But in *Citizens United v. Federal Elections Commission* (2010), the Supreme Court of the United States made clear that the First Amendment forbids Congress from silencing corporate political speech.[56] As long as *Citizens United* is good constitutional law, shareholder primacy will be bad corporate theory.

THE NIGHT WATCHMAN STATE COUNTER

Leading proponents of the prevailing system do not agree that *Citizens United* poses a show-stopping problem for shareholder primacy.

---

[54] *See* Hanson & Yosifon, *The Situation, supra* note 26.

[55] *See* FRED S. MCCHESNEY, MONEY FOR NOTHING: POLITICIANS, RENT EXTRACTION, AND POLITICAL EXTORTION 140–41 (1997); *see also* Robert H. Sitkoff, *Corporate Political Speech, Political Extortion, and the Competition for Corporate Charters,* 69 U. CHI. L. REV. 1103, 1136 (2002).

[56] 130 S. Ct. 876 (2010).

Professor Stephen Bainbridge has advanced a set of responses that aim to bolster the canonical approach against this challenge.[57] For starters, Bainbridge thinks that the scale of corporate political influence is overstated. The *amount* of money being spent is just not that much. The combined spending of corporations and unions on politics pales in comparison to product advertising by corporations, he notes. This observation brings skeptics of shareholder primacy little comfort, however, as the work of that shareholder-serving commercial advertising is part of the problem we are trying to solve. Further, the reason that politics is such an attractive investment for corporations is because it is so cheap, relative to other forms of influence. The fact that corporations do not have to spend a lot to gain political influence is the problem.

Bainbridge also doubts that the regulations corporations are able to stunt through political involvement are worth having anyway. "In the absence of a showing that the benefits of foregone regulations exceed their costs, there is *no reason* to assume that corporate political spending increases the extent to which corporations can externalize costs."[58] But there *is* reason to assume that. The reason is supplied by the logic that shareholder primacy theorists have traditionally accepted: firms charged with profit maximization will seek to, and often succeed in, externalizing costs to non-shareholders. It would be great if responsive regulations were cost-effective, but whether they are or not has nothing to do with the fact that in their absence firms externalize costs to non-shareholders. Even if regulatory benefits do not exceed their costs on net, they may nevertheless

---

[57] Stephen M. Bainbridge, *Corporate Social Responsibility in the Night-Watchman State*, 115 COLUM. L. REV. SIDEBAR 39 (2015). Bainbridge's reply to these arguments was in direct response to Leo E. Strine, Jr. & Nicholas Walter, *Conservative Collision Course?: The Tension Between Conservative Corporate Law Theory and Citizens United*, 100 CORNELL L. REV. 335 (2015). I was honored (ok, thrilled) that Strine and Walter referenced my scholarship as contributing to this *Citizens United* gambit in corporate theory. *See id.* at 72 n. 189 (citing David G. Yosifon, *The Law of Corporate Purpose*, 10 BERKELEY BUS. L. J. 181, 228 (2013) and quoting David G. Yosifon, *The Public Choice Problem in Corporate Law: Corporate Social Responsibility After Citizens United*, 89 N. C. L. REV. 1197, 1237 (2011) ("shareholder primacy is not viable unless one is prepared to restrict corporate political activity").

[58] See Bainbridge, *Corporate Social Responsibility in the Night-Watchman State, supra* note 57 at 47 (emphasis added).

be justified on distributional grounds. We cannot usually just add up regulatory costs and benefits to reach anything like a math answer. The economy is too vast, and the impact of regulations too uncertain. That is why we must have theory to guide our thinking about institutional designs. After *Citizens United*, our theory must predict that under shareholder primacy, government regulations will tend to serve rather than restrict the externalizing tendencies of firms.

As to the problem of firms not just *avoiding* regulation but actually using government to *get* profit-maximizing, anti-competitive regulation, Bainbridge proposes a sweeping solution. If we are really panicked about corporations capturing regulation for their own advantage, he says, then we should just do without big government altogether, neither relying on it to curb corporate abuse nor leaving it vulnerable to corporate use. This is the "Night Watchman state," a libertarian utopia in which the state has very little authority, and, as Robert Nozick put it, is "limited to the function of protecting all its citizens against violence, theft and fraud, and to the enforcement of contract, and so on."[59] Bainbridge concludes that "even in the proverbial Night Watchman state"[60] in which corporations were free "to externalize social costs subject only to limited prohibitions on force, fraud, and the like, conservative corporate law theorists would still oppose permitting – let alone requiring – corporate directors and managers to make tradeoffs between the welfare of shareholders and that of nonshareholder constituencies."[61] To escape the *Citizens United* problem in shareholder primacy theory, Bainbridge is now content to whistle past the problem that the system's advocates had long admitted, that shareholder primacy firms have the incentive and power to exploit non-shareholding stakeholders. The "Night Watchman" move retreats to the position that it is better to have

---

[59] ROBERT NOZICK, ANARCHY, STATE, AND UTOPIA 26–27 (1974), quoted in Bainbridge, *Corporate Social Responsibility in the Night-Watchman State, supra* note 57 at 49 n. 51.

[60] *See* Bainbridge, *Corporate Social Responsibility in the Night-Watchman State, supra* note 57 at 39.

[61] *Id.*

shareholder primacy in corporate governance even if government cannot be expected to curb the excesses it inspires.[62]

But even if this kind of Night Watchman state were desirable (which I doubt), I do not think it is even possible as long as we have *Citizens United*. The public choice problem haunts shareholder primacy theory all the way down. Look at it this way: despite insisting that the state will be unobtrusive, the Night Watchman move promises that contract "fraud" will be policed. Tremendous conflict hides in this libertarian promise. Everything depends upon whether we are to have a narrow or a broad idea of what counts as fraud. Some people (and most corporations) adopt a view of human decision-making that makes it hard to conclude that someone has been defrauded, while others have a much more capacious idea of what counts as fraud. Whether you are going to have a broad or a narrow *legal* definition of fraud depends on which of these opinions is embraced by the government. The government's opinion on the matter will be subject to the influence of shareholder primacy corporations working to secure higher profits, even in a Night Watchman state, if *Citizens United* is to remain good constitutional law. And corporations will not just push their preferred definition of fraud. Shareholder primacy firms will recognize that profits can be made by pushing for the growth of government and influencing its operation. Corporations will not leave the Night Watchman to her lax rounds, but will pay her overtime to create competition-impeding regulations that yield abnormal profits at the expense of non-shareholders. The problem posed to shareholder primacy theory by *Citizens United* cannot be evaded by positing shareholder-oriented corporations operating in a Night Watchman state, because while

---

[62] Conspicuously absent from Nozick's list of the Night Watchman's duties is the provision of corporate charters. There are no corporations in the Night Watchman state if all the government does there is enforce contracts and stop fights. Henry Hansmann and Reinier Kraakman have persuasively shown that crucial attributes of corporate legal existence (most importantly, segregation of the firm's assets from the personal creditors of its shareholders) cannot be achieved through ordinary contract and property law. Henry Hansmann & Reinier Kraakman, *The Essential Role of Organizational Law*, 110 YALE L. J. 387 (2000). To have a corporation, you need corporate law. The question, then, is whether the Night Watchman should be hired on for one further task, the provision of corporate charters governed by shareholder primacy, if she is not to *also* be retained to regulate the corporations she charters.

Citizens United and shareholder primacy both reign, you will not get a Night Watchman state.[63] You will get a shareholder-centric Leviathan.[64]

THE SOCIAL RESPONSIBILITY SOLUTION, AND THE PBC NON-SOLUTION

If we cannot keep corporations out of our democracy, then we must have more democracy in our corporations. To make our corporations more socially responsible, we should alter our corporate governance law so that firms are not managed in the exclusive interests of shareholders, but instead operate under a standard that requires directors to actively attend, openly, honestly, and in good faith, to the interests of multiple stakeholders in firm governance. This standard should be mandatory for our largest corporations, while smaller businesses could continue to operate under shareholder primacy if they desire. This diversity of organizational form will ensure that stakeholder concerns are actively addressed by decision makers inside the most powerful firms, while also ensuring that experimentation and entrepreneurial verve are not compromised in the overall economy.

A multi-stakeholder corporate governance system would constrain the excesses that shareholder primacy firms exhibit both in business and in politics. Shareholder primacy pushes firms to deal sharply in the market and in politics when doing so will benefit shareholders. A multi-stakeholder standard would forbid such conduct as a matter of fiduciary duty. A multi-stakeholder governance standard would ameliorate

---

[63] This is a challenge for libertarians generally. Their insight, that a powerful state is more likely to be used to advance private interests than public ones, shows that we are likely to end up with a powerful state whether we want it or not. I asked my colleague David Friedman how anarcho-capitalists (like he) expect to get a world of limited or no government, given that their own theory predicts that self-interested individuals will find it useful to create and expand government. His reply: "It is a problem." He answered that what he understood himself, and his father before him, to be doing was generating "free knowledge" about what state power does, such that people would find it cheaper to overcome collective action problems to prevent its formation.

[64] *Cf.* Bob Dylan, *Visions of Johanna*, Blonde on Blonde (1966) ("We can hear the night watchman click his flashlight / Ask himself if it's him or them that's really insane.").

the worst problems associated with *Citizens United*, without requiring or allowing the government to censor corporate political speech. To the extent that corporations do continue to engage in political activity under a multi-stakeholder system, they will do so on behalf of numerous stakeholders, rather than for shareholders alone. Honest, searching deliberation in corporate governance about the consequence of corporate operations for multiple stakeholders might also generate knowledge that will inform the work of external regulatory institutions. If particular conflicts between corporate stakeholders can sometimes be managed at the level of firm governance, then there may even be less need for external regulation by distant bureaucrats.

I will explore this multi-stakeholder corporate governance reform proposal in detail in the final chapter, but a word must be said here about a kind of solution to the problem of shareholder primacy that will not suffice. In the last decade, many states have begun to offer charters for a new kind of business entity called the "public benefit corporation" (PBC). The PBC offers limited liability for investors and has other valuable attributes of the corporate form, but it explicitly charges directors with *balancing* the interests of shareholders and non-shareholders in corporate operations. To see the urgency of the critique and reform program pursued in this book, it must be understood that this PBC innovation is not a solution to the irresponsible social disruptions occasioned by the work of shareholder primacy corporations in our society. No state has substituted the PBC for its basic corporate law. You can now either get the conventional shareholder primacy charter, *or* you can get a PBC charter if you want one. But shareholders clearly prefer the superior profits that are available in the shareholder primacy firm to the more "balanced" profits promised by the PBC.[65] Capital is not racing, nor even crawling, to divest from shareholder primacy corporations in favor of PBCs. The PBC will not

---

[65] The fact that the capital markets evinced not the slightest shutter when Delaware adopted the PBC statute, which included a provision allowing shareholder primacy firms to become PBC's upon a 90 percent shareholder vote, nor even blinked a year later when the statute was amended to allow for adoption of PBC status by a 2/3 shareholder vote, suggests that the capital markets understood the PBC innovation to be unimportant. *See* David G. Yosifon, *Opting Out of Shareholder Primacy*, 41 DEL. J. CORP. L. 461, 499–501 (2017).

displace for-profit corporations or their socially deleterious effects.[66] We need a more serious reform if we are to ease the corporate friction in our society.

Indeed, the PBC innovation may make matters worse, by encouraging managers of for-profit firms to behave *more* rapaciously, on the theory that benefit corporations are there for shareholders who want socially responsible investing.[67] The benefit corporation model also threatens to create a "mirage" of social policy responsiveness to the problems attendant to shareholder primacy firms.[68] By appeal to this mirage, legislators can tell the public, and themselves, that they have responded to the problems associated with shareholder primacy. Already it is common to see jurists and policymakers indulge this non sequitur, pointing to the PBC when critics lament the destructive features of shareholder primacy law. In this sense, creating benefit corporations was worse than doing nothing, because if nothing had been done, at least nobody could think something significant had been done.

I will further develop and field criticism of my multi-stakeholder corporate governance reform in the final chapters. Before getting there, the next several chapters will first deepen my critical examination of shareholder primacy theory. In the next chapter, I explore in further detail the challenge that the Supreme Court's *Citizens United* decision poses to shareholder primacy theory and corporate social responsibility.

---

[66] *See, e.g.,* Kent Greenfield, *A Skeptic's View of Benefit Corporations*, 1 EMORY CORP. GOV. & ACCOUNTABILITY REV. 17 (2015); Dana Brakman Reiser, *Benefit Corporations—A Sustainable Form of Organization?*, 46 WAKE FOREST L. REV. 591 (2011) (doubting the efficacy of the public benefit corporations to respond to the problems occasioned by the operation of ordinary corporations).

[67] *See* Lyman Johnson, *Pluralism in Corporate Form*, 25 REGENT U. L. REV. 269, 295 (2013).

[68] *See* Ronald Chen & Jon Hanson, *The Illusion of Law, supra* note 26.

3   THE *CITIZENS UNITED* GAMBIT IN CORPORATE THEORY

INTRODUCTION

The last chapter showed that traditional shareholder primacy theory, by its own terms, depends upon robust government regulation to restrain the predictable externalizing tendencies of shareholder primacy firms. This is a core problem for shareholder primacy because corporate influence is endogenous to the political system. The profit imperative that makes corporations a threat in their dealings with workers, consumers, and other stakeholders, also makes them a dangerous partisan of narrow shareholder interests in the realm of government. Shareholder primacy theory cannot rely on government to restrain corporations, because shareholder primacy compels corporations to restrain government. One straightforward solution to this wrench in the works of shareholder primacy theory would be to keep corporations out of politics: allow firms to pursue profits, but forbid them from interfering in the regulatory process. But the First Amendment to the United States Constitution forbids that response, according to the Supreme Court in the *Citizens United* case.[1]

A coherent retort to this analytic dead end, for proponents of shareholder primacy, would be to insist that *Citizens United* be overturned. That would clear the way for shareholder primacy in the boardroom, backed with non-shareholder protection by the government. But the most prominent supporters of shareholder primacy do

---

[1] Citizens United v. Federal Elections Commission, 130 S. Cᴛ. 876 (2010). This chapter is based on material that was first published in David G. Yosifon, *The Public Choice Problem in Corporate Law: Corporate Social Responsibility after Citizens United*, 89 N. C. L. Rᴇᴠ. 1197 (2011).

not favor getting rid of *Citizens United*. For collateral political and theoretical reasons, supporters of shareholder primacy tend to support that decision. They do not want to invite the restrictions on free speech that overturning it would entail. I do not support shareholder primacy in corporate governance, but I, too, am opposed to overturning *Citizens United*. I think there are better ways to achieve corporate social responsibility that are more consistent with broader constitutional and moral interests in free speech.

I have two central aims in this chapter. First, I want to make the case that we should not allow government to censor corporate political speech. Then, I want to use that conclusion to build my case in favor of altering our corporate governance law from shareholder primacy to a regime that requires directors to manage firms in the interests of multiple stakeholders, not just shareholders. This reform, I argue, is both normatively desirable and constitutionally permissible. My ambition is to develop an approach to socially responsible corporate operations that does not require censure of political speech to make it work.

A STRONG PRESUMPTION IN FAVOR OF FREE SPEECH

The First Amendment does not grant the freedom of speech. It memorializes it. The principle that a human being has a fundamental right to speak and express herself is basically inseparable from commitment to the idea that a human being is a person. Speech is a core means of self-discovery and expression, and of relating to other people. It is the only legitimate means we have to establish and maintain orderly social arrangements. Either we are persuaded by speech, or we are subdued by force. Speech is "the supreme pragmatic imperative."[2] We must keep speaking, every generation to itself, and each generation to the next, if we hope to discover and maintain the will and the ways to improve this civilization. So crucial is this tool that our Constitution ordains: "Congress shall make no law ... abridging the freedom of speech."[3]

---

[2] *See* Bruce Ackerman, *Why Dialogue?*, 86 J. PHIL. 5, 10 (1989).
[3] United States Constitution, Amendment 1.

Freedom of speech must mean more than the right to talk across a campfire or shout in a public park. It must contain the right to publish and broadcast one's views – to run them in newspapers, tweet them, broadcast them over the airwaves and through the cables, and bounce them off the satellites. Some people say that "money is not speech," and therefore it does not offend free speech principles to allow the government to restrict the amount of money that can be spent on political speech, so long as speech itself is not restricted.[4] This is sophistry. Money is not speech, but money is not abortion, or a lawyer, or a gun, either. Nobody who accepts that abortion is a fundamental constitutional right would think that right was secure if the government could pass a law forbidding the spending of money to procure one. Or that the Sixth Amendment right to counsel in a criminal proceeding was not fundamentally compromised by a law prohibiting the accused from paying an attorney. Or that the Second Amendment right to keep and bear arms did not involve the right to use money to acquire them. The right to spend money to express speech is at the heart of the freedom of speech and cannot be separated from it.[5]

Despite a broad social consensus about the importance of free speech, many people believe we can and should restrain the political speech of corporations. People are incensed by the outsized power that corporations have in our political process, and they see regulation of corporate speech as a legitimate solution. I do not think that speech censorship is the right way to deal with the problem of adverse corporate influence in our government. Part of what motivates the work of this book is my frustration that the theoretical and practical failures of our corporate law are leading many Americans to doubt not the worth of shareholder primacy, but the worth of *free speech*, and maybe the whole democratic political system itself. Unfettered operation of shareholder primacy in corporate governance combined with unfettered

---

[4] Justice Stevens was sympathetic to this idea: "I have taken the view that a legislature may place reasonable restrictions on individuals' electioneering expenditures in ... recognition of the fact that such restrictions are not direct restraints on speech but rather on its financing." Citizens United, 130 S. Ct. at 972 (dissenting opinion)(internal citations and quotations omitted).

[5] *See* Buckley v. Valeo, 424 U.S. 1, 19 n. 18 (1976) ("Being free to engage in unlimited political expression subject to a ceiling on expenditures is like being free to drive an automobile as far and as often as one desires on a single tank of gasoline.").

operation of the First Amendment creates a social problem. But it is shareholder primacy that should yield, not the First Amendment. This is not to say that we must do away with corporations. To the contrary, we need them. But we can have corporations without structuring them in a way that makes them attack our democracy, or that requires us to allow censorship to stop them from doing so.

Aggravation about corporate political speech has yielded a host of bad arguments for why the government should be allowed to censor it. These arguments were developed against corporate political speech, but if they prevail, they cannot logically or practically be contained there. If accepted, in the hearts of citizens and the rulings of courts, they would countenance more expansive speech regulation and compromise core speech values. This is why I advocate a change to corporate governance law as a way of dealing with pernicious corporate operations, rather than trying to do it through speech regulation.

Citizens United v. Federal Election Commission

In 2002, Congress enacted the Bipartisan Campaign Reform Act (BCRA), which, among other things, prohibited corporations and labor unions from spending any money or broadcasting any speech in support of or against a candidate for political office within thirty days of a primary election or sixty days of a general election. The legislation did not limit campaign expenditures by natural persons.[6]

Citizens United was a non-profit corporation that received funding from business corporations. In 2008, Citizens United Productions produced a film called *Hillary: The Movie*, which was deeply critical of Hillary Rodham Clinton, who was then a United States Senator from New York. Citizens United wanted to show its film in theaters and make it available "on-demand" through cable television within thirty days of a primary election in which Senator Clinton was running (against then-Senator Barack Obama) to become the Democratic Party's candidate in the 2008 presidential election. Fearing their plans

---

[6] Bipartisan Campaign Reform Act of 2002, Pub. L. No. 107–155, §§201, 203, 116 Stat. 81, 88–89, 91 (codified at 2 U.S.C. §§434(f)(3)(A), 441b(b)(2) (2006)), invalidated by Citizens United, *supra* note 1.

would leave them vulnerable to civil and criminal penalties under BCRA, Citizens United sought a judicial ruling that BCRA could not legally be applied to them. During oral argument before the Supreme Court on this "as applied" challenge, Deputy Solicitor General Malcolm Stewart stumbled into an assertion that the government could, under proper legislation, prohibit a corporation from publishing or circulating *a book* favoring or opposing a candidate for office in advance of an election.[7] After this, the Court called for full briefing on the facial validity of the statute. Then, in a 5–4 ruling, the Court invalidated the BCRA, holding that the First Amendment forbids Congress from censoring political speech, irrespective of whether the speaker is a natural person or a corporation.[8]

We should be clear, since the matter is sometimes confused in conversations about the case, that *Citizens United* did not hold that corporations or anyone else can make unlimited cash contributions to candidates for political office. In the 1975 case of *Buckley v. Valeo*, the Supreme Court held that because exorbitant campaign *contributions* pose a genuine threat of "quid pro quo corruption," Congress could restrict such contributions without offending the First Amendment.[9] The *Citizens United* opinion does not alter this *Buckley* rule. Instead, *Citizens United* holds that the First Amendment prohibits the government from punishing corporations for spending their own money to express their own political opinions about candidates (through ads, movies, or whatever). Many people think the Court's distinction between contributions and expenditures takes too narrow a view of what can constitute "corruption." But the Court has steadfastly maintained this jurisprudential line in the sand. Our examination of arguments for and against *Citizens United* can, in a sense, be understood as an inquiry into whether that line is properly drawn.

The basic arguments made by proponents of overturning *Citizens United* and restricting corporate political speech are, first, that corporate speech is only directed at advancing corporations' narrow profit-making agenda, not the machinery of democracy, and second, that corporations gain disproportionate influence in the political arena

---

[7] *See* Transcript of Oral Argument at 27–37 (No. 08–25), Citizens United, *supra* note 1.
[8] Citizens United, 130 S. Ct. at 900.   [9] 424 U.S. 1 (1976).

because of advantages bestowed on them by the state. Because these two arguments ultimately fail to rebut the strong moral and constitutional presumption in favor of free speech, a third argument is at last convened: the government should have the power to regulate the political speech of powerful actors, whether corporate or not, in order to provide greater space for other, less powerful actors to participate in the political process. I will treat these distinct (but overlapping) arguments in serial (but overlapping) fashion.

POLITICAL SPEECH WITH A PROFIT PURPOSE

Some argue that business corporations should not enjoy First Amendment protection because their speech is always calculated only to make profit, not to contribute to the effective functioning of democracy. This critique reflects a hallowed idea in our political tradition called the "norm of public reason." The idea is that for a pluralistic, liberal democracy to function effectively, we must have not just robust political speech, but a particular kind of ethical, restrained political speech. Political speakers must restrict themselves to only advancing positions on political matters that they sincerely believe to be in the "public interest" generally, rather than fighting for positions that would only advance their personal interests or worldview.[10] The norm of public reason enjoins us to articulate and defend our public policy positions with reference to areas of overlapping consensus among different outlooks. Widespread adherence to this norm is crucial to generating *acceptance* of the democratic process and democratic outcomes, especially in a heterogeneous society such as ours. And none of this can be mere acting. For civic discourse to be believable, listeners must be disposed to think that others are speaking to them sincerely and not secretly preferring a policy only because it advances their sectarian agenda.

   Shareholder primacy firms cannot comply with the norm of public reason because they must always support a point of view that is in the interests of their shareholders, irrespective of the consequence to other

---

[10] Ackerman, *supra* note 2 at 17.

groups or the nation as a whole. Because the norm of public reason (as a *principle*) is so strong in the American political tradition, firms do speak *as if* they are adhering to it. Indeed, they often do so more scrupulously than natural people. For example, as worry about an American "obesity epidemic" spread in the early years of this century, junk food corporations spent millions of dollars to fund political speech through advocacy groups, advertising, and lobbying efforts in order to forestall a profit-leveling public policy response to the problem.[11] In these efforts, the industry did not argue against restrictive junk food regulations on the grounds that they would harm shareholders. Instead, the industry adopted a public interest idiom focused on the idea that restrictions on junk food purveyance would undermine individual responsibility and diminish consumer choice.[12] Corporations are good at maintaining the appearance of propriety in their political speech precisely because, unlike natural people, they do not actually care about the issues. Indeed, if directors were to spend corporate money to express political views because they were concerned about the public interest, *that* speech would be illegitimate from a corporate law perspective, at least when such speech conflicts with the interests of shareholders. There may sometimes be harmony between the public interest and the shareholder interest, but such coincidence does not satisfy the sincerity requirement in the norm of public reason.

The juxtaposition of this professed public spirit in corporate political speech, with the bias that we otherwise know corporations have, is particularly galling. It generates cynicism about both corporations and politics.[13] Corporate political speech thus impoverishes the mission of civic discourse, just to advance the firm's mission of profitability.

---

[11] *See generally* MARION NESTLE, FOOD POLITICS: HOW THE FOOD INDUSTRY INFLUENCES NUTRITION, AND HEALTH (Darra Goldstein ed., 2002) (reviewing efforts to influence food regulation); MICHELE SIMON, APPETITE FOR PROFIT (2006) (reviewing food industry influence on political process).

[12] *See* Adam Benforado, Jon Hanson, & David Yosifon, *Broken Scales: Obesity and Justice in America*, 53 EMORY L. J. 1645, 1769–1802 (2004); David Burnett, *Fast-Food Lawsuits and the Cheeseburger Bill: Critiquing Congress's Response to the Obesity Epidemic*, 14 VA. J. SOC. POL'Y & L. 357, 365 (2007).

[13] It may be that the obviousness of this hypocrisy in corporate political speech exposes the implausibility of the norm of public reason in political discourse more generally. We know that corporations only speak to advance private interest, regardless of what they actually say, and we then assume, maybe correctly, that natural people do the same thing. In an

But what are you going to do about it?

The First Amendment does not prescribe the norm of public reason or protect only speech that complies with it. If it did, the country would be quiet indeed. A lot of political speech by natural persons is undertaken for selfish reasons, often just to make a buck. The profit motive is the "but-for" cause of a great deal of valuable political speech. Many authors would not write books or articles, or speakers give keynote addresses, without it. As Dr. Johnson said: "No man but a blockhead ever wrote, except for money."[14] The profit-not-public-interest argument for censoring corporate speech proves too much.

Perhaps the norm of public reason is the best kind of speech for a democracy. But nonsense is better than censorship. The Devil himself, by speaking his lies, can help discerning listeners to better understand the nature of truth, morality, or sound fiscal policy. Who but a chump could trust that God's ways were best if Satan were forbidden to state his case? Speech may be valuable to the *listener*, in forming her own opinions about what to think and value, irrespective of the identity or motive of the speaker.

The Supreme Court adopted this "listener interests" view of the First Amendment in an important corporate political speech case decided long before *Citizens United*. In *First National Bank of Boston v. Bellotti* (1978), a 5–4 decision, the Court struck down a Massachusetts statute forbidding business corporations from making campaign expenditures in referendum elections. In that case, the Court said it was unnecessary to decide whether corporations "have" First Amendment rights. The statute was unconstitutional because the state was seeking to silence speech about political matters, precisely the kind of speech that

important article, Dan Kahan argues that the problem with the norm of public reason is that as a cognitive matter, we humans cannot really pull it off. *See* Dan M. Kahan, *The Cognitively Illiberal State*, 60 STAN. L. REV. 115 (2007). We all process policy debates through the biased cognitive frameworks dictated by our "world-views" (i.e., our private "preferences about how society should be organized"). Since we are cognitively incapable of conforming to the norm of public reason, even good-faith efforts to conform to it only antagonize our opponents, who must contend not only with an adversary whose world-view they oppose, but also an adversary who fails to see the relationship between their worldview and the polices they support. This antagonizes social strife.

[14] JAMES BOSWELL, THE LIFE OF SAMUEL JOHNSON 529 (David Womersley ed., 2008) (1791).

the First Amendment was meant to keep free from state censure. What is crucial is not so much that corporations have the right to speak, but rather that the government does not have the right to silence.[15]

CORPORATIONS BENEFIT FROM ADVANTAGES BESTOWED BY THE STATE

Another justification that is given for restricting corporate political speech is that corporations are creatures of the state, and the advantages bestowed on them by the state give them a disproportionate, distorting power in the political arena. Since it is the government's action that leads to this distortion, the government should be able to cure it by restricting corporate political activity.

The Supreme Court actually adopted this idea in 1990, in *Austin v. Michigan State Chamber of Commerce*,[16] a case that followed *Bellotti* but preceded *Citizens United*. In a 6–3 decision, the Court let stand a Michigan statute forbidding corporations from spending money "in support of, or in opposition to, any candidate in elections for state office."[17] The Michigan Chamber of Commerce, which challenged the prohibition, was a non-profit corporation, funded by for-profit corporations. Justice Thurgood Marshall wrote for the majority that states had a legitimate interest in stemming "the corrosive and distorting effects of immense aggregations of wealth that are accumulated with

---

[15] A variant on the "profit motive" justification for limiting speech is the "foreign motive" justification or, combining the two, the "foreign profit motive" justification. Many American corporations have a substantial foreign shareholder base. Critics say that allowing foreign interests to participate in American elections disrupts the domestic political process. Such concerns were academic when *Citizens United* was decided, but the problem has become an acute concern since evidence of Russian interference in the 2016 American presidential election has come to light.

Professor Richard Hasen, a leading authority on election law, predicts the Supreme Court will *not* hold that the First Amendment forbids the government from restricting foreign spending on domestic politics, despite the contradiction this would pose to the "listener interests" pillar of the Court's First Amendment jurisprudence. *See* Richard Hasen, *Citizens United and the Illusion of Coherence*, 109 MICH. L. REV. 581 (2011).

[16] Austin v. Mich. State Chamber of Commerce, 494 U.S. 652, 656 (1989).

[17] *Id.* at 654.

the help of the corporate form and that have little or no correlation to the public's support for the corporation's political ideas."[18]

This justification is superficially enticing. But the free speech gag reflex kicks in before it goes all the way down. It is true that corporations are powerful because of state conferred advantages. But state conferred benefits are widespread. Many speakers enjoy economic advantages stemming from, for example, inheritance laws, the home mortgage interest deduction, or access to courts for contract enforcement. The government grants patents that make it easier to produce typewriters, computers, microphones, and amplifiers. A state-conferred benefits justification for restricting corporate political speech would justify a lot of speech regulation that had little or nothing to do with corporations.

The government may sometimes condition the grant of benefits on the recipient agreeing to comply with regulatory commands or restrictions that compromise core interests. The Supreme Court's rule on this is that the government can condition benefits on a waiver of rights only where the demand for the waiver is closely related to achieving the government's legitimate purpose in granting the benefit.[19] For example, the federal government can condition highway construction grants on a state's willingness to limit speeds on their highways to a specified standard. This is a legitimate condition of the grant because the speed limit is reasonably related to the government's purpose in funding highways: the creation of safe, efficient, interstate travel. But the government could not condition use of the highways on a traveler's willingness to keep political bumper stickers off of their vehicles. Similarly, requiring the forfeiture of hallowed free speech rights is not related to any legitimate purpose that the government has in granting corporate charters. The government's purpose in chartering firms is to facilitate productive business enterprise, or maybe just to fill its coffers with chartering fees. Prohibiting political speech does not advance these goals. It thus violates the "unconstitutional conditions" doctrine

---

[18] Austin, 494 U.S. at 660.

[19] *See* International Development v. Alliance for Open Society International, Inc., 133 S. Ct. 2321 (2013) (adumbrating unconstitutional conditions doctrine).

for the government to condition the grant of a corporate charter on a willingness not to engage in political speech.[20]

If you are not convinced, consider that many media entities are organized as business corporations. For example, the *New York Times*, CNN (a subsidiary of Time Warner, Inc.), Fox News (News Corp.), Facebook, and Twitter are all publicly traded corporations. The government-conferred advantage argument would allow the state to regulate the political speech of these organizations. A special First Amendment status for the institutional press, if it ever was plausible, no longer makes any sense, given that many Americans get their news predominately, or even exclusively, from social media companies. Political organizations, such as the NAACP, NOW, and the NRA, are organized as non-profit corporations and enjoy state-conferred benefits, including limited liability to members for the debts of their organizations, the right to hold and sell property, and tax advantages. The First Amendment would be a weak guard against censorship if outfits such as these could be silenced on the grounds that they enjoy the benefits of state-conferred corporate status. The government does not have to allow corporations to exist, but having occasioned their existence, it cannot censor the political messages they express.

Austin stood on clay feet and *Citizens United* explicitly overturned it. Incredibly, or tellingly, in arguing the *Citizens United* case, the Obama administration's lawyers largely abandoned *Austin*'s "state conferred benefits" justification and instead focused on two other arguments: a narrow "shareholder protection" justification for limiting corporate speech, claiming that the government had a legitimate interest in protecting *shareholders* from wasteful or disloyal spending of their assets on political campaigns, and a very broad argument that government should have the prerogative to regulate corporate speech in order to keep it from overwhelming the discursive environment and wrecking the sound operation of the market in social and political ideas. The former can be dealt with quickly. The latter will take more doing.

---

[20] *See* Citizens United, 130 S. Ct. at 905 ("It is rudimentary that the State cannot exact as the price of those special advantages the forfeiture of First Amendment rights.") (internal citations omitted).

From a corporate law perspective, the idea that shareholders need to be protected from corporate political spending is nonsense. Corporations spend money on politics for the same reason they assay land for its mineral content: they are trying to make money. If shareholders were harmed by corporate political speech, then we would expect firms looking to raise capital to promise in their charter that they would not do it. We would expect to see shareholders pushing bylaws forbidding firms from spending money on political speech. There has been some gadfly shareholder activism of that sort, but it has not attracted widespread support among capital investors. Shareholders of any one firm, and shareholders as a class, are not interested in binding their agents' hands (or tongues, as it were). Corporate political speech tends to benefit shareholders, not harm them. Where directors spend on behalf of candidates who are family members or friends, or on behalf of causes that are pet projects unrelated to the corporate purpose, then corporate law provides a remedy through loyalty suits that put the onus on directors to show that such spending was in the corporate interest. And such regulation poses no First Amendment problem.

CORPORATE POLITICAL SPEECH IS OVERPOWERING

Having failed to find a corporation-specific justification for curbing corporate political speech, what remains is the claim that the speech of the powerful, whether corporation or not, should be subject to restriction in order to keep them from dominating the discursive playing field. The logical thrust of this argument is powerful. Humans are finite creatures. We have limited cognitive capacity, limited strength, and a limited time on Earth. We can only take in and make sense of a discrete amount of stimuli. Our voices can be drowned out by other voices around us, and our minds can be overwhelmed if one speaker or group can dominate a space or time to the exclusion of other speakers. The First Amendment is meant to enable individual and group expression, and to engender the robust production and circulation of ideas that are useful to a well-functioning, free, and democratic society. Given the scarcity that plagues the human cognitive condition, these aims are frustrated if some speakers can overwhelm others.

Justice Stevens captured this idea in his dissenting opinion in *Citizens United.* He wrote: "All of the majority's theoretical arguments turn on a proposition with undeniable surface appeal but little grounding in evidence or experience, 'that there is no such thing as too much speech.'"[21] He continues:

> If individuals in our society had infinite free time to listen to and contemplate every last bit of speech uttered by anyone, anywhere ... then I suppose the majority's premise would be sound. In the real world, we have seen, corporate domination of the airwaves prior to an election may decrease the average listener's exposure to relevant viewpoints, and it may diminish citizens' willingness and capacity to participate in the democratic process.[22]

In Chapter 2, I insisted that in analyzing corporate theory we must use a realistic picture of human decision-making, one that is sensitive to the limitations of human cognition and decision-making. We surely cannot just abandon such critical realism in thinking through First Amendment theory.

But what are you going to do about it?

Justice Stevens knows what he would do, and what he would allow. In his *Citizens United* dissent, Stevens embraced the view that the government should be permitted to restrain the speech of disproportionately powerful speakers *irrespective* of whether they were natural people or corporations. He wrote:

> legitimate and substantial government interests can justify the imposition of reasonable limitations on the expenditures permitted

---

[21] Citizens United, 130 S. Ct. at 975 (Stevens, J., concurring and dissenting) (quoting Austin, 494 U.S. at 695 (Scalia, J., dissenting)). First Amendment law in a few narrow places is responsive to the problem of scarcity and drown out. For example, states can limit ballot access to candidates with a bona fide chance of winning an election, and state-run television can broadcast campaign debates that allow only candidates with substantial support to take part. *See* Ark. Ed. Television Comm'n v. Forbes, 523 U.S. 666 (1998) (upholding restrictions allowed on televised debates). The government can also impose content-neutral, and speaker-neutral, time, place, and manner restrictions. It does not violate the First Amendment, for example, for the government to stop anyone (as long as it is anyone) from blasting loudspeakers in open space at all hours or covering every inch of land with billboards. *See* Rowan v. U.S. Post Office Dep't, 397 U.S. 728, 738 (1970) ("[N]o one has a right to press even 'good' ideas on an unwilling recipient.").

[22] Citizens United, 130 S. Ct. at 975–76 (Stevens, J., concurring and dissenting)

during the course of any single campaign... In my judgment, such limitations may be justified to the extent they are tailored to 'improving the quality of the exposition of ideas' that voters receive, 'free[ing] candidates and their staffs from the interminable burden of fundraising,' and 'protect[ing] equal access to the political arena.'[23]

Coherence is only hard where it must conform with principle.

Our society evinces vast disparities in power, along many dimensions. Some people are well connected, others are isolated. Some are smart and articulate. Others are not as smart, and are less articulate. Power disparities are born of genes, the Creator, or luck. There are historic inequities in the distribution of power along race, gender, age, and other categories, that lend the power of privilege to the speech of some speakers and muffle the speech of others. These power dynamics are every bit as real as the advantages of the corporate charter, inherited money, or other prerogatives, and the views of those, like Justice Stevens, who would allow government to restrict political speech based on wealth and institutional advantage, would also countenance the limitation of speech based on the disproportionate social, cultural, or ideological power of a speaker.

The point is not just that the censoring response to disparities in discursive power fails to admit of a limiting principle. Just as worrisome is that if provisional limiting principles are subject to ordinary political processes, ordinary public choice dynamics will infect their operation. Once the state is empowered to censor as a mode of ordinary regulation, that censoring power will undoubtedly be deployed not to enhance the voices of the relatively powerless, but rather to consolidate the prerogatives of the powerful. A government that is broadly authorized to restrict speech will exercise that power on behalf of those who can most effectively influence government. This is why it is so crucial that free expression be understood as a pre-political right that is merely codified as a constitutional principle.

The religious speak of a leap of faith. In that domain, for myself, I am always toeing the edge, measuring the wind, waiting to decide. On that precipice, it seems to me, there is no rush to decide. Indeed,

---

[23] Citizens United, 130 S. Ct. at 963 n. 65 (internal citations and quotations omitted).

it seems that a rushed leap of faith is no leap of faith at all. But the institutional design of civilization waits on no such contemplation. A leap of faith must be made to the principle of free speech, despite the incoherence of the psychological presumptions pulling on the ankle, or else we stay and take our chances against Leviathan already thundering over the hill with its regulatory force. "One fast move or I'm gone," Kerouac wrote in *Big Sur*.[24] The power of speech prohibition is too great to give to the government.[25] It would therefore be prudent to search for another solution to the problem of corporate influence in government.

IMPLICATIONS FOR CORPORATE THEORY

One of the strange things in Justice Stevens's dissent in *Citizens United*, and in popular opposition to the case, is the implicit assumption that the *only* thing Congress can do to protect democracy from being hijacked by corporate power is to stem corporate political speech. That is not true. If corporations are behaving in a socially destructive way, government has many avenues available to it other than speech regulation to solve that problem. Congress could forbid corporations altogether. Congress could tax corporate operations until capital, labor, and consumers prefer to deal with each other through common law partnerships rather than through the corporate form. The problem with those kinds of solutions to the problem of corporate political influence is that we do not want to lose the jobs-and-goods producing capacities that corporations can provide.

---

[24] JACK KEROUAC, BIG SUR 7 (1962).

[25] *See* Martin H. Redish & Howard M. Wasserman, *What's Good for General Motors: Corporate Speech and the Theory of Free Expression*, 66 GEO. WASH. L. REV. 235, 290 (1988) ("[O]ne cannot construe the First Amendment to allow the government conclusively to determine either how citizens process information or when the fear of an information overload dictates a need for governmental intervention."). In an early article of mine, I repudiated Redish and Wasserman's view, criticizing it for it refusal to confront the reality of the human psychological predicament. *See* David Yosifon, *Resisting Deep Capture: The Commercial Speech Doctrine and Junk Food Advertising to Children*, 39 LOY. L.A. L. REV. 507, 599–601 (2006). As is clear in the text, I am less confident now that such concerns should license censorship. *Cf.* Bob Dylan, *My Back Pages*, on ANOTHER SIDE OF BOB DYLAN (1964) ("I was so much older then, I'm younger than that now.").

There is, however, a way of dealing with the troubling political squawks of the Golden Goose that neither requires silencing it nor slitting its throat. We can instead teach the corporate bird to sing a more melodious – or rather, a more harmonious – tune. We should replace shareholder primacy with a system of multi-stakeholder governance that can reign in socially destructive corporate behavior without overturning *Citizens United*.

CONSTITUTIONAL CONSTRAINTS ON MULTI-STAKEHOLDER GOVERNANCE

I will address critiques of multi-stakeholder corporate governance when I fully explore that alternative design in the final chapter. However, in light of the First Amendment focus here, I want to say a word about the constitutionality of a multi-stakeholder system before concluding this chapter.

The reader may have noted (and if not, I will now admit) that my overall argument so far employs two distinct ways of thinking about speech and influence that are at least in some tension with each other. When it comes to corporate theory, I insist that shareholder primacy falters because "powerful" corporations will "capture" government to stem the regulatory architecture that shareholder primacy theory itself insists is necessary to curb corporate "manipulation" of non-shareholders. I therefore conclude that as a matter of social policy, we should use a different, more directly socially responsible corporate governance standard. On the other hand, when it comes to *constitutional* theory, I embrace the "listener interests" idea that speech is (or can be) socially valuable irrespective of who is speaking it, or why they are speaking it. I also claim that giving government the authority to censor speakers because they are "powerful" would undermine, rather than advance, First Amendment values, and would ultimately result in speech regulation that aids the strong, not the weak. It is interesting to note this tension between how public choice theory thinks about power and influence and how First Amendment theory thinks about it. But I think there is ultimately no deep contradiction here. We should care about the kind of speech we are making. Just because no speech should be censored does not mean that all speech should be encouraged, or that we should be indifferent to the kind of speech that our institutional design is creating. It is precisely because of the problem of cognitive scarcity, coupled with the commitment to not censor any speech, that we should care very much about what kind of speech our institutional designs are encouraging. We can and should think very carefully when creating our economic and business entities about how they will interact with our core constitutional values, so that we are not tempted to compromise those core values when bad business structures begin exploiting them.

The winds that set the *Citizens United* ship to sail would not sink an effort to impose multi-stakeholder governance commands on large business corporations. Government does not have the authority to censor political speech, regardless of who is uttering it. On the other hand, I think the government does have, and should have, the authority to dictate the structure and purpose of corporate governance when granting corporate charters to business firms. While the government cannot condition the grant of a charter on a firm's willingness to stay silent on political matters, the government can condition the charter on the firm using a prescribed mode of governance. This is a subtle, but principled, and jurisprudentially sound distinction.

The federal government already extensively regulates corporate governance standards for large publicly traded companies. For example, the Sarbanes-Oxley reforms of 2002 impose on all publicly traded corporations the requirement that the audit committee of the board of directors be composed *completely* of independent directors who do not work for the company in any other capacity. The same regulation grants such audit committees *exclusive* governance authority over the firm's financial audits.[26] Sarbanes-Oxley also prompted the national stock exchanges to develop governance standards that

---

[26] *See generally* Roberta S. Karmel, *Realizing the Dream of William O. Douglas – The Securities and Exchange Commission Takes Charge of Corporate Governance*, 30 Del. J. Corp. L. 79 (2005).

require all publicly traded companies to have their boards composed of a majority of independent directors. Commentators debate the wisdom of these rules, but nobody has raised a serious claim that they violate any constitutional free speech or association rights. State law also imposes *mandatory* governance rules on business corporations. Delaware, for example, forbids firms from including provisions in their charter that would excuse directors from having to pay money damages for violations of the duty of loyalty, as the state defines that duty.[27] These rules do not offend constitutional protections, and neither would a multi-stakeholder governance standard imposed on large business firms. Under my multi-stakeholder governance proposal, there is no demand that any constitutional right be turned over in exchange for a charter, let alone one that is unrelated to the government's purpose in offering charters. A multiple-stakeholder system imposes a fiduciary norm aimed at promoting socially useful business activity, without censoring political speech.

With respect to expressive associations and corporations formed to advance the aims of such associations, the situation must be different. Organizations that are formed to advance associational interests, such as pursuing civic or legal reforms, advancing ideological, spiritual, or intellectual agendas, or celebrating communal affinity, have a constitutional right to associate for such purposes.[28] Strict multi-stakeholder governance prescription could not, and should not, be imposed on expressive associations, even if they are organized through the corporate form, as many are. It would impose an unconstitutional condition to require associational groups to compromise their self-determination in exchange for the corporate charter, since the very purpose of

---

[27] *See* 8 DEL. GEN. CORP. L. § 102(b)(7).

[28] *See* Hosanna-Tabor Evangelical Lutheran Church and School v. Equal Opportunity Employment Commission, 132 S. Ct. 694 (2012) (First Amendment right of free association protected Church from being forced to rehire a minister that the government claimed it had fired in violation of the anti-retaliatory discharge provisions of the Americans with Disabilities Act); Boy Scouts of America v. Dale, 120 S.Ct. 2446 (2000) (holding unconstitutional a New Jersey law forbidding discrimination against gay people as applied to a civic association with anti-gay beliefs, because "[f]orcing a group to accept certain members may impair [its ability] to express those views, and only those views, that it intends to express.").

imposing such a restriction would be to constrain or alter the efficacy of the associational activity as the group defines it.[29]

---

[29] The right that expressive associations enjoy to determine their membership and governance structure does not involve a constitutional right to be free from other generally applicable laws that would bear on the organization's activity. *See* Employment Division, Dept. of Human Resources of Oregon v. Smith, 110 S. Ct. 1595 (1990). In some cases, however, statutory protections do provide for exemptions from laws that would substantially burden an organization's sincerely held religious commitments. Such exemptions could be maintained in the corporate governance reforms I am advocating here. *See* Burwell v. Hobby Lobby Stores, Inc., 134 S. Ct. 2751 (2014). Hobby Lobby successfully argued that the Religious Freedom Restoration Act (RFRA) entitled it to an exemption from elements of a health care law (the provision of abortion-inducing birth control to its employees) that substantially burdened its religious obligations. In Chapter 8, I argue that the multi-stakeholder system should, anyway, only be applied to very large corporations, so most hybrid, religiously oriented firms would not be touched by it. The Hobby Lobby corporation, a large, religiously oriented firm, is an anomaly both among large firms and among religious firms.

4   THE ACTUAL LAW OF CORPORATE PURPOSE

"[T]he shareholder wealth maximization norm ... indisputably is the law in the United States."[1]

– Stephen M. Bainbridge

"The notion that corporate law requires directors ... to maximize shareholder wealth simply isn't true."[2]

– Lynn Stout

INTRODUCTION

So far, I have been concerned with critiquing shareholder primacy theory, and subsequent chapters will deepen that critique and explore alternative corporate law designs. In this chapter, I want to make clear that my critique is directed at the system of corporate governance that actually does prevail in the United States today.[3]

Some readers may be surprised to learn that there is controversy over what the law of corporate purpose *is* in the United States. Many scholars take it as given that corporate boards are supposed to pursue profits for shareholders and that directors have neither the obligation nor the right to pursue other interests. This view also seems to be widely accepted in broader social and political discourse about corporate operations. Readers of corporate law scholarship, however, are

---

[1] STEPHEN M. BAINBRIDGE, THE NEW CORPORATE GOVERNANCE IN THEORY AND PRACTICE 53 (2008).

[2] LYNN STOUT, THE SHAREHOLDER VALUE MYTH: HOW PUTTING SHAREHOLDERS FIRST HARMS INVESTORS, CORPORATIONS, AND THE PUBLIC 29 (2012).

[3] This chapter is based on material that was first published as David G. Yosifon, *The Law of Corporate Purpose*, 10 BERKELEY BUS. L. J. 181 (2013).

continually confronted with the claim, voiced by some of the field's most accomplished academics, that the law allows directors to steer the corporate ship in service of non-shareholding stakeholders, including employees, consumers, and the public generally, even when shareholder interests are compromised by such pursuits. Social activists also sometimes proffer the view that corporate law does not require directors to advance only the shareholder interest. Getting this point wrong does not help their cause. It impedes it.

The normative agenda of this book is to critique and replace shareholder primacy law. But no reformative project can be coherent or effective unless it first accurately describes the state of the world as it is. Confusion in our literature about the law of corporate purpose in the United States is not just embarrassing, it is disempowering.[4]

In this chapter, I endeavor to clarify what the law of corporate purpose is, and to explain the missteps that other scholars have made in interpreting this doctrine, in order to help advance conversations about what the law of corporate purpose ought to be. Scholars who think the law *is* shareholder primacy tend also to believe that shareholder primacy is desirable.[5] Scholars who believe the law *is* that directors need not always put shareholders first tend to think that multi-stakeholder governance is preferable. It would be reasonable to suspect that there might be some motivated reasoning going on in these two camps. I am somewhat of an outlier in thinking that shareholder primacy *is* the law but that it should not be.[6] My thinking is therefore

---

[4] While scholars and activists get this issue wrong, business lawyers usually get it right. *See, e.g.,* CHRISTOPHER M. FORRESTER & CELESTE S. FERBER, FIDUCIARY DUTIES AND OTHER RESPONSIBILITIES OF CORPORATE DIRECTORS AND OFFICERS 9 (5th ed. 2012) (a handbook produced by Morrison & Foerster, LLP, for use by its corporate clients, stating: "One of the most difficult tasks for a board ... is to balance the competing interests of multiple constituents of a business... The difficulty arises when decisions do not affect all parties equally... [T]here is a clear legal answer to the question: a corporation's board and management owe a fiduciary duty as their primary obligation, above all others, to the stockholders, to maximize the value of the equity of the corporation.").

[5] Scholars who believe that shareholder primacy is the law typically treat the proposition as self-evident and do not rigorously make the case for it in their scholarship. *See* Stout, THE SHAREHOLDER VALUE MYTH, *supra* note 2, at 115 (collecting prominent examples of this). This chapter therefore also serves to flesh out an important, but unproven, premise in such scholarship.

[6] I agree with the Chief Justice of the Delaware Supreme Court, Leo Strine, who put it simply in a recent law review article: "Directors must make stockholder welfare their sole

completely objective and free of the distorting influence of subconscious bias.[7]

I focus here exclusively on Delaware law because, for reasons described in Chapter 1, Delaware dominates the corporate landscape in the United States.

THE STATUTE ITSELF IS UNCLEAR

Corporations are created by statute. To find the purpose of Delaware corporations, therefore, it would seem appropriate to look at Delaware's statute. Unfortunately, the statute provides no crisp declaration on this point. It does require that every firm's articles of incorporation must "set forth ... the nature of the business or purposes to be conducted or promoted."[8] However, this requirement can be satisfied if the articles state "either alone or with other business purposes, that the purpose of the corporation is to engage in any lawful act or activity for which corporations may be organized."[9] So, while the code feints towards clarity by requiring a statement of purpose, it lands with obscurity by allowing the purpose to be stated generally as the pursuit of "any lawful act." In fact, most business corporations use this "any lawful act" language in the purpose section of their charter.[10]

---

end." Leo E. Strine, Jr., *The Dangers of Denial: The Need for a Clear-Eyed Understanding of the Power and Accountability Structure Established by the Delaware General Corporation Law,* 50 WAKE FOREST L. REV. 761, 768 (2015).

[7] Of course, my whole project of repudiating shareholder primacy and arguing for multistakeholder governance reforms would be pretty pointless if the law was not presently shareholder primacy. So, be skeptical of me along with everyone else.

[8] 8 DEL. GEN. CORP. L. § 102(a)(3).   [9] *Id.*

[10] David Millon has argued that, historically, corporate law statutes did not speak to corporate purpose because they were formulated against a business background in which firms were closely held by shareholders who were actively in control of corporate operations. It was unnecessary for the statute to say what should be done with corporations, because the shareholders could say so for themselves. This explains the absence of clear purpose in the corporate statute and highlights the need for the authority of the "gap filling" case law that Delaware courts have undertaken to provide a default law of corporate purpose for modern firms with dispersed shareholders who do not control the firm. *See* David Millon, *Two Models of Corporate Social Responsibility,* 46 WAKE FOREST L. REV. 523 (2011).

Once a corporation is formed, the code requires that it be managed: "The business and affairs of every corporation organized under this chapter *shall be managed* by or under the direction of a board of directors."[11] But what should the directors of a corporation formed to undertake "any lawful act" do with the firm they command? Should they undertake lawful acts in a random fashion, without intent to serve any particular interest? Or may directors run the firm with the purpose of serving beneficiaries of their own choosing?

Indirectly, the Delaware code indicates that directors owe fiduciary duties to the corporation and its stockholders. I say indirectly, because the only explicit reference to this obligation comes in a section of the statute, adopted in 1986, stating that "the certificate of incorporation may also contain ... a provision eliminating or limiting the personal liability of a director to the corporation or its stockholders for monetary damages for breach of fiduciary duty."[12] This section also *forbids* charter terms limiting personal liability "for any breach of the director's duty of loyalty to the corporation or its stockholders" or "for acts or omissions not in good faith."[13] (Disinterested transactions may thus be exculpated from liability, but not interested transactions). This language implies that directors *do*, by default, owe fiduciary obligations of care, loyalty, and good faith to the corporation and its stockholders.[14]

But to say that a person owes fiduciary obligations is only the start of a meaningful conversation, it does not conclude it.[15] What *goal* is the fiduciary to pursue on behalf of the corporation and its stockholders carefully, loyally, and in good faith? The statute does not specify. We are not told whether it is profits, profits with a conscience, profits balanced against the interests of other parties, short-term profits, long-term profits, or something else. All we know from the statute is that directors owe the corporation and its stockholders fiduciary

---

[11] 8 Del. Gen. Corp. L. § 141(a).   [12] *Id.* at § 102(b)(7).   [13] *Id.*

[14] Even if a charter contains an exculpation provision, the duties themselves are not obviated. It is just that one is excused from paying money damages for a breach.

[15] *See* Securities and Exchange Commission v. Chenery Corp., 318 U.S. 80, 85 (Frankfurter, J.) ("[T]o say that a man is a fiduciary only begins analysis; it gives direction to further inquiry. To whom is he a fiduciary? What obligations does he owe as a fiduciary?").

obligations. Fortunately, a rich body of case law deepens the conversation and gives answers.

CASE LAW

I am explaining Delaware law, but no review of corporate purpose can be properly undertaken without at least a ceremonial first pitch from the venerable old Michigan case of *Dodge v. Ford.*[16] In the first fifteen years of its existence, the Ford Motor Company was hugely successful and paid tens of millions of dollars in dividends to its stockholders. In 1916, however, Henry Ford, the majority stockholder, chairman, and dominant personage of the company, announced that the firm would no longer pay discretionary dividends. Instead, profits would be reinvested in the company for the avowed purpose of increasing wages for workers and lowering prices for consumers. "My ambition," Ford declared, "is to employ still more men, to spread the benefits of this industrial system to the greatest possible number, to help them build up their lives and their homes."[17] The Dodge brothers, minority shareholders in the company, sued Ford for violating his fiduciary obligations to them. The Michigan Supreme Court famously admonished Ford:

> A business corporation is organized and carried on primarily for the profit of the shareholders. The powers of the directors are to be employed for that end. The discretion of directors is to be exercised in the choice of means to attain that end, and does not extend to a change in the end itself.[18]

The Michigan Court cited no statute or case law for this decisive statement about its corporate law. It is as if they considered it obvious.

This quote from the *Dodge* case is familiar to just about anyone who has taken a class in corporate law.[19] The lines have been cited in the law review literature more than 800 times. However, *Dodge* has been cited only sixty-eight times by subsequent state and federal courts. It

---

[16] 170 N.W. 668 (Mich. 1919).   [17] *Id.* at 683.   [18] *Id.*
[19] *But see* Lynn A. Stout, *Why We Should Stop Teaching Dodge v. Ford,* 3 VA. L. & BUS. REV. 163 (2008). I address Stout's arguments below.

has been cited just three times, and never for the crucial issue of corporate purpose, in Delaware cases. It is a decision about *Michigan* corporate law, and Michigan corporate law is today not even very important in Michigan. The Ford Motor Company is itself now a Delaware corporation. *Dodge* is a great case because of its interesting facts and elegant language. And it does express the rule that also binds Delaware directors. But it is not a great *doctrinal* reference for Delaware law.

Ceremony concluded, then, let us turn to the most important Delaware cases on this issue. Many Delaware cases, old and new, give language stating that directors have a duty to pursue the interests of shareholders. But only a few cases have litigated the issue of whether directors are allowed to balance shareholder interests against the interests of other stakeholders. The touchstone jurisprudence on this question comes from a series of "hostile takeover" cases from the 1980s. (A hostile takeover involves an effort by one entity – or person – to gain control of a "target" corporation against the wishes of the target's incumbent board of directors.) Hostile takeovers present myriad legal questions. For our purposes, what is most important is the occasion these cases provide for courts to clarify the nature of directors' obligations, and, specifically, whether or not directors may sacrifice shareholder value in favor of other interests.

The first and most mischievous case in this line (for what it has been *misread* to have said about corporate purpose) was *Unocal v. Mesa Petroleum Co.* in 1985.[20] The oil magnate T. Boone Pickens, through his Mesa corporation, sought to gain control of Unocal, Inc., an oil company, by appealing directly to Unocal's shareholders and inviting them to tender their stock to him.[21] Unocal's board believed Mesa's tender offer was inadequate and coercive, despite the fact that it offered

---

[20] 493 A.2d 946 (Del. 1985).

[21] Mesa's tender offer was "structurally coercive," in that Mesa made clear that once it gained control of the firm it would "cash-out" any remaining shareholders at a price lower than what it was offering to gain control of the firm. Since nobody wanted to be caught getting less on the "back end" if Mesa succeeded in gaining control, all shareholders had an incentive to tender their shares on the "front end." The "coercive" nature of the Mesa threat was important to the Court's conclusion that Unocal's board should have the discretion to disrupt Mesa's offer. However, in later cases, the Court would give boards latitude to resist hostile takeovers even where the threat was not "structurally" coercive but

a premium over the prevailing stock price, because the board itself was bullish on the *long-term* prospects of the company under its own management. The Delaware Supreme Court was called on to decide whether it was permissible for Unocal's board to deploy aggressive, costly measures to stymie Mesa's takeover bid. The Court concluded that anti-takeover measures adopted by a board would be permitted if they were "reasonable in relation to the threat posed."[22] In its written opinion, the Court, per Justice Andrew Moore, appeared to hold that consideration of non-shareholder interests could be a legitimate component of the directors' thinking. Crafting a reasonable anti-takeover plan, Moore wrote,

> entails an analysis by the directors of the nature of the takeover bid and its effect on the corporate enterprise. Examples of such concerns may include: inadequacy of the price offered, nature and timing of the offer, questions of illegality, *the impact on "constituencies" other than shareholders (i.e., creditors, customers, employees, and perhaps even the community generally)*, the risk of nonconsummation, and the quality of securities being offered in the exchange.[23]

Remarkably, the Court cited no cases or statutory authority for this proposition.[24]

---

would nevertheless interfere with the incumbent board's long-term plans for the firm. *See, e.g.,* Paramount Comm., Inc. v. Time Inc., 571 A.2d 1140, 1142 (Del. 1989).

[22] *Id.* at 949. This standard is known as the "enhanced business judgment rule." *Id.* at 954.

[23] *Id.* at 955 (emphasis added).

[24] Perhaps even more remarkably, immediately after this famous passage, the Court did cite an obscure piece of unpublished scholarship by two corporate law practitioners that made reference to directors appropriately giving attention to multiple stakeholders in a takeover context: Martin Lipton and Andrew R. Brownstein, *Takeover Responses and Director Responsibilities: An Update*, A.B.A. NAT'L INST. ON THE DYNAMICS OF CORP. CONTROL 7 (Dec 8, 1983) (on file with author). *See* Unocal, 493 A.2d at 955. The Lipton and Brownstein piece was later published under the same title but in substantially altered form, at 40 BUS. LAW. 1403 (1985). Still more remarkably, the published version of Lipton and Brownstein's article omitted the crucial "constituencies other than shareholders" language that the Court had borrowed from the unpublished version of the piece for its infamous passage in Unocal. *Id.* Neither Lipton nor Brownstein recall any specific reason for dropping the "constituencies other than shareholders" language between the draft and the published version. E-mail from Martin Lipton & Andrew R. Brownstein, to David G. Yosifon, Professor, Santa Clara University School of Law (Jun 22, 2012) (on file with author).

This passage from *Unocal* has been cited many times by scholars claiming that Delaware allows directors to attend to constituencies other than shareholders in firm governance. But that is wrong. The Delaware Supreme Court *clarified* its *Unocal* opinion that same year in another prominent takeover case, *Revlon, Inc. v. MacAndrews & Forbes Holdings, Inc.*, and made clear that sacrificing shareholder profits for other groups is not permissible.[25] Follow this closely.

Revlon was the target of a hostile takeover bid by a prominent corporate raider, Ronald Perelman. The Revlon board responded with a series of defensive maneuvers. One of the things it did was offer its shareholders the opportunity to exchange shares of Revlon stock for debt notes with a high interest rate. Like many debt instruments, the notes came with certain promises (covenants) restricting the firm's subsequent business dealings. The covenants were meant to assure that the debt would be paid. The company offered to exchange these debt notes for up to 10 million shares, and the exchange was fully subscribed. The board hoped the exchange would both pacify frustrated shareholders (who, like Perelman, believed their Revlon stock was underperforming) and ward off Perelman, who they hoped would no longer want the company after it was burdened by the debt and the debt covenants.

Perelman was not dissuaded. He continued to increase his offer price for Revlon. Intent on not allowing the company to fall into Perelman's hands, the directors cut a deal to sell the firm to the board's preferred suitor, Forstmann Little & Company, a private equity firm. Forstmann, the board concluded, had offered a fair price for the company, and had also promised to support at full value the debt notes that the board had recently exchanged for outstanding stock. Perelman's bid contained no such promise. Perelman and other Revlon shareholders filed suit to enjoin the Forstmann deal, claiming that it violated the board's obligations to the shareholders by unnecessarily ending an active bidding war for the company (between Perelman and Forstmann) that was driving up the price shareholders would receive for their stock. Revlon's board admitted that its deal with Forstmann was in part motivated by a desire to protect the noteholders, who they thought might suffer under a Perelman regime. The board argued that

---

[25] Revlon, Inc. v. MacAndrews & Forbes Holdings, Inc., 506 A.2d 173 (Del. 1985).

its motive was proper under *Unocal,* which stated that when confronting a takeover, directors could consider an offer's "impact on 'constituencies' other than shareholders (i.e., *creditors,* customers, employees, and, perhaps, even the community generally)."[26]

The Delaware Supreme Court took this opportunity to clarify (or walk back, if you prefer) its *Unocal* language. The introduction to the *Revlon* opinion states that the Court would "address *for the first time* the extent to which a corporation may consider the impact of a takeover threat on constituencies other than shareholders."[27] This framing undermines the view that the Court had already addressed the other-constituencies issue dogmatically in *Unocal.* The *Revlon* opinion then asserts that "while concern for various corporate constituencies is proper when addressing a takeover threat, that principle is limited by the *requirement that there be some rationally related benefit accruing to the shareholders.*"[28] The Court reiterates this later in the opinion:

> The Revlon board argue[s] that it acted in good faith in protecting the noteholders because *Unocal* permits consideration of other corporate constituencies. Although such considerations may be permissible, there are fundamental limitations upon that prerogative. *A board may have regard for various constituencies in discharging its responsibilities, provided there are rationally related benefits accruing to the stockholders.* However, such concern for non-stockholder interests is inappropriate when an auction among active bidders is in progress, and the object no longer is to protect or maintain the corporate enterprise but to sell it to the highest bidder.[29]

Revlon thus clearly states the law in Delaware. Boards can attend to the interests of non-shareholders when the board believes that doing so is rationally related to serving the shareholders. However, boards may not attend to the interests of non-shareholders when doing so is not rationally related to shareholder interests. That is, they may not attend to non-shareholder interests when doing so will cost the shareholders money.[30] Remarkably, the Delaware Supreme Court cites no authority for its

---

[26] Unocal, 493 A.2d at 955.   [27] Revlon, 506 A.2d at 176 (emphasis added).

[28] *Id.* (emphasis added).   [29] *Id.* at 182 (emphasis added).

[30] *Cf.* City Capital Assocs. Ltd. v. Interco, Inc. 551 A.2d 787, 902 (Del. Ch. 1988) ("Revlon ... can be seen an application of traditional Delaware law: a fiduciary cannot sell for less when more is available on similar terms.").

"rationally related benefits accruing to the shareholders" proposition, other than *Unocal*.[31]

Let us look back on what happened in *Unocal* through the clarifying lens provided by *Revlon*. In *Unocal*, the board was allowed to repel a hostile takeover bid in order to pursue its own plans for the future of the company. The board believed its long-term plans would prove more profitable to shareholders than the short-term gains offered by Mesa's tender offer. In deciding to fight Mesa, it was appropriate for Unocal's board to consider how its entrenchment plan would impact workers, creditors, customers, even the community at large, since all those constituencies were relevant to the firm's long-term prospects for advancing *shareholder* interests. Consideration of such constituencies is entirely appropriate for a going concern, since you cannot make profits without them. However, the only permissible *reason* for considering those constituencies is if doing so is related to advancing shareholder interests.

In contrast to the Unocal situation, the Revlon board accepted that there would be no future, no tomorrow, for its shareholders. The company was going to be bought by either Perelman (the board feared) or Forstmann (the board hoped). Whoever took over, the shareholders were going to get cash for their stock and would have no future stake in the company. In this scenario, it was entirely *irrelevant* how the board's actions would impact non-shareholding constituencies like creditors, workers, or customers because the impact on those constituencies would not bear on any future shareholder interest. Consideration of non-shareholders in that context could not be "rationally related" to the directors' obligation to serve the shareholders. The command to maximize *present* value followed from the fact that having made the decision that their shareholder would be cashed out, there was no future left about which discretion might be exercised.

Revlon left no doubt on this subject. But a more recent case, *eBay v. Newmark*, decided in 2010 by the Delaware Court of Chancery, makes the point in language that is even more explicit.[32] One of the three founders of craigslist, Inc., the online classifieds site, sold his craigslist stock to eBay Inc., in a complicated transaction that the other two

---

[31] *Id.*   [32] eBay Domestic Holdings, Inc. v. Newmark, 16 A.3d 1 (Del. Ch. 2010).

craigslist founders had allowed. Later it became clear that while eBay expected to be actively involved in shaping craigslist's future, the two remaining founders wanted eBay to be a passive investor. In their capacity as directors, the remaining founders undertook a series of maneuvers seeking to limit eBay's influence in craigslist, and to assure that control of the company remained in their hands and would pass to their heirs. eBay sued. Using a litigation playbook they may have found on their own website, the craigslist founders defended their machinations as necessary to protect the public-service orientation of craigslist and keep it from becoming too focused on profit-making.

Not on Chancellor Chandler's watch. He wrote:

> Having chosen a for-profit corporate form, the craigslist directors are bound by the fiduciary duties and standards that accompany that form. Those standards include acting to promote the value of the corporation for the benefit of its stockholders. The "Inc." after the company name has to mean at least that. Thus, I cannot accept as valid for the purposes of implementing the Rights Plan [i.e., the entrenchment plan] a corporate policy that specifically, clearly, and admittedly seeks not to maximize the economic value of a for-profit Delaware corporation for the benefit of its stockholders.[33]

Remarkably, Chandler did not cite a single case, statute, or piece of scholarship to support his conclusion. As with the *Dodge* court in Michigan, the proposition seemed so obvious and fundamental to Chandler that it needed no citation. Those who prefer to have one now have *eBay*.

Crucially, *eBay* made clear both that shareholder primacy is the rule, *and* that corporate "persona," public statements, routine self-descriptions, and board policies are not sufficient to alter that rule. I believe that shareholder primacy could be accomplished by a clear provision specifying so in the charter, but absent that, directors are obliged to abide by shareholder primacy.[34]

---

[33] *Id.* at 34.
[34] David G. Yosifon, *Opting Out of Shareholder Primacy: Is the Public Benefit Corporate Trivial?*, 41 DEL. J. CORP. L. 461 (2017) (arguing that deviation is possible through charter provision or through use of a public benefit corporation).

The clarity of Delaware case law on the law of corporate purpose gives meaning to the near total silence on the issue in the Delaware statute. With the help of its active Corporate Law Committee, the Delaware Legislature is very alert to developments in the interpretation of its corporate code and has not been shy about responding to unsatisfactory judicial holdings with legislative amendments.[35] The failure of the legislature to do so in the area of corporate purpose must be read to express legislative acquiescence in shareholder primacy.

INTERPRETIVE CONFUSION

I now want to address the major arguments made by scholars and activists who deny that Delaware law requires shareholder primacy in firm governance. To be effective, this must be done in detail. It is my hope that the stakes will make it worth the pain (in the reader's brain and bottom) of following this staking all the way down. I do not attempt to review every piece of scholarship that has wrongly interpreted Delaware law on corporate purpose. But I do seek to cover all of the kinds of arguments that come up on this issue. Before beginning this review, I want to sincerely acknowledge my intellectual debt to every one of the scholars referenced here. On many other issues, I agree with them entirely. Much of what I know about corporate law I have learned from these authorities. In other arts, the sincerest form of flattery is imitation. In ours, it is critique.

"ANY LAWFUL ACT" DOES NOT DESCRIBE DISCRETION AS TO BENEFICIARY

As noted at the start of this chapter, the Delaware statute requires every corporation to specify its purpose in its charter, but the statute

---

[35] For example, in 1986 the Delaware legislature adopted the exculpatory provisions of §102(b)(7), allowing firms to opt out of duty of care liability for its directors in direct response to the Delaware Supreme Court (seemingly) expanding such liability in Smith v. Van Gorkom, 488 A.2d 858 (Del. 1985).

says this requirement can be satisfied by stating that "the purpose of
the corporation is to engage in any lawful act or activity for which
corporations may be organized."[36] Most Delaware business corporations today are in fact formed with the catch-all purpose to engage
in "any lawful act." Sometimes scholars interpret this "any lawful
act" language as countenancing management of a firm in favor
of some goal other than shareholder wealth maximization.[37] This
is wrong.

The statutory "any lawful act" provision, used without further
qualification in a corporate charter, refers to the *type of activities* a
company may undertake, not its purpose for undertaking them. The
"any lawful act" language gives directors the widest possible latitude in
deciding *how* to go about advancing shareholder interests. This interpretation is supported by the history of the statute. In the eighteenth
and nineteenth centuries, states granted corporate charters only by
specific legislative action for particular undertakings or "purposes,"
such as building a harbor or a hospital. Starting in the late nineteenth
century, states (including Delaware) adopted "general" incorporation
statutes, which made corporate charters available by routine administrative action to all comers.[38] The new incorporation statutes still
required corporate promoters to specify the purpose or type of
business their corporation would undertake. At this stage, however,
the stipulation of "purpose" in the charter became less a limitation on
corporate power imposed by a jealous state, and more a protection
afforded to corporate investors, to give them some certainty about the
kind of business they were investing in. Soon it became evident that
what investors really wanted was for their firms to enter whatever
fields of endeavor might prove profitable. Promoters therefore started
stuffing long lists of permissible purposes into corporate charters,
which could reach cumbersome and absurd lengths. Solicitous
legislatures responded by reforming general incorporation statutes

---

[36] *Id.*

[37] *See, e.g.,* Lyman Johnson & David Millon, *Corporate Law After Hobby Lobby*, 70 Bus. Law.
1, 13 (2014).

[38] *See generally* S. Samuel Arsht, *A History of Delaware Corporation Law*, 1 Del. J. Corp. L 1
(1976).

to allow firms to specify that their purpose was to undertake "any lawful act or activity."[39]

No Delaware Court has ever held that the "any lawful act" language describes or causes a deviation from shareholder primacy. In fact, the *eBay* case must be read as a direct rejection of such an interpretation. craigslist's certificate of incorporation states that its purpose was to "engage in any lawful act or activity for which corporations may be organized under the General Corporation Law of Delaware."[40] Yet Chancellor Chandler held that craigslist's corporate purpose was profit maximization. In fact, the expansive "any lawful act" language played *no role whatsoever* in Chandler's assessment of corporate purpose in *eBay*.

In my view, it would be permissible for corporate promoters to specify in their charter that they desire to deviate from shareholder primacy and operate under some other governance norm.[41] But stipulating, as the statute invites, that you are forming a firm that is authorized to undertake "any lawful act" does not accomplish such deviation. It merely specifies that firms may use any lawful means to pursue the default goal of corporate operations, which is to advance the interests of the shareholders.[42]

---

[39] *See* David G. Yosifon, *Corporate Aid of Governmental Authority: History and Analysis of an Obscure Power in Delaware Corporate Law*, 10 U. St. Thomas L. Rev. 1086 (2013) (distinguishing between corporate purposes, corporate powers, and corporate beneficiaries).

[40] Certificate of Incorporation of Craigslist, Inc., Oct 13, 2004. On file with author.

[41] *See generally* Yosifon, *Opting Out of Shareholder Primacy*, *supra* note 34.

[42] In Burwell v. Hobby Lobby Stores, Inc., 134 S. Ct. 2751, 2770–2772 (2014), the United States Supreme Court sloppily combined reference to the "any lawful act" provisions of the Oklahoma and Pennsylvania corporate law statutes used to charter the firms in that case, with non-charter "declarations of principles" and other corporate statements by these firms, to support the Court's conclusion that the firms were organized to pursue religious aims in addition to profit. This was an important step in the Court's determination that Hobby Lobby could claim protections against otherwise generally applicable law under the Religious Freedom Restoration Act (RFRA). The Court's looseness on the law of corporate purpose was not put at issue in that case because *all* of the shareholders of the closely held Hobby Lobby corporation were agreed that the firm should temper its pursuit of profits in service of religious values. If a shareholder was present and complaining about this deviation from shareholder primacy, the analysis would have looked quite different, or anyway it would have under Delaware law. As noted above, the craigslist case makes clear that corporate "persona" is not sufficient to change the rule of shareholder primacy. It has to be in the charter.

MISINTERPRETING *UNOCAL*, *REVLON*, AND THEIR PROGENY

The most common mistake that scholars make in arguing that Delaware does not require shareholder primacy is misinterpreting *Unocal* and *Revlon*. A prominent example is seen in Lynn Stout's 2012 book, *The Shareholder Value Myth.*[43] Citing *Unocal*, Stout declares: "the Delaware Supreme Court has stated that in weighing the merits of a business transaction, directors can consider 'the impact of "constituencies" other than shareholders.'"[44] But, incredibly, Stout never follows up on this *Unocal* invocation with *Revlon*'s clarification. Her book *never* quotes the Delaware Supreme Court's crucial statement in *Revlon* that there must be "rationally related benefits accruing to the stockholders" before the considerations noted in *Unocal* would be permissible. This is a common error.

When Stout does get to *Revlon,* she misreads it. Like many scholars, Stout argues that *Revlon* stands for the proposition that directors are *only* obligated to maximize shareholder value when shareholders are being cashed out of their equity interest in a firm. Since in *Revlon* the shareholders were going to receive cash for their shares, she acknowledges "[t]hat meant there would be no public corporation whose long-term interests the board might consider."[45] She also rightly states that the "Delaware Supreme Court held that, under the circumstances, the business judgment rule did not apply and Revlon's directors had a duty to get the public shareholders (soon to be ex-shareholders) the best possible price for their shares."[46] But from this she draws the non sequitur that, "[i]n other words, it is *only* when a public corporation is about to stop being a public corporation that directors lose the protection of the business judgment rule and must embrace shareholder wealth as their only goal."[47]

In terms of formal logic, Stout has committed the fallacy of "denying the antecedent."[48] From the statement, "if A, then B" it is a fallacy

---

[43] STOUT, THE SHAREHOLDER VALUE MYTH, *supra* note 2.   [44] *Id.*   [45] *Id.* at 31.
[46] *Id.*   [47] *Id.* (emphasis added).
[48] *See* HOWARD KAHANE, LOGIC AND PHILOSOPHY: A MODERN INTRODUCTION 300 (6th ed. 1990).

to conclude "not A, therefore not B." From the statement, "if it rains, then Jane is required to work from home," one cannot conclude that if it is sunny, Jane is not required to work from home. She might be required to work from home on sunny and rainy days, or on rainy days and Wednesdays. In *Revlon*, the Delaware Supreme Court held that if [A] the firm is for sale, then [B] directors must maximize profits. Stout concludes from this that if the firm is not for sale, directors do not have to maximize profits. But that does not follow as a matter of logic, and it is not *Revlon*'s teaching.

As I showed above, *Revlon*'s "rationally related benefits accruing to the stockholders" rule is explicitly presented as a clarification of what the Delaware Supreme Court had said about "other constituencies" in *Unocal*. And *Unocal* was *not* an auction case. Unocal's directors were resisting a takeover in order to continue as a going concern. Therefore, the "rationally related benefits" rule applies to firms that are intent on continuing as a going concern. It is only *after* connecting the "rationally related benefits" language to *Unocal* that the Revlon Court moves on to explain how this rule operates in Revlon's auction setting.

There is some sloppiness in the scholarship denying that shareholder primacy is the law in Delaware. Consider Professor Einer Elhauge's use of a different fragment of *Unocal* to support his view that shareholder primacy is not required in corporate governance.[49] He writes (quoting *Unocal*, the quoted language put in italics here): "Delaware case law ... explicitly states that '*stockholder interests*' are '*not a controlling factor*.'"[50] That seems like persuasive evidence against shareholder primacy as positive law. But the full sentence from which these phrases are pulled reveals that they have nothing at all to do with the Court's view of the relative standing of shareholder and non-shareholder interests. The complete sentence from which Elhauge plucked his phrases reads:

> While not a controlling factor, it also seems to us that a board may reasonably consider the basic stockholder interests at stake,

---

[49] *See* Einer Elhauge, *Sacrificing Corporate Profits in the Public Interest*, 80 N.Y.U. L. REV. 733, 817 (2005). Elhauge also reiterates Stout's mistaken reading of *Unocal* and *Revlon* "'constituencies' other than the shareholders" language reviewed above.

[50] *Id.* at 764–65.

including those of short term speculators, whose actions may have
fueled the coercive aspect of the offer at the expense of the long
term investor.[51]

The "basic" "stockholder interests" the Court is referencing here
are the different interests between a long-term investor and a short-
term speculator. It "seems" to the Court that directors "may" consider
the different interests of the two groups when deciding what to do
about a takeover threat. To accept Elhauge's interpretation of this
sentence – that it is saying that shareholder interests are "not controlling" as against the interests of non-shareholders – would require us to
believe that the Court was announcing that it "seems" to them that the
board "may" consider *stockholder* interests in such a situation. As if
anyone ever doubted whether it was permissible for corporate directors
to consider the *stockholder* interest. My interpretation is better. The
Court is saying that it "seems" appropriate to consider the relative
interests of short-term as against long-term investors, although those
relative interests are not "controlling." In a footnote to this passage, the
Court cites studies finding that some target companies that resisted
takeovers eventually traded at a higher price than the price offered in
the hostile bid.[52] This buttresses my interpretation that the phrase is
about short-term vs. long-term shareholder interests, not shareholder
vs. non-shareholder interests.

Compounding this folly, Elhauge also pursues a strained interpretation of another important case to argue that *even when the company is
up for sale,* Delaware authorizes directors to consider the interests of
non-shareholders. He examines the 1989 auction sale of RJR Nabisco,
in which a disinterested board chose to sell the company to the investment firm KKR (Kohberg, Kravis, Roberts & Co.), rather than to a
group of competing bidders comprised of the firm's incumbent managers. After a tense, complicated bidding process, the board weighed
KKR's best offer, which the board's investment bankers valued at

---

[51] Unocal, 493 A.2d at 955–56.

[52] *Id.* at 956 n. 11 ("There has been much debate respecting such stockholder interests. One
rather impressive study indicates that the stock of over 50 percent of target companies,
who resisted hostile takeovers, later traded at higher market prices than the rejected offer
price.").

"approximately \$108 to \$108.50 per share,"[53] against the management team's best offer, which the firm's bankers "were of the view ...
had a value of approximately \$108.50–\$109 per share."[54] The Court
also stated that "the Company's bankers ... were of the view ... that
the two bids, were, so far as financial analysis could determine, substantially equivalent."[55] Nevertheless, Elhauge looks to make hay of the
fact that Delaware sanctioned the board's decision to accept the KKR
bid and reject the management team's bid. He writes:

> the fact is that, even as valued by the corporation itself, the two bids
> were not equal: The accepted bid had a value of \$108–108.50 and
> the rejected bid a value of \$108.50–\$109.00... The decision effect-
> ively holds that, even in the auction context, management can go
> beyond considering only those nonshareholder interests that bear a
> rational relationship to shareholder value.[56]

This analysis would hold up if it were true, as Elhauge writes, that
"as valued by the corporation itself, the rejected bid had a higher price
range."[57] But that is not true. The "Company's bankers" may have
given the rejected bid a higher upper range than the accepted bid, by
50 cents. But the bankers also said the bids were "substantially equivalent," so their words conflicted with their numbers, unless 50 cents per
share is insubstantial, which is really not their call. And that is the
point. It is not their call. Under Delaware law, neither bankers nor law
professors determine the value of a bid. The directors do that. Only by
substituting "the corporation" for the "Company's bankers" can
Elhauge claim that the directors believed there was no chance the
winning bid was worth more than the rejected bid. The board was
under no obligation to accept the investment bankers' word – or
numbers – as final. Indeed, the board was obligated to make its own
decision. Reading Chancellor Allen's summary of the byzantine attributes and contingencies that went into valuing the extremely complicated securities that comprised each bidder's offer – which included
predictions about future market conditions – even the layperson can
see that any dollar, or fraction of a dollar, figure put on the value of the

---

[53] In re RJR Nabisco, Inc. S'holder Litig., *Unpublished Opinion*, 14 Del. J. Corp. L. 1132,
1137 (1989).
[54] *Id.*   [55] *Id.* at 1138.   [56] Elhauge, *supra* note 49 at 851–52.   [57] *Id.*

securities was highly speculative. Determining the value of deals of that complexity requires more than a calculator. It requires judgment. That judgment was the board's to exercise.

Unlike Revlon's board, the Nabisco directors "disclaim[ed] any motivation other than one to pursue the special duty that fell to them with diligence for the best interests of the shareholders."[58] Chancellor Allen saw good faith. There was no "inference that those who made such a choice must have had some motivation other than the honest pursuit of the corporation's welfare."[59] Therefore, nothing in this jurisprudence implies that it was alright for the board to choose the KKR bid because it was better for other stakeholders, as Elhauge would have us believe.

In the first period, in ordinary times, and in the final period, Delaware requires and allows directors to serve only the shareholders.

MAXIMIZATION IS THE STANDARD

Another common confusion about the law of corporate purpose involves the question of whether directors are required always to "maximize" corporate profits or whether they are permitted to do something less than that, even if one concedes that directors must pursue shareholder interests to *some* extent. Most Delaware cases that touch on corporate purpose describe the directors' duty as an obligation to "maximize" profits or pursue the "best" interests of the shareholders.[60] In some cases, however, the obligation is described as a duty

---

[58] Nabisco, *supra* note 53 at 1138.   [59] *Id.*

[60] *See*, e.g., Paramount v. Time, 1989 WL 79880, 58 USLW 2070 (Del. Ch. 1989) ("The legally critical question this case presents then involves when must a board shift from its ordinary long-term profit *maximizing* mode to the radically altered state recognized by the Revlon case in which its duty, broadly stated, is to exercise its power in the good faith pursuit of immediate *maximization* of share value") (emphasis added); eBay Domestic Holdings, 16 A.3d at 35 ("I cannot accept as valid . . . a corporate policy that specifically, clearly, and *admittedly* seeks not to *maximize* the economic value of a for-profit Delaware corporation for the benefit of its stockholders.") (second emphasis added); Katz v. Oak Industries, 508 A.2d 873, 879 (Del. Ch. 1986) ("It is the obligation of directors to attempt, within the law, to *maximize* the long-run interests of the corporation's stockholders") (emphasis added); Mills Acquisition Co. v. Macmillan, Inc., 559 A.2d 1261, 1287 (1989) ("Thus, like any other business decision, the board has a duty in the design and

to manage the corporation "for the benefit of the shareholder owners," with the maximization or "best" qualifier dropped. And then there is *Revlon's* language, which states that attention to non-shareholders is allowed when there are "rationally related"[61] benefits to shareholders. Some shareholder primacy skeptics claim that the inconsistent application of the "maximization" qualifier, and the "rationally related" language, means that in the going-concern condition directors may steer the corporate ship in a way that attends to non-shareholder concerns, so long as *some* profits are involved for shareholders. On this view, Delaware allows directors to choose a less profitable course over a more profitable one, so long as the course does benefit shareholders.

This is not a plausible interpretation of Delaware law. To clarify this particular confusion we should first recognize that human beings "maximize" their performance in any area when they "do the best they can." We have limited cognitive capacity and limited willpower. We cannot hope to "maximize" anything the way a strictly rational actor, or a computer, would. All we can do is try. So to say that the law requires directors to maximize profits, we must understand that it means directors must do their best to maximize profits. What Delaware directors may not do, however, is slack on satisfying the interests of shareholders in order to have cognitive capacity, time, or corporate wealth left over to serve the interests of non-shareholders. Consideration of non-shareholder interests is only permitted to the extent that it is "rationally related" to shareholder interests.

Suppose a board of directors was confronted with a decision to set the price for a particular product. The directors believe in good faith that they can set the price at $100 and produce a yearly profit of $10 per share. They also believe that they could instead set the price at $90 and produce a yearly profit of $8 per share, with the extra $10 staying in the consumer's pocket, to be put to other uses, like buying candy or some life-saving medicine. Setting the price to produce the $8 profit might superficially be said to take into consideration the consumer interest in a way that is "rationally related" to advancing shareholder

---

conduct of an auction to act in 'the *best* interests of the corporation and its shareholders.'") (emphasis added).

[61] Revlon, 506 A.2d at 176 (emphasis added).

interests, since shareholders will make *some* profit out of the decision. But the directors here have to choose between setting the price to make a $10 or an $8 profit. They have both contingencies in mind, and must make a good faith choice between them. The decision to choose an $8 profit instead of a $10 profit is not "rationally related" to the shareholder interest. It advances the consumer interest at the expense of shareholders, and is thus forbidden.

Directors obviously may choose to make $8 now instead of $10 now if they believe it will establish better relationships with consumers and result in more profits in the long run. But that is a different issue. We should be clear about what we are talking when we are talking about discretion. There is no duty to maximize short-term value. There is a duty to try to get shareholders the best deal possible, over whatever time horizon directors believe will be best for shareholders.

"THE CORPORATION AND ITS SHAREHOLDERS" NAMES ONLY ONE STAKEHOLDER

In several places, both in Delaware's statute and in its case law, we read that directors owe fiduciary obligations to "the corporation *and* its shareholders."[62] Scholars and activists who insist that shareholder primacy is not bedrock corporate law see in this formulation a foothold for their position that directors can (or even must) manage firms to serve interests other than the shareholders.

But the "corporation and its shareholders" formulation offers no support for that proposition. To say that directors owe fiduciary duties to "the corporation" is simply to say that they must deal with the corporation carefully and loyally. They may not abuse the corporation, neglect it, or use its assets for their own purposes. They must care for the corporation because doing so is *how* they serve the shareholders. That is the best way to read the "corporation and its shareholders" language consistently with the rest of the case law I have reviewed here.

---

[62] *See, e.g.*, Mills Acquisition, 559 A.2d at 1287 ("[T]he board has a duty ... to act in 'the best interests of the corporation and its shareholders.'").

There is no independent interpretation of the phrase in any case, but my view of it is expressed in *TW Services Inc. v. SWT Acquisition Corp.*, where Chancellor Allen wrote, "directors may be said to owe a duty to shareholders as a class to manage the corporation within the law, with due care and in a way intended to maximize the long run interests of shareholders."[63]

The phrase "the corporation and its shareholders" is a linguistic habit of the Delaware judiciary, but it has never been made to do any work or played any role in any Delaware court's working through a corporate purpose controversy. If it was meaningful, if it was useful, then surely the courts would have made reference to it, one way or the other, in *Unocal*, *Revlon*, or *eBay*. But it played no part at all in those cases. There are no cases that use the "corporation and its shareholders" to express the view that directors may pursue their obligations to the "corporation" in a manner that privileges the interests of non-shareholders at the expense of shareholders.

Scholars who doubt that shareholder primacy is the law reference "the corporation and its shareholders" formulation but fail to show any instance in which the phrase is used to describe distinct or competing obligations.[64] Here again the devil in the scholarly mistake can be seen by looking closely at the details. In a law review article, Professor Eric Gouvin wrote:

> Well-established law in Delaware and other jurisdictions holds that the directors of corporations owe fiduciary duties to both the corporation and its shareholders. The Delaware Supreme Court has recently stated that these duties are "*of equal and independent*

---

[63] TW Services Inc. v. SWT Acquisition Corp., 1989 WL 20290 (Del. Ch. 1989).

[64] *See, e.g.*, Millon, *Two Models of Corporate Social Responsibility*, *supra* note 10 at 526 (referencing the recurring "corporation and its shareholders" phrasing as a justification for his view that "Delaware law is not committed to shareholder primacy."); Christopher M. Bruner, *Corporate Governance in a Time of Crisis*, 36 J. CORP. L. 309, 325 (2011) (asserting that the "formulation reflect[s] deep-seated ambivalence regarding the degree to which shareholders' interests ought to dominate corporate decision-making in the United States); Andrew S. Gold, *Theories of the Firm and Judicial Uncertainty*, 35 SEATTLE U. L. REV. 1087, 1097 (2012) (pointing to the phrase and arguing that "[b]ecause the interests of shareholders and the interests of the corporation will sometimes conflict this amounts to an indeterminate standard" regarding corporate purpose).

significance," but case law reveals that the directors' duty to the corporation as an entity usually predominates over their duty to the shareholders.[65]

Gouvin's paragraph has been referenced in other influential scholarship, including in a law review article by a former Chief Justice of the Delaware Supreme Court.[66] But when you chase down the case Gouvin is quoting here, *Cede v. Technicolor*,[67] you find that the phrase "of equal and independent significance" is *not* being used to describe the relationship between directors' obligations to the corporation, on the one hand, and its shareholders, on the other. Instead, it specifies a distinction between the directors' duty of *care* and the directors' duty of *loyalty*. The full passage from *Cede* reads as follows:

> Duty of care and duty of loyalty are the traditional hallmarks of a fiduciary who endeavors to act in the service of a corporation and its stockholders. Each of these duties is of equal and independent significance. In decisional law of this Court applying the rule ... this Court has consistently given equal weight to the rule's requirements of duty of care and duty of loyalty.[68]

The *Cede* Court was repudiating the Chancery division's confusing conflation of the care and loyalty analysis in the *Cede* litigation. The discussion had *nothing* to do with any disjunction between duties owed to the corporation and those owed to its shareholders. It is one thing to model a dinosaur on a single cracked tooth found ossified in a jurisprudential swamp. That is fair play in the archeology of legal knowledge. But dinosaurs reconstructed out of fossilized cranberries mislabeled as teeth construct only mythical creatures, and mistaken jurisprudence.

---

[65] Eric J. Gouvin, *Resolving the Subsidiary Director's Dilemma*, 47 HASTINGS L. J. 287, 294–95 (1996) (quoting Cede & Co. v. Technicolor, Inc., 634 A.2d 345, 367 (Del. 1993))(emphasis added by me).

[66] *See* E. Norman Veasey and Cristine Di Guglielmo, *How Many Masters Can a Director Serve? A Look at the Tensions Facing Constituency Directors*, 63 BUS. LAW. 76, 764 n. 8 (2008); *see also* Gold, *supra* note 64 at 1098 n. 43 (citing Veasey & Di Guglielmo on this issue).

[67] Cede & Co. v. Technicolor, Inc., 634 A.2d 345, 367 (Del. 1993).

[68] Cede & Co., 634 A.2d at 367.

The repeated judicial reference in Delaware case law to director duties to "the corporation and its shareholders" is a linguistic convention that has no relevance to the question of corporate purpose. It certainly cannot support the view that directors are allowed to sacrifice shareholder value for other stakeholders. Indeed, the better reading of "the corporation and its shareholders" formulation is that it emphasizes rather than detracts from the conclusion that the law is shareholder primacy. Shareholders are the only stakeholder group that is singled out. We never see the phrase, "the corporation and its workers," "the corporation, its shareholders, and its workers," or "the corporation and its stakeholders." It is always, "the corporation and its shareholders." The better interpretation of this phrase is that it expresses a unified, coherent set of obligations rather than serial or disjunctive ones. The directors' attention is to be devoted to doing things aimed at increasing the value of the corporation *for* the shareholders.

CHARITABLE GIVING: NOT REALLY AN EXCEPTION TO THE RULE

There is a provision in the Delaware statute which gives every corporation the "power to ... [m]ake donations for the public welfare or for charitable, scientific or educational purposes, and in time of war or other national emergency in aid thereof."[69] When I began this inquiry, I was prepared to treat the corporate charitable giving power as an exception that proved the general rule of shareholder primacy in corporate governance. After all, if the general powers granted corporate directors already include the power to advance the public interest, then they would already have the power to make charitable donations. The charitable giving exception thus brings the default rule of shareholder primacy into clearer focus.

But after study, I am convinced that the charitable giving power, as interpreted in Delaware case law, represents no real exception or deviation from the fundamental rule of shareholder primacy. For starters, the provision granting firms the power to make charitable

[69] 8 DEL. GEN. CORP. L. § 122(9).

contributions comes ninth in a list of seventeen specifically enumerated powers that corporations "shall have."[70] Other powers in the list include: the power of "perpetual succession"; the power to "[s]ue and be sued"; the power to "appoint ... officers and agents ... and provide for them suitable compensation"; and the power to "make contracts."[71] These are powers that all corporations have, but the question remains as to what principle governs the *exercise* of these powers. Although the corporation has the power to make contracts, directors cannot cause the corporation to make contracts that advance the interests of suppliers at the expense of shareholders. Similarly, while the corporation has the power to make charitable contributions, it may not use that power in a way that deviates from the abiding purpose of corporate governance: the interests of the shareholders. Often it will benefit shareholders for firms to contract with suppliers, and it will also frequently serve shareholders when the firm makes charitable donations (by improving its reputation, for example). In the nineteenth century, when corporations could only be formed for narrowly specified purposes, there was contradictory case law on the question of whether firms had the power to make charitable contributions or whether such acts were *ultra vires*. Modern corporate law statutes clarify that firms do have the power to make charitable donations. When and how they exercise that power, however, is governed by background fiduciary principles.[72]

The key Delaware cases interpreting the charitable giving power clearly express this view. *Theodora v. Henderson* (1969) involved a complaint that the directors of Alexander Dawson, Inc., a holding company, had violated their duties to shareholders when they made a corporate gift of $528,000 to a charity that ran a camp for underprivileged boys.[73] After quoting the statutory power, the Court framed its inquiry into the propriety of the gift like this:

---

[70] 8 DEL. GEN. CORP. L. § 122.   [71] *Id.*

[72] For comprehensive treatment of the policy issues involved in corporate charitable giving, see Faith Stevelman Kahn, *Pandora's Box: Managerial Discretion and the Problem of Corporate Philanthropy*, 44 U.C.L.A. L. REV. 579 (1997).

[73] Theodora Holding Corp. v. Henderson, 257 A.2d 398, 404 (Del. Ch. 1969). The case actually involved myriad allegations of directorial shenanigans, but the charitable giving issue is the only one relevant here.

> [C]ontemporary courts recognize that unless corporations carry
> an increasing share of the burden of supporting charitable and
> educational causes that the business advantages now reposed in
> corporations by law may well prove to be unacceptable to the
> representatives of an aroused public.[74]

The Court's emphasis is not on what charitable giving might do for
the public, but rather, what corporate giving, or the absence of it, might
mean for the public's tolerance of the "advantages" that corporations
enjoy.[75] After this framing, the Court leapt to its doctrinal conclusion:
"the test to be applied in passing on the validity of a gift such as the one
here in issue is that of reasonableness, a test in which the provisions of
the Internal Revenue Code pertaining to charitable gifts by corporations furnish a helpful guide."[76] (At the time the Internal Revenue
Code allowed charitable contributions to be deducted up to 5 percent
of taxable income; today it allows for deductions of up to 10 percent of
income, although the average corporation contributes just 1.5 percent
of its income to charity.)[77] Applying this standard to the Dawson
firm's donation to the boys' camp, the Court again returns to the issue
of purpose and situates that purpose squarely in the idiom of shareholder primacy. Because of the tax benefits associated with the gift, the
Court concludes that "the contribution under attack can be said to
have 'cost' all of the stockholders of Alexander Dawson, Inc. including
plaintiff, less than $80,000."[78] But why does the Court put the term
"cost" in shock quotes? If it is a cost, even just a small one, then why
not just write the word? The reason is that the Court views the
contribution to be no cost at all, but rather a gain, to the shareholders:

> It is accordingly obvious, in my opinion, that the relatively small
> loss of *immediate* income otherwise payable to plaintiff and the

---

[74] Id. at 404.

[75] The Court also discussed a famous New Jersey case, A.P. Smith Mfg. v. Barlow, 13
N.J. 145, 98 A.2d 581 (1953), in which New Jersey corporate law was held to countenance a small gift that the Smith corporation had made to Princeton University. The
Theodora court approvingly observed that the *Barlow* court "noted that the gift tended
to bolster the free enterprise system and the general social climate in which [the firm] was
nurtured." Theodora, 257 A.2d at 404.

[76] Theodora, 257 A.2d at 405.   [77] *See* Elhauge, *supra* note 49, at 836–37.

[78] Theodora, 257 A.2d at 405.

corporate defendant's other stockholders, had it not been for the gift in question, is far out-weighed by the overall benefits flowing from the placing of such gift in channels where it serves to benefit those in need of philanthropic or educational support, thus providing justification for large private holdings, *thereby benefiting plaintiff in the long run.*[79]

As with attention to non-shareholders in ordinary business decisions, the corporate charitable contribution is acceptable because of the long-term benefits it may bring to shareholders. The *Theodora* "reasonableness" standard for charitable giving must therefore be construed as having two components. The first requires a reasonable relation to the shareholder interest, which explains the Court's repeated reference to long-term shareholder interests. The second component of reasonableness is magnitude, which explains the Court's reference to the tax code as guidance.

A hypothetical. Directors of a firm decide to make a charitable contribution of less than 10 percent of taxable income after deliberating and expressly concluding that the donation *would not* advance shareholder interests. In fact, the directors decide to make the donation after expressly determining that the donation would *undermine* shareholder interests over all possible time-horizons. Suppose that the donation were made to a camp that was dedicated to teaching underprivileged children about the inadequacy of capitalism and democracy as means to overcoming the suffering of the American poor. If shareholders challenged such a contribution, the directors' action would surely be held unreasonable, not because of the size of the charitable gift, but because the gift was not even intended to be rationally related to the shareholder interest. The exercise of the power to make charitable contributions is circumscribed by the fiduciary obligations that directors owe to the corporation and its shareholders.

More frequently cited than the seminal *Theodora* opinion is the more modern charitable giving case of *Kahn v. Sullivan.*[80] *Kahn* involved a challenge to a decision by the directors of an energy company, Occidental Petroleum Corp., to donate $50 million for the construction of a museum to house the art collection of Occidental's

[79] *Id.* (emphasis added).   [80] 594 A.2d 48, 51 (Del. 1991).

retiring CEO. The Delaware Supreme Court accepted that the donation likely would pass the reasonableness test it established in *Theodora*. Crucial to the Court's analysis was the Occidental board's explicit determination that the charitable contribution would benefit the corporation by improving its reputation in the local community and around the world. The charitable contribution was not selfless giving. It was a studied extension of a long-standing business plan:

> Through Occidental's financial support and sponsorship, the Art Collection has been viewed by more than six million people in more than twenty-five American cities and at least eighteen foreign countries. The majority of those exhibitions have been in areas where Occidental has operations or was negotiating business contracts. Occidental's Annual Reports to its shareholders have described the benefits and good will which it attributes to the financial support that Occidental has provided for the Art Collection.[81]

In considering funding the museum, the board was informed by a law firm's ninety-six page memorandum that "included an analysis of the donation's effect on Occidental's financial condition, [and] the potential for good will and other benefits to Occidental."[82] After deliberation, a special Committee of the board, comprised of independent directors (i.e., non-officer directors), "concluded that the establishment of the Museum, adjacent to Occidental's corporate offices in Los Angeles, would provide benefits to Occidental for at least the thirty-year term of the lease."[83]

Occidental made its charitable contribution only after concluding that the donation was beneficial to the corporation. And *that* determination was relevant to the Supreme Court's upholding of the Chancery Court's assessment of the reasonableness of the donation. Neither Chancery nor the Supreme Court considered "reasonableness" to be merely a matter of dollar figure. Purpose remains relevant in the inquiry, and the purpose must be to advance the overarching charge of the directors: serve the shareholders.

---

[81] *Id.*   [82] *Id.* at 53–54.   [83] *Id.* at 54

CORPORATE AID OF GOVERNMENTAL AUTHORITY

The section of the Delaware statute that contains the charitable giving "power" also contains a provision stating that "[e]very corporation ... shall have power to ... [t]ransact any lawful business which the corporation's board of directors shall find to be in aid of governmental authority."[84]

This oddly worded language has been in the Delaware code for more than forty years. Yet no reported cases reference it, and scholars have ignored it almost entirely.[85] This lack of attention is surprising, given that by its own terms the provision seems to implicate fundamental questions about corporate purpose and corporate social responsibility. Does the corporate power to aid governmental authority authorize directors to sacrifice shareholder value in favor of non-shareholder interests? The history of the provision provides some guidance.[86]

The original version of section 122(12), adopted as part of a sweeping modernization of the Delaware statute in 1967, was far more limited in scope than the present version of the power. The 1967 version stated:

> Every corporation ... shall have power ... *[i]n time of war or other national emergency,* to do any lawful business in aid thereof, notwithstanding the business or purposes set forth in its certificate of incorporation, at the request or direction of any apparently authorized governmental authority.[87]

The 1967 reforms were developed by a Corporate Law Revision Committee, which took its cues from Professor Ernest Folk, III, a corporate law scholar hired to serve as the Committee's Reporter. Folk's work for the Committee was heavily informed by the American Bar Association's Model Business Corporation Act (MBCA). The

---

[84] 8 DEL. GEN. CORP. L. § 122(12).

[85] One interesting exception is Robert J. Rhee, *Fiduciary Exemption for Public Necessity: Shareholder Profit, Public Good, and the Hobson's Choice During a National Crisis,* 17 GEO. MASON L. REV. 661 (2010).

[86] This subsection draws on material first published in Yosifon, *Corporate Aid of Governmental Authority, supra* note 39.

[87] 8 DEL. GEN. CORP. L. § 122(12) (1967) (emphasis added).

Model Act, published in 1950, with memories of the Second World War still vivid and the reality of the Cold War becoming clear, stipulated that firms should have the power "in time of war to transact any lawful business in aid of the United States in the prosecution of the war."[88] The official annotation to the Model Act, published by the ABA in 1960, contained this important comment: "The section explicitly recognizes that in time of war a corporation may validly assume *responsibilities* that it would not normally undertake in peacetime."[89] Folk acknowledged that he was influenced by the Model Act when he suggested a "wartime or emergency" power in a comprehensive report he made in 1967 to Delaware's Revision Committee. What is less clear is whether he, the Committee, or the Delaware legislature shared the Model Act's view that this power authorized an expansion of ordinary corporate "responsibilities."

There is evidence that Folk himself considered the section 122(12) power merely to extend the permissible kinds of activities in which a corporation could engage if its charter expressed a purpose narrower than to undertake "any lawful act."[90] In his report, Folk wrote:

> Many statutes ... specifically authorize a corporation, irrespective of the purposes stated in the certificate of incorporation, to do any lawful business in time of war or other national emergency. Its effect is to eliminate the necessity for a formal amendment of the certificate, by shareholder action; and in war or emergency times, especially in a nuclear age, this may be important.[91]

Having completed its work, the Revision Committee forwarded its draft statute to the Delaware legislature. No public hearings were held. The Delaware legislature adopted the entire new statute in July 1967,

---

[88] MODEL BUS. CORP. ACT ANN. § 4(n) (West 1960).

[89] *Id.* (emphasis added). This annotation listed fourteen states as having statutory versions of this provision (not yet Delaware) but indicated that there were no cases "of general interest" interpreting the power.

[90] 8 DEL. GEN. CORP. L. § 102(a)(3) (allowing a corporation to specify that its purpose is to undertake "any lawful act").

[91] Ernest L. Folk, III, REVIEW OF THE DELAWARE CORPORATION LAW 40 (1967), http://law .widener.edu/LawLibrary/Research/OnlineResources/DelawareResources/DelawareCor porationLawRevisionCommittee.

without amendment, without debate, and without any formal legislative history.

Two years later, in 1969, the section 122(12) power was significantly expanded by amendment. The new version, which still stands today, reads: "Every corporation ... shall have power to ... [t]ransact any lawful business which the corporation's board of directors shall find to be in aid of governmental authority."[92] The original section 122 (12) power was only operable during time of "war or other national emergency," whereas under the revised version it is *always* available. The other change is just as striking. Under the 1967 version, the power to aid war or national emergency was only triggered after a government agent "request[ed]" or "direct[ed]" it.[93] Thus, in the original version, the discretion to use the power had to come in the first instance from outside of the corporation. After the change, the authority became fully vested at all times in every corporation's board of directors.

There is no formal legislative history for this amendment. Nevertheless, the change can be connected to a change to the Model Act undertaken at about the same time. In 1969, the ABA's Committee on Corporate Laws amended the Model Act and, among other changes, expanded the "wartime power," dropping the reference to "war" and now generally authorizing, "any corporate business which the board of directors shall find to be in aid of governmental authority."[94] The formal annotations to the Model Act's 1969 revisions provided two remarkable explanations for the change:

> The first was the waging of undeclared wars and engagement in varying forms of hostilities, leaving uncertain the legal basis for exercise of the power. The second was the emergence of other equally important areas of government support in the elimination of poverty, disease and civil strife. Hence, the adoption in 1969 of the existing provision, which is intended to enlarge the corporate powers in support of governmental policy.[95]

The Committee that developed those changes to the Model Act had nineteen members, including Samuel Arsht of Wilmington, Delaware.

---

[92] 8 Del. Gen. Corp. L. 8, § 122(12) (1969).

[93] 8 Del. Gen. Corp. L. 8, § 122(12) (1967).

[94] Model Bus. Corp. Act Ann. 2d. § 4(n) (1969).   [95] *Id.* at P 2.

Arsht was an influential corporate lawyer and had served on the Delaware Revision Commission which overhauled Delaware's statute in 1967. While I have found no "smoking gun," the most likely scenario is that Arsht brought the changes his ABA committee was making to the "wartime" powers in the Model Act home to Delaware in 1969.[96]

In 1972, Folk published a comprehensive treatise on the revised Delaware General Corporation Law that he had been so deeply involved in shaping. In it, Folk seems to double down on his view that section 122(12), even in its 1969 form, merely expands the kinds of activities that a corporation may undertake and does not expand the permissible purpose for undertaking them:

> Section 122(12), as amended in 1969, broadly authorizes any corporation to transact any lawful business which the board of directors finds to be in aid of governmental authority. Such statutory power would override provisions in the certificate of incorporation specifying the permissible purposes of the corporation, although it is likely that corporations will increasingly take advantage of the "all purpose" clause authorized in 1967 by § 102(a)(3), so that the chance of conflict between declared charter purposes and the new statutory provision is markedly diminished.[97]

A similar hypothetical to the one that guided our analysis of the charitable giving power must test the meaning of the power to aid governmental authority. Suppose the board of a corporation chartered generally to undertake "any lawful act" deliberated and explicitly determined that it would sacrifice shareholder profit over all time horizons in order to aid governmental authority in advancing fair housing policies, or mitigating climate change. Would this be permissible? If Delaware were to interpret section 122(12) consistently with the rest of its jurisprudence, I think the answer must be no. Of course, directors taking the long view may conclude in good faith that it is desirable for the corporation to advance government policies, lest it alienate constituencies crucial to sustaining the operation's profitability. But directors are required to take whatever view they sincerely

---

[96] See Yosifon, *Corporate Aid of Governmental Authority*, *supra* note 39 at 1096.
[97] FOLK, THE DELAWARE GENERAL CORPORATION LAW, *supra* note 91, at 37–38.

believe is in the best interests of the shareholders. Delaware courts are unlikely to hold that the long-dormant power to "aid governmental authority" changes that.

THE FALLACY OF NORMATIVE INDIFFERENCE IN THE BUSINESS JUDGMENT RULE

A final interpretive move that has bred confusion on the law of corporate purpose is conflation of what the law requires with speculation about what directors can get away with. Some scholars claim that corporate boards can easily attend to non-shareholders at the expense of shareholders without getting caught or punished. This may be true. But sometimes getting away with something is by no means the same thing as being always allowed to do it. A system in which directors can get away with non-shareholder attention will produce very different results than a system that includes de jure permission to attend to non-shareholders.

The source of this obfuscation is found in one of corporate law's most potent doctrines: the "business judgment rule." This is a rule of judicial design, which holds that courts will not interfere with or second guess a board's decision, so long as the directors were personally disinterested in the decision (i.e., had no conflict of interest) and the decision was informed, deliberate, made in good faith, and legal.[98] If these simple conditions are met, directors will be insulated from personal liability for strange, negligent, or even disastrous business decisions. A shareholder whose only complaint is that directors pursued the wrong business plan is bounced right out of Chancery.

Because of the business judgment rule, directors have near total discretion to run firms the way they see fit. It is true, therefore, that it is nearly impossible to enforce the shareholder primacy norm through litigation, absent, essentially, an explicit statement by directors that they are managing the firm towards some other goal. Absent, that is, a confession that negates the *presumption* of good faith that the business

---

[98] *See* JAMES D. COX & THOMAS L. HAZEN, BUSINESS ORGANIZATIONS LAW 197–216 (2011) (discussing business judgment rule).

judgment rule supplies. But just because shareholder primacy cannot be easily enforced through lawsuits does not alter the fact that it *is* the prevailing command of corporate governance law. In *The Shareholder Value Myth*, Lynn Stout blithely collapses this distinction when she writes: "The notion that corporate law requires directors … to maximize shareholder wealth simply isn't true. There is no solid legal support for the claim that directors … in U.S. corporations have an enforceable legal duty to maximize shareholder wealth. The idea is a fable."[99] There is indeed little precedent showing courts enforcing the shareholder primacy norm, but the paucity of such actions stands beside a jurisprudence that clearly specifies that Delaware's law requires shareholder primacy in firm governance. Of course, it really is a fable to say that the enforceable duty is a fable, instead of more accurately saying that enforcement is rare. *Revlon* and *eBay* and are both cases where Delaware courts enforce the shareholder primacy obligation.[100]

The fallacy of normative indifference in the business judgment rule is a recurring problem in the academic literature. Christopher Bruner, after first promising that his article, "The Enduring Ambivalence of Corporate Law," would "describe … explicit deviations from shareholder wealth maximization" as being "common both in takeover law and with respect to charitable donations,"[101] finally acknowledges (in his footnotes) that he can draw only a "de facto"[102] conclusion about the current state of these things in Delaware. I emphasize here with italics the word Bruner puts into a parenthetical: "the board enjoys … considerable latitude to deviate (*tacitly*) from shareholder wealth maximization."[103] The enduring ambivalence that Bruner purports to describe is therefore not a statement about Delaware law, but about what lawless directors might get away with.

---

[99] STOUT, THE SHAREHOLDER VALUE MYTH, *supra* note 2 at 25.

[100] Stout claims that Revlon is an "exception that proves that rule," *id.*, and so it is for her not fable-busting. In every case where directors have acknowledged serving some other interest at the expense of shareholder, Delaware courts have concluded that the directors broke the law.

[101] Christopher M. Bruner, *The Enduring Ambivalence of Corporate Law*, 59 ALA. L. REV. 1385, 1401 (2008).

[102] *Id.* at 1400 n. 84.   [103] *Id.* at 1412 (emphasis added).

With no good cases to substantiate his claim that Delaware disavows shareholder primacy, Einer Elhauge is similarly left calling fraud a freedom. Where non-shareholder interests are threatened in a takeover bid, Elhauge argues, "[m]anagement need only, if it wants to do so, make sure that the winning bid is structured to include some securities whose future value can be claimed to bear some rational relationship to effects on other constituencies."[104] In his essay describing ambivalence on the question of corporate purpose in Delaware, David Millon says that Delaware's rule that non-shareholder interests have to be rationally related to shareholder value is "of no practical importance, because shareholders lack the ability to challenge management policies that favor nonshareholder interests even if the result is reduction of profits."[105] If the president wants to make war on Vietnam without congressional authorization he can merely claim, if he wants to, that there was an attack on an American ship in the Gulf of Tonkin.[106]

We must distinguish between plausible assertions, duties easily ignored, and tacit undertakings – which faithless servants may abide – and sincere, good faith deliberation and decision-making – which honest men and women will strive for when they are true to their duty. Haphazard, unethically infected skim may come from the former; strong, decisive leadership in social responsibility can only come from the latter. In this vein, Delaware's pronouncements about directors' obligations running solely to shareholders are most certainly of practical importance. Within a corporate governance system that explicitly avows process, loyalty, and honesty, it is wholly inapposite to conclude that anything "tacit" should play a crucial role in an accurate or desirable conception of proper corporate governance.

Obscurity, or obscurantism, on this issue is one of the core frictions of our corporate law conversation. In the smoke of the business judgment rule, shareholder primacy's critics see cover to slip into corporate governance social responsibility norms that are formally prohibited

---

[104] Elhauge, *supra* note 49, at 852   [105] Millon, *supra* note 10, at 527.
[106] *See* MARILYN B. YOUNG, THE VIETNAM WARS, 1945–1990, 117–23 (1991) (reviewing President Lyndon Johnson's duplicity in escalating the Vietnam War based on erroneous reports of a North Vietnamese attack on United States ships in the Gulf of Tonkin).

from operating there, and which can only operate so long as the smoke stays thick and nobody sees very clearly anything about the truth of what corporate law commands and what corporations are really doing.

The law of purpose in the United States is shareholder primacy, and the consequences of that law are serious. The next two chapters return to thematic inquiry into the frictions of the shareholder primacy norm, beginning next with the problem of corporate patriotism.

5   CORPORATE PATRIOTISM

In July 2014, President Barack Obama gave a speech to a "rowdy crowd" in California, in which he condemned corporations that recharter from the United States to foreign jurisdictions in order to avoid American tax liability as "economic deserters."[1] Obama's scorching epithet presaged what would become a central theme of Donald Trump's 2016 presidential campaign: a charge that domestic corporations were undermining the national interest. Such suspicions have been evident in American political discourse for generations, but they are especially pressing in our era of widespread international corporate operations.[2] In the mainstream political conversation, the problem of corporate patriotism is never connected to the fundamental law of corporate governance. It will be connected here.[3]

In the course of doing business, domestic corporations can and do send jobs and tax revenues overseas, devastating local communities even as they boost the prospects of workers in a foreign land, and the interests of capital across the globe. American firms also disperse across the border valuable resources, and control over resources, that

---

[1] *See* Jeff Mason, *Obama Rails Against Corporate Maneuver to Evade U.S. Taxes*, REUTERS (Jul 25, 2014), www.reuters.com/article/2014/07/25/us-usa-tax-obama-inversions-idUSKBN0FT13K20140725.

[2] Before the second half of the twentieth century, even large corporations typically were chartered, produced, and sold goods in only one country. But corporate operations went global in every sense – capital, labor, consumer – after World War II. By the 1990s, multinational corporations controlled one-third of all private-sector assets. In the early twenty-first century, multinational corporations have become dominant social, economic, political, and cultural forces throughout the world. *See* Linda A. Mabry, *Multinational Corporations and U.S. Technology Policy: Rethinking the Concept of Corporate Nationality*, 87 GEO. L.J. 563, 569 (1999).

[3] This chapter is based on material first published in David G. Yosifon, *Is Corporate Patriotism a Virtue?*, 14 SANTA CLARA J. INT'L L. 265 (2016).

could otherwise be nationalized or made available to the homeland in times of crisis or war. The shareholder primacy norm at the heart of American corporate governance law may compel directors to do these things, or at least consider doing them. Shareholder primacy sees no need and leaves no quarter for other values, such as patriotic conscience, in the boardroom. This may be a problem.

Patriotism is love for one's country. Felt strongly, it motivates action as powerfully as any other kind of love. Like other modes of loving, patriotism is nontransactional. A patriot is willing to *sacrifice* in service to their nation. This is often conceived as putting the nation before one's self-interest. But human lives are deeply interconnected. Love for family, for example, often means we put our family above our friends, or our community, or business. Patriotic self-sacrifice may also involve sacrifice of not just one's self-interest, but also one's other responsibilities, to a spouse, or child, or shareholders, in favor of serving the nation.

The legitimacy of the patriotic impulse has been scrutinized by some of the most important modern ethicists, including George Orwell, Alasdair MacIntyre, and more recently, Martha Nussbaum.[4] But neither these thinkers nor their followers have given any serious attention to the problem of patriotism as it relates to corporate operations. Corporate law scholarship, for its part, has filled volumes dissecting problems of corporate "social responsibility" but has been curiously unfocused on the question of patriotism as an element of this concern. The aim of this chapter is to bridge these two literatures, add something to each, and continue to build the case that multistakeholder governance should replace shareholder primacy in our corporate law.

The corporate law command to always put shareholders first would seem to be in tension with the idea of patriotism, or at least the idea of corporate patriotism. Nevertheless, canonical justifications for prevailing corporate law, which I reviewed in Chapter 1, insist that shareholder

---

[4] *See* STEPHEN NATHANSON, PATRIOTISM, MORALITY, AND PEACE (1993) (book-length study, summarizing literature); MARTHA C. NUSSBAUM, FOR LOVE OF COUNTRY: DEBATING THE LIMITS OF PATRIOTISM (Joshua Cohen ed., 1993) (collection of essays by leading intellectuals discussing patriotism).

primacy is only *superficially* about shareholders. Its proponents say it turns out to be the rule that best serves all stakeholders, and society generally. We must test this view against the commands of patriotism.

WHAT IS AN AMERICAN CORPORATION?

To ask about corporate patriotism requires some idea of corporate nationality. This is not a straightforward matter. Is a firm that is chartered in the United States, but produces with workers in China, and sells its products in France, on behalf of Russian investors, an American company? In an important sense, it is. Corporations do not exist without the law of the sovereignty that creates them. My first point of departure, therefore, is to consider firms that are chartered in the United States under American law (Delaware law), to be American corporations. This is not an exhaustive conception, but it is an important starting place. If patriotism is an American value, then we should expect our corporate law to prudently reflect patriotic concerns. And, of course, if patriotism is an important Irish, German, or Japanese value, then the Irish, Germans, and Japanese should expect the issue to be prudently reflected in their corporate law. As a secondary consideration, I also think that we should regard as "American" corporations, for the purposes of this inquiry, firms that have their principle place of business, their "real seat of power," in the United States. Such firms have special influence in the United States and thus are rightfully subjects of an inquiry concerned with patriotic conscience in corporate operations.[5]

IS CORPORATE PATRIOTISM A VIRTUE?

American corporations in a few specific industries (fewer than in the past) are subject to specific charting, ownership, and governance

---

[5] The "real seat" doctrine prevails in Europe, where firms are governed by the corporate law that obtains in the nation where the firm has its "real seat" of power. In the United States, at present, the law of the chartering place determines the rules that will apply to the firm's corporate governance. I discuss this important difference further in Chapter 8.

regulations aimed at forcing them to operate in ways that serve American interests.[6] But I am concerned with the default rules that govern corporate operations generally. It may be difficult to know ahead of time what kinds of companies are, or will suddenly become, of acute national importance. And when that knowledge does arrive, it may be too late for ordinary or extraordinary political processes to take effect to force (or allow) the firm to serve the nation. For example, a global pharmaceutical company could become of vital national interest during an international pandemic, which might spread across the globe too chaotically for ordinary political processes to operate effectively. In such a case, a patriotic company might direct emergency resources disproportionately to the United States. Absent a patriotic conscience, it might not. The same could be true of an American technology company in the context of a global computer virus accidently or intentionally attacking computer systems across the globe. And this

---

[6] American anxiety about foreign influence in domestic affairs dates to the colonial era, but early American thirst for capital rendered restrictions on foreign investment in the United States relatively anemic until after World War I. *See* Detlev F. Vagts, *The Corporate Alien: Definitional Questions in Federal Restraints on Foreign Enterprise*, 74 HARV. L. REV. 1489 (1961) (landmark and still essential study). The advent of the Great War revealed extensive foreign ownership of enterprise in the United States, as billions were repatriated from the United States to fuel European armies. In response, "[t]he 1916–1930 period saw a proliferation of legislation restricting alien participation in such areas as radio, aircraft, shipping, and petroleum production." *Id.* at 1493. After World War II, the growing wealth of the United States and its new role as a global investor dampened concerns about foreign investment in domestic enterprise. Writing in 1961, Vagts correctly predicted that, "the future portends contraction . . . of restrictive legislation except in defense industries." *Id.* at 1494. The last several decades have seen relaxation of foreign ownership restraints in most industries. Nevertheless, there are continuing ebbs and flows. In 1975, President Gerald Ford issued an executive order establishing the Committee on Foreign Investment in the United States (CFIUS), which he charged with making recommendations regarding foreign investment activity that could undermine American interests. *See* Paul Connell & Tian Huang, *An Empirical Analysis of CFIUS: Examining Foreign Investment Regulation in the United States*, 39 YALE J. INT'L L. 131, 135–36 (2014). In 1988, Congress granted the president the power to block foreign investment deemed a threat to national security. This power was delegated to CFIUS, making it a powerful administrative entity. CFIUS's initial charge was limited to reviewing investment in just a few industries, but its authority continually expanded over ensuing decades and increased dramatically after the attacks of September 11, 2001. *See id.* at 132–33, 137. CFIUS and other federal regulations restricting foreign influence in American business are important interventions, but for present purposes they are the exceptions that prove the rule: the vast majority of corporations are not subject to laws that encourage or require them to be governed in a manner that privileges American interests over the interests of other nations.

"time of crisis" angle may just provide a salient way of thinking through how we want corporate decision-making to operate at more routine margins. We may want corporations to be patriotic in the ordinary course.

I have so far in this book been addressing people in terms of subcategorizations such as "workers," "consumers," "shareholders," and sometimes, "communities." Firms with international operations have stakeholders of those types who are citizens of many different nations. Should we also be concerned with the category "America" or "Americans" in our thinking about corporate social responsibility? To know if corporate patriotism is desirable, we should first think through whether patriotism itself is ethically defensible. A positive reply would not in itself be sufficient to vindicate a normative command for corporate patriotism, but it would be a necessary step to such vindication. If patriotism is a vice, then so is corporate patriotism. If patriotism is a virtue, then corporate patriotism *may* be desirable.[7]

PATRIOTISM AS VICE, CORPORATE LAW AS VIRTUE

George Orwell endeavored to distinguish "patriotism" and "nationalism."[8] Patriotism he saw as benign "devotion to a particular place and a particular way of life," involving no desire to impose those commitments on others. He thus considered patriotism to be "defensive," in contradistinction to nationalism, which he saw as characterized by a "desire for power," and which is therefore aggressive towards other people and ways of life.[9] Both strains are treated in Orwell's voluminous writings. He despised imperialism, and his brief work on its behalf as a British policeman in Burma in the 1920s so filled him with disgust that it motivated his whole journey as the conscience of the twentieth

---

[7] The analysis here could be applied to the patriotic concerns of any nation, and any nation's corporate law. I write about the United States here because that is the nation I love, and whose interests I aim to advance in a way that is ethically harmonious with my concomitant love of all humanity. To write seriously about patriotism, one must write about it literally.

[8] GEORGE ORWELL, *Notes on Nationalism*, collected in SUCH, SUCH WERE THE JOYS 74 (1948, 1953).

[9] *Id.*

century. On the other hand, Orwell loved England and the English way of life, and he celebrated it poetically, warmly, routinely.[10] But I think Orwell's categories, the passive legitimate patriotism and the active illegitimate nationalism, are not sustainable in a global economic age where patriots cannot remain isolated, but must continually decide whether to *favor* their nation in their business dealings *or not*. Being patriotic does not require that a person be prepared to go to *any* lengths for their nation, or be willing to treat foreigners in *any* way, in favor of their countrymen. But we must insist on the hard logical and practical truth that in an international era devotion to a particular nation implies discrimination at some margin against people of other nations. And that is the margin at which patriotism is an important moral problem.

Patriotism is in fact pervasive. In mainstream political discourse, it operates as orthodoxy and assumption. It abides in the conscience of most ordinary men and women to different degrees and in different ways. The World Values Survey finds patriotism to be common among the peoples of the world, with Americans among the most patriotic.[11]

---

[10] *See, e.g.*, GEORGE ORWELL, *England Your England*, collected in SUCH, SUCH WERE THE JOYS 252 (1941, 1953). Much of the misery emphasized in Orwell's *1984* involves deprivation of the ordinary habits of everyday English life. Bad tea, bad chocolate, and the absence of little shops are used to paint the dystopian picture. George Orwell, 1984 (1948).

[11] "The United States indeed has the highest percentages of 'very proud' nationals over 25 years [of survey data]." Jerome Karabel & Daniel Laurison, *An Exceptional Nation? American Political Values in Comparative Perspective* 22 (Institute for Research on Labor and Employment, Working Paper No. 136–12, 2012), http://irle.berkeley.edu/workingpa pers/136–12.pdf. Another group of researchers concludes that, generally, "Europe and Asia are less patriotic than the Americas, Africa, and the Middle East." Adair Morse & Sophie Shive, *Patriotism in Your Portfolio*, 14 J. FIN. MARKETS 411, 414 (2011). Morse and Shive argue that there is a capital-allocation bias that results from investors privileging national firms over foreign ones. "Asset pricing theory predicts that investors should hold the world market portfolio, not a portfolio primarily of domestic stock. Country portfolios with small domestic holdings are, however, simply not observed." *Id.* They find a signifi-cant impact: "The economic magnitude of patriotism's effect is large: an average country invests 3–5% more for its aggregate portfolio abroad with a one standard deviation drop in patriotism." Now that's econometrics. The claim that capital has a preference for patriot-ism might suggest a reason for expanding, beyond wealth maximization, the permissible bounds of what it means to serve shareholder interests, even under a shareholder primacy regime. But serving the patriotic preferences of capital becomes difficult in firms with globally dispersed stockholders. To the extent that national diversity in shareholder base undermines nonpecuniary common denominators, then shareholder wealth maximization inevitably becomes the more exclusive focus of corporate governance. *Cf.* Edward B. Rock, *Shareholder Eugenics in the Public Corporation*, 97 CORNELL L. REV. 849 (2012). I do not pursue the question of shareholders' preferences for patriotism here, because I am less

Yet even among those who recognize within themselves a patriotic sentiment, the impulse is suspect. The patriotic conscience is haunted by the worry that it may be stupid or corrupt, or both. Stupid, because, except for immigrants, one's homeland is an accident of their birth. It seems immoral to base a special regard, a motivating affection, on such happenstance, at least when it comes to important matters. Most people consider it morally acceptable to privilege their own family, another accident of birth, over the interests of strangers.[12] But this begs the question: do compatriots deserve to be treated specially, like family, or is it capricious to treat them better than one treats other kinds of strangers? Enlightened, liberal morality requires us to treat all people equally and to consider them to be equally valuable and worthy unless they have shown themselves for some good reason not to be. From this perspective, "patriotism is like racism."[13] Worse than being stupid, patriotism may be corrupt, and corrupting. It is a dangerous kindle, threatening always to blaze into discrimination, xenophobia, and imperialism.

From the point of view of liberal morality, then, patriotism is a vice. And if patriotism by natural people is pernicious, corporate patriotism would obviously be undesirable. We would do well to organize a corporate law that ignores or excludes it. This we appear to have done. If patriotism is a vice, then the exclusion of patriotic sentiment from corporate decision-making is a morally desirable feature – *a bonus feature* – of shareholder primacy in corporate governance law.

Consider an illustrative episode concerning the response of American corporations to the OPEC oil embargo of 1973–1974.[14] In retaliation for western support of Israel during the Arab-Israeli War of 1973, Arab nations threatened to nationalize the property of major oil

---

interested in the narrow question of what capital wants from corporate governance than I am in the more fundamental question of what society wants, or should want, and can expect to get from it.

[12] *See,* e.g., Adam Swift, How Not to Be a Hypocrite: School Choice for the Morally Perplexed Parent (2003) (examining the legitimacy of and moral limits to parents' preferences for their own children).

[13] *See* Paul Gomberg, *Patriotism Is Like Racism,* 101 Ethics 144 (1990).

[14] *See* Mabry, *supra* note 2, at 620–22 (relying on Staff of S. Comm. on Multinational Corporations, 93d Cong., Rep. On Multinational Oil Corporations and U.S. Foreign Policy 67 (Comm. Print 1975)).

companies if they supplied oil obtained from the Middle East to the United States, several European countries, or South Africa. American corporations complied, which was perhaps not in itself unpatriotic since the choice was comply or be nationalized by foreigners. However, the Arab nations imposing the boycott did not seek to control the way companies distributed oil they obtained from other parts of the world. American oil companies could have privileged American interests and shipped all available oil to the homeland, given the shortages caused by the embargo. Indeed, the federal government was "urging U.S.-origin oil companies to bring as much oil as possible into the United States."[15] Instead, what American corporations decided to do was apportion their oil equally among countries affected by the embargo. That decision could fit into a "just so" shareholder wealth maximization story, since the firms may have been aiming to maintain good relations across their global customer base in anticipation of a return to normal business dynamics. But it surely was not patriotic in the sense of putting the United States first, especially in a time of crisis. In effect, it was a choice that treated all the peoples of the world as being of equal dignity. If patriotism is a vice, then shareholder primacy may be virtuous, or at least virtue's servant. Shareholder primacy may even be virtue inducing by encouraging in corporate elites a habit of disregarding national identity in their decision-making. It may further be useful in disabusing workers, consumers, and others of any expectation that their national identity will or should be relevant to how they are treated by others.

There is an ironic or "strange bedfellows" implication to this analysis. The kind of people who regard themselves as advocates of universal humanism and who are generally suspicious of treating people differently on the basis of nationality probably also tend to be people who regard themselves as suspicious of the shareholder primacy norm in corporate operations. (I do not have survey evidence for this claim, but I would wager good money – or at least money from my faculty research budget – on the correlation.) But if shareholder primacy excludes and undermines patriotic conscience in favor of a more even-handed treatment of people across the planet, then proponents of

[15] Mabry, *supra* note 2, at 622 n. 236.

universal humanism might be more attracted to shareholder primacy law than they would have thought. Irony being a two-way street, proponents of shareholder primacy in corporate governance might be more committed to the pursuit of universal humanism, and the denigration of national difference, than they would have expected.

PATRIOTISM AS VIRTUE, CORPORATE LAW AS VICE

There is available, however, a sophisticated argument which vindicates patriotism as virtuous.

A thoughtful approach to justifying patriotism was supplied by the great moral philosopher Alasdair MacIntyre, in his seminal lecture: "Is Patriotism a Virtue?"[16] MacIntyre argues that the starting place of liberal morality that I just summarized – treat everyone equally unless there is good reason to do otherwise – mistakenly approaches morality as if it were like mathematics, or chemistry, or mechanical engineering: something that can be taught, learned, and acted upon without reference to the particulars of human culture and experience. Morality is not like that. To the contrary, MacIntyre argues, leaving aside whether moral *principles* are themselves objective, *becoming a moral person* always involves the specific, subjective experience of being in relationship to a specific society. For the human animal, "an essential characteristic of the morality which each of us acquires [is] that it is learned from, in, and through the way of life of some particular community."[17] Even if the moral standards of many cultures end up being similar, learning to embrace those standards must be grounded in experience of and allegiance to a distinct "social order."[18] A special commitment to *our* community, a sense of identification with it – the kind of identification that spurs a willingness and desire to serve its interests and sacrifice for it – is psychologically necessary for any of us to learn any morality. If this is true, then patriotism is perhaps not only acceptable but commendable, or even imperative, if humans are to be moral creatures.

[16] *See* Alasdair MacIntryre, *Is Patriotism a Virtue?: The Lindley Lecture* (1984).
[17] *Id.* at 8.   [18] *Id.* at 8–9.

It may be tempting to think that even if patriotism undergirds moral *development*, it does not necessarily follow that patriotism must be, or can be, a component of a resultant, fully developed morality. Once matured, a person may be able to push away the scaffolding of patriotic sentiment, in order to regard and treat all humans equally. But I think that view is inconsistent with MacIntyre's conjecture. If the morally mature person looks past her own community, seeing and treating all others in a scrupulously universalist fashion, then her own conduct threatens to undermine the maintenance of the moral community, replete with specific devotion, on which moral development for others depends. By acting in a morally "superior" fashion herself, the supposedly mature universalist undermines the conditions of morality for others.

Before MacIntyre crystallized his insight for an assessment of patriotism, the basic idea had a long pedigree which sometimes emphasized rougher dimensions. Sigmund Freud, for example, wrote that the impulse to animosity is a core feature of the human psyche. He claimed that fraternity could be an effective organizing principle in society, but only if the anger impulse had some outgroup to focus on. "It is always possible to bind together a considerable number of people in love, so long as there are other people left over to receive the manifestations of their aggressiveness."[19] We, on this account, implies them. Freud thought that feuds and ridicule between people of adjoining regions or nations, which can be sustained for generations without erupting into war, could be a "convenient and relatively harmless satisfaction of the inclination to aggression,"[20] which could enable nationals internally to make productive use of the coalescing power of patriotism. A more pernicious fulcrum of outgroup designation that Freud noted was European anti-Semitism, which allowed nations to self-regard affectionately through an "othering" that did not even directly threaten war with other nations.

Even if patriotism is necessary, it need not be – indeed, rightly understood, it must not be – dogmatic. A blind devotion to one's country, an unwillingness to see and address its faults, would make national pride a childish fiction, instead of a rich source of

---

[19] Sigmund Freud, CIVILIZATION AND ITS DISCONTENTS 60 (1930, 1961).   [20] *Id.*

community-based morality making. A nation's domestic critics are often just as motivated by patriotic love as are its boosters. Dissidents often express themselves in terms of shame, disappointment, or embarrassment at their country – emotions that could only be felt by one who adores the object of their appraisal.[21] Critical assessment of one's social order is evidence that the morality-making powers of patriotism are working. According to MacIntyre, instead of blindly accepting one's nation as it is, what a morally functional patriotism requires is commitment to the nation "as a project."[22]

This argument makes a compelling case that parochialism may be necessary to achieve moral development. But there is little in it that explains why the *nation* should describe the contours of that parochialism. Why not race or creed? Or something simpler. Reading in the patriotism literature, I felt I had found some vindication for the pleasure, which I have often regarded as a guilty one, of being a sports fan. Here is a passage from Jonathan Lethem's 2015 novel, *Dissident Gardens*. A morose professor, Cicero, slouches in front of the TV after a day's work:

> Contemptuous of the pull of tribal nationalism in the human psyche ... Cicero could humble himself contemplating his own irrational lifetime affiliation with the Mets. A thread of Fascist susceptibility lay in how Cicero fought the pull of sleep each summer night, blood quick to the chance of seeing men triumph in the same orange and blue that had limned Tom Seaver's thighs. Leni Riefenstahl, alive and well on DirecTV.[23]

Perhaps fandom is not just saccharine consumption or foolish rallying around arbitrary team identity. Maybe it generates an openness to solidarity that is crucial to the development of morality in more important matters. Loyalty to a team, fake as the whole thing is, may be good for us. Understanding himself in terms of MacIntyre's conjecture, Cicero might see in his arousal for the Mets not the seeds of fascism but the wellspring of something that could crush fascism.

---

[21] This is succinctly expressed by Leonard Cohen in his 1992 anthem, *Democracy*: "I love the country but / I can't stand the scene." Leonard Cohen, *Democracy*, on THE FUTURE (Sony Records, 1992).

[22] MacIntyre, *supra* note 16, at 13.

[23] JONATHAN LETHEM, DISSIDENT GARDENS 200 (2013).

Love of sports and love of nation perhaps engage the same psychological mechanics in the human animal. But we are here concerned with the legitimacy of corporate *patriotism*, and for good reason. The legal philosopher Martha Nussbaum explains why the nation, rather than some other group, should serve the motivating function that MacIntyre indicated. The nation, Nussbaum argues, is the largest organizational structure that can plausibly sustain the sentiments of devotion that serve community-based, efficacious morality.[24] Patriotic love is a sweet spot at the intersection of size and effectiveness. Smaller groups like families are highly motivating but too small to have substantial cooperative utility. All of humanity is a great size but requires too much abstraction, and is too bereft of the power of othering, to induce more than "watery motivation" to pursue collective projects.[25] The nation is a community that can be plausibly imagined, and it is a potent kind of imagining.

Indeed, Orwell said that love of country is unequaled as a motivating force, compared to other sources of public emotion. It is stronger than sports or more serious things: "Christianity and international socialism are as weak as straw in comparison with it."[26] The Second World War, Orwell argued, showed that class conflict within nations was not inevitable, and class consciousness across nations was not necessary, to do horrible or great things.[27] Patriotism was sufficient to both. Hitler and Mussolini could not have risen to power without the power of patriotism. And Hitler and Mussolini could not have been put down without it.

More than potent, Nussbaum insists, the nation is also at least potentially a politically *legitimate* way of orchestrating a moral

---

[24] *See* Martha C. Nussbaum, *Teaching Patriotism: Love and Critical Freedom*, 79 U. CHI. L. REV. 213, 232 (2012). Curiously, unlike most contemporary scholars writing about patriotism, Nussbaum does not address her arguments to MacIntyre's treatment. Nevertheless, her contributions build nicely on MacIntyre's framework.

[25] *Id.* Nussbaum's use of "watery" motivation draws on Aristotle's critique of the idea, discussed in Plato's *Republic*, of raising children by the polity, rather than in families. *Id.* (citing ARISTOTLE, THE POLITICS OF ARISTOTLE 1262b (Ernest Baker trans., 1958)).

[26] GEORGE ORWELL, *England Your England*, in SUCH, SUCH WERE THE JOYS 200 (1941, 1953).

[27] *See* GEORGE ORWELL, *Writers and Leviathan*, in SUCH, SUCH WERE THE JOYS 68 (1948, 1953).

community, for example, if it is democratically organized. A constitutional democracy can also build countermajoritarian safeguards into the national project to counter the worst impulses of patriotism. For example, free speech guarantees can provide foreigners and minorities protections against the malignant out-group scapegoating that patriotism can feed.[28] If our institutional designs can ward off what is ill in patriotism, then we can be free to tap what is good in it.

Yes, patriotism can be "the last refuge of a scoundrel,"[29] masking self-serving conduct and spurring mistreatment of out-groups. But Nussbaum thinks the danger can be managed by the critical, self-reflective impulses that patriotism also ignites. It must be managed. There is no alternative. Human society cannot be organized in strictly rational ways. Emotion is going to operate in civic life. It is better to confront that reality directly so that emotion's constructive aspects can be harnessed and its destructive tendencies contained. We had better do it in the cause of liberty, democracy, and justice, or else, Nussbaum warns, it will surely be done on behalf of "less appetizing aims."[30]

Patriotism and Canonical Corporate Theory

If patriotism is a virtue, then perhaps our corporate law, which excludes patriotic conscience, is not virtuous. Sometimes doing right by the nation will be best for shareholders, but not always. There are many examples, small and large, of how firms disregard or undermine the national interest in furtherance of the profit maximand. The OPEC case described above suffices to illustrate the point for now.

Proponents of the shareholder primacy norm would be quick to argue (they are never slow to argue) that even if patriotism is a virtue, it does not necessarily follow that patriotism should be pursued through

---

[28] *See* MARTHA C. NUSSBAUM, POLITICAL EMOTIONS: WHY LOVE MATTERS FOR JUSTICE 214 (2013).

[29] James Boswell attributed this enduring quip to Dr. Johnson in JAMES BOSWELL, THE LIFE OF SAMUEL JOHNSON 615 (1799, 1953). Christopher Hitchens always insisted that Johnson was here referring to a specific political party in his own day that went by the name "Patriots," and that he was not making a general point about patriotism as we know it. No matter. Moral discourse has needed the point, and Dr. Johnson, even if apocryphally, is always welcome in polite conversation.

[30] NUSSBAUM, POLITICAL EMOTIONS, *supra* note 28, at 256.

corporate operations. For these thinkers, patriotism may be like envir-onmentalism: an important goal, but one best pursued through means other than corporate governance.

The standard account promises that predictable overreach by shareholder primacy firms can be constrained or compensated by the operation of external governmental regulation. This asserted escape hatch has special problems as it pertains to concerns about patriotism. First, as stated earlier, firms work within the political process to stunt such regulatory intervention. Once patriotism is recognized as an important value in and of itself, this public choice problem looks particularly gross, as the machinery of our constitutional democracy is sullied by the poor corporate law design. And the consequence is not just adverse to ideals but also to practical arrangements. Firms capture legislation that would otherwise be aimed at advancing not just "worker" or "consumer" or "environmental" interests, but *American* interests – the national interest. Firms with large international share-holding bases are doing these things on behalf of foreign shareholders.

Shareholder primacy theory's reliance on "external" government regulation to curb corporate excesses is further undermined by the mismatch between the cross-border operations of international firms and the decidedly national limit of political arrangements. American firms with international operations employ foreign workers, sell to foreign consumers, and impact foreign ecosystems. The American electorate would likely be less concerned to protect those stakeholders than they would be to look after their own compatriots or homeland. Indeed, American shareholders and some American stakeholders, like consumers of products produced abroad, may be benefitting from international overreach, and so will be even less motivated to remedy it. The foreign stakeholders who suffer sharp dealing by American shareholder primacy firms have no access to the American political system to seek the governmental regulation that shareholder primacy theory prescribes. And their own governments may not recognize the right to petition for redress of grievances. Indeed, an American firm may have set up shop in a foreign place precisely *because* it is not a democracy, and regulatory redress to exploitation is not available. This is primarily a humanist critique, but there is also a narrow patriotic vantage to it, as doing these things is harmful to our national character and reputation. It may antagonize foreigners against the United States because it is our law that compels our corporations to behave this way.

Bainbridge argues that American corporations, made powerful by shareholder primacy, stand as an effective bulwark against "the slavering maw" of the state.[31] Corporations efficiently organize production, distribution, and consumption, and so there is no call to create a large, powerful state to do those things. To the extent that shareholder primacy makes corporations powerful, this creates a crucial resource in the constant struggle to *stop* the state from trying to intrude into the life and affairs of the citizenry where it has no rightful business operating. Corporate power thus keeps alive a vital civil society that stands between the people and a too powerful, commanding state. This space of *voluntary* action is where authentic patriotism flourishes. Without shareholder primacy, corporations will not flourish, the state will necessarily become stronger and more pervasive for want of such private organization, and voluntary love of the nation gives way to mandatory obedience to the state. Behavior compelled by the state can never be called patriotic.

But there is a conflict between the canonical account's call for the creation of external government regulation to restrain the predictable overreach of shareholder primacy in corporate operations, and the view that one of the benefits of shareholder primacy is that it helps create powerful corporations that stand as a shield against an otherwise encroaching Leviathan. A large state is *implied* by shareholder primacy, not negated by it. And this large state, critics of shareholder primacy insist, cannot be relied upon to do what shareholder primacy advocates call on it to do. Instead, the state will be used by corporations to extend their pursuit of profits on behalf shareholders. As I reviewed in Chapter 3, it will not suffice for libertarian advocates of shareholder primacy to insist that the solution to the problem of corporate capture of the regulatory state is to make sure that the state is small, because shareholder primacy firms will see to it that the state is *not* small but is made big, the better to serve shareholders.

---

[31] Stephen M. Bainbridge, *Community and Statism: A Conservative Critique of Progressive Corporate Law Scholarship*, 82 CORNELL L. REV. 856, 895 (1997).

More subtly, American firms operating internationally without the constraints of patriotic conscience may be undermining the domestic cultural conditions upon which a healthy patriotism can flourish. International corporate operations threaten to marginalize the importance of national community, and the consequent depth of patriotic sentiment, of people in any one country. For example, international corporate operations disaggregate production and consumption across national borders, severing important social relationships that might otherwise form the basis of patriotic connection. I have in mind the community that is created by the production of food in the American heartland and its consumption on the American coasts. The production of durable goods in Michigan for consumption in Mississippi. As production and consumption are separated across national borders, the patriotic imagination thins. And a thin imagination is a dangerous one.[32]

In summary then, if patriotism is a virtue, corporate law may be a vice. Shareholder primacy excludes patriotic conscience from the boardroom, leading firms to make decisions without regard to the national interest. For firms operating in the international arena, this may often cause them to make decisions that undermine American interests or advance the interests of competing nations. Government regulation cannot be counted on to curb such antipatriotic corporate abuses, in part because shareholder primacy corporations will operate politically to stunt regulatory efforts, in continued service to their shareholders. Such political activity also pollutes the waters of legitimate political discourse, poisoning a crucial but fragile environment in which authentic patriotism may otherwise be nurtured, and nurturing.

---

[32] The expansion of consumerism and the rise of global corporate operations have perhaps made patriotism a more routine issue in the lives of ordinary people than it was in earlier eras. For previous generations, the question of patriotism emerged as a decisional matter only episodically, for example, when deciding whether to volunteer for military service in times of war. In previous eras, consumer goods, being generally nationally produced, did not implicate the question of national advantage. "Marginal patriotism," if I may, is a feature of consumer culture under global capitalism. Consumers must continually decide whether to favor American or universal interests in their consumption behavior. In this way, patriotism becomes a commoditized, routine problem instead of an exceptional encounter that is not reducible to dollars. I examine the relationship between consumer culture and corporate law in the next chapter.

By disaggregating the corporate nexus of ownership, control, production, and consumption across national borders, firms with international operations also compromise the conditions of community identification that are necessary to the effective operation of patriotic impulse.

PATRIOTISM AND THE CORPORATE BOARD

The law provides that "the business and affairs of every corporation . . . shall be managed by or under the direction of a board of directors."[33] Therefore, crucial places to focus in assessing the threat or promise of patriotic conscience in corporate operations are inside the hearts and minds of corporate directors. Like all humans, directors have limited cognitive capacity and self-restraint. While the law requires directors to manage firms solely in the interest of shareholders, they do not always do so. Sometimes, consciously or subconsciously, they serve their own interests, and sometimes they serve the interests of other stakeholders at the expense of shareholders. If we assume that directors, like most people, are patriotic, then we must assume that directors' patriotic conscience will at some margin influence corporate decision-making. This "patriotic slacking" may be desirable, or it may be pernicious, depending on your view of the broader issues. Either way, it compels us to think about the consequences of the nationalities of directors serving on our corporate boards.

Now hold on a minute. We must stand guard against the known devils of patriotic discourse: stereotyping and xenophobia. And the unknown ones about which conscience warns. The reader should be wary, as is the author. Yet we should ask. If directors cannot be trusted to always restrain their patriotic impulse where the law calls for shareholder primacy, or if I am wrong in my depiction of corporate law and it already countenances non-shareholderist impulses on corporate boards,[34] then the patriotic commitments of corporate directors to the United States or another country become an issue of real concern.[35]

---

[33] 8 DEL. GEN. CORP. L. § 141(a).   [34] I am not wrong. *See* Chapter 4.

[35] We might expect the magnitude of "patriotic slack" on a corporate board to be a function of the strength of directors' patriotism, on the one hand, and the strength of corporate law,

So we must proceed, suspicious of ourselves and our reasoning, and only ever provisionally committing to our conclusions. I heed Judge Learned Hand's expression of the searching self-skepticism that must be at the core of patriotic inquiry: "What is the spirit of liberty? I cannot define it; I can only tell you my own faith. The spirit of liberty is the spirit which is not too sure it is right."[36]

If patriotism is a vice, then it may be desirable to encourage large firms, especially those with international operations, to populate their boards with directors reflecting a broad array of nationalities. Each director's personal patriotic instincts might counterbalance their fellow director's instincts, with no national bias prevailing. But if corporate patriotism is a virtue, then it might be desirable to ensure that the boards of American firms operating internationally are dominated by at least a critical mass of American nationals, such that inevitable directorial slack manifesting in the patriotic dimension will privilege American interests, rather than those of some foreign country.

Little is known, empirically, about the nationality composition of corporate boards or the implications of director nationality on corporate governance dynamics.[37] Neither Delaware, the federal securities laws, nor the major American stock exchanges require firms to report

---

on the other. Because American corporate law is typically viewed as the "best," in the sense that it most effectively reduces shareholder agency costs, we might expect American corporations dominated by American directors to be relatively less patriotic for America, and foreign corporations dominated by foreign citizens to be relatively more patriotic for foreign countries. *See* Lars Oxelheim & Trond Randoy, *The Impact of Foreign Board Membership on Firm Value*, 27 J. BANKING & FIN. 2369, 2370 (2003) ("The Anglo-American system is commonly regarded as the most demanding corporate governance system."). However, Americans start out with a more patriotic baseline, so this may counterbalance the strength of American corporate law, resulting in similar rates of patriotic slack as are seen in nations with less patriotism but weaker corporate law. Perhaps Morse & Shive can run the numbers. *See supra* note 11. I compare the American corporate governance system to less shareholder-centered models in other nations in Chapter 7.

[36] LEARNED HAND, THE SPIRIT OF LIBERTY 190 (1952).

[37] Surveying the literature, one group of researchers concluded that "[d]espite extensive ongoing research on boards of directors ... the internationalization of corporate boards remains relatively unexplored." Oxelheim & Randoy, *The Impact of Foreign Board Membership on Firm Value, supra* note 35 at 2370. One group of researchers did document a correlation between internationalization of shareholder-base and diversification of nationalities in Nordic boardrooms. Lars Oxelheim et al., *On the Internationalization of Corporate Boards: The Case of Nordic Firms*, 44 J. INT'L BUS. STUD. 173–76 (2013) ("foreign shareholders may be more confident that directors from their own country will represent their interests more forcefully.").

the nationality or citizenship of directors who are serving on their boards or running in corporate elections. Likewise, biographies of directors in annual reports generally do not include this information, an omission that is remarkable whatever the normative purchase.

There are, however, economic and legal reasons to expect that American corporations with global operations will increasingly have higher proportions of foreign national directors serving as corporate directors. Firms might find this profitable for several reasons. If an American company is operating in another country, a citizen of that country may be better placed than American directors to monitor the firm's foreign operations. A foreign national may have special, subtle knowledge about how to effectively reach customers in their homeland. They might have a network of contacts and resources in the foreign country that will make it easier for the firm to attract capital and workers, or manage relationships with the foreign government or local communities. These "connections" can be among the main benefits that a foreign director brings to a board.[38]

Delaware corporate law and federal securities regulations may also be pushing American firms with global operations to put foreign nationals on their boards. Leo Strine, now Chief Justice of the Delaware Supreme Court, made clear in one of his last cases as Chancellor of the Delaware Court of Chancery that corporate boards with

---

[38] One interesting study, however, found that corporations with foreign independent directors performed worse than firms without such directors. *See* Ronald W. Masulis et al., *Globalizing the Boardroom: The Effects of Foreign Directors on Corporate Governance and Firm Performance*, 53 J. ACCT. & ECON. 527, 529 (2012). This study found that for S&P 1500 companies from 1998 to 2006, FIDs (foreign independent directors) accounted for about 13 percent of all independent directors, and that for boards with at least one FID, they accounted for 18 percent of all independent directors. *Id.* at 529. The authors conclude that while individual firms in given years can benefit substantially from FIDS, on net, these gains do not compensate for the losses otherwise associated with FID presence on the boards of U.S. corporations. *Id.*

The principle explanation these researchers gave for their findings is the high transactions costs FIDs bear in traveling long distances for board meetings and other corporate functions. *Id.* FIDs are "nearly three times more likely" to miss 25 percent of board meetings than are non-FIDs. Id. This explanation seems inadequate to me. As the authors note, Delaware allows attendance at board meetings by telephone. *Id.* at 535 n.22. The authors do allow as a secondary explanation the influence on the FIDs of their homeland's law, culture, and norms, which are often more lax on corporate governance standards than those that prevail in the United States. *Id.* at 551.

operations in foreign countries must have directorial eyes and ears in those countries if they are to satisfy their monitoring obligations.[39] *In Re Puda Coal, Inc. Stockholders Litigation* was a case alleging that a Chinese national, independent director of a Delaware corporation doing business in China, had stolen assets belonging to the company. When two other U.S.-based independent directors learned of the theft, they resigned. Shareholders brought suit against the thieving director and against the directors on whose watch the thieving occurred. After entering a default judgment against the absent Chinese director,[40] Strine refused to dismiss the case against the American directors. From the bench, he said:

> If you're going to have a company domiciled ... in Delaware and the assets and operations of the company are situated in China that [sic], in order for you to meet your obligation of good faith, you better have your physical body in China an awful lot ... You better have the language skills to navigate the environment in which the company is operating.[41]

Strine goes on:

> [I]f the assets are in Russia, if they're in Nigeria, if they're in the Middle East, if they're in China ... you're not going to be able to sit in your home in the U.S. and do a conference call four times a year and discharge your duty of loyalty. That won't cut it. That there will be specific challenges that deal with linguistic, cultural and others [sic] in terms of the effort that you have to put in to discharge your duty of loyalty.[42]

---

[39] *See* Oral Argument and the Court's Ruling, In re Puda Coal, Inc., Stockholders Litigation, C.A. No. 6476-CS (Del. Ch., Feb 6, 2013) at 17–18, www.delawarelitigation.com/files/2013/02/puda-case.pdf [hereinafter Puda Coal].

[40] *Id.* Strine recognized that the default judgment he was entering against the Chinese national director was going to be difficult to enforce, given that the defendant was in China. *Id.* at 26. This is another dimension of concern in the effective regulation of corporate governance where there is increased service of foreign nationals on the boards of domestic corporations.

[41] *Id.* 21.

[42] *Id.* at 21–22. This case has limited formal precedential value and Strine may be engaging here more in aspirational suasion than legal line drawing. Nevertheless, such talk from a Delaware jurist, now the Chief Justice of the Delaware Supreme Court, is influential even where it is not, strictly speaking, making law. *See* Edward B. Rock, *Saints and Sinners: How Does Delaware Corporate Law Work?*, 44 UCLA L. Rev. 1009, 1103 (1997) (arguing that

Strine is signaling that for corporations with international operations, at least some directors need implicit cultural knowledge of the
foreign societies in which their firms are doing business. He showcases
the magic words that bring hope to plaintiffs and fear to defendants in
shareholder litigation. Having deep knowledge of the countries in
which their firm is operating is a matter of directorial "good faith." It
is a matter of "loyalty." Under Delaware law, corporate charters may
insulate corporate directors from having to pay damages for violations
of their duty of care, but exposure to damages for violations of good
faith and loyalty always remains.[43] All of the real action in shareholder
litigation today, therefore, is over what counts as loyalty and good faith.
For firms with international operations, knowledge of foreign places,
mores, and ways of life is part of the action. This may have the effect of
pushing boards with international operations to appoint more foreign
nationals as directors.

Beyond Delaware, there are implications for board nationality
demographics in the relentless push by the federal government and
the national stock exchanges to get independent directors on the
boards of large corporations. The Sarbanes-Oxley reforms of
2002 required for the first time that the boards of publicly traded
corporations be comprised of a majority of independent directors.
After the subprime mortgage crisis of 2008, "the trend toward board
independence accelerated as Congress and other regulators appointed
independent directors as the capitalist cavalry and charged them with
riding to the system's rescue."[44] This insistence on independent directors, coupled with increasingly strict definitions of what counts as
"independent," may have the unintended consequence of sending
executive search firms more regularly looking for qualified foreign
nationals as candidates to serve on domestic boards of directors.
As one group of analysts put it, in arguing against "term limits" for
existing directors (another hobbyhorse of regulators): "[G]ood

---

even as Delaware courts usually decline to formally hold directors liable for violating their
fiduciary obligations to shareholders, Delaware jurists nevertheless endeavor to influence
directorial conduct by signaling best practices and shaming poor conduct).

[43] 8 DEL. GEN. CORP. L. §102(b)(7).

[44] STEPHEN M. BAINBRIDGE, CORPORATE GOVERNANCE AFTER THE FINANCIAL CRISIS 78 (1st
ed. 2012).

directors are hard to find ... only a limited number of people possess both the management experience and industry knowledge required to serve capably as public company directors. Further restrictions on board service dramatically shrink that limited pool of talent."[45] And it may cause corporations to look in other pools, across the seas.

If corporate patriotism is a vice, then the economic and legal dynamics that seem to be compelling the internationalization of the boards of American companies should be celebrated and extended. If corporate patriotism is a virtue, then these dynamics may need to be critically assessed in terms of their impact on the patriotic impulses of domestic firms.

PRESCRIPTIVE CORPORATE PATRIOTISM

Despite marginal opportunities for slacking, of the patriotic or more selfish variety, the law of fiduciary duty, incentive-based pay structures, and corporate culture keep directors of American corporations working "hard and honestly,"[46] for the most part, on behalf of their shareholders. If we presume that directors largely restrain their patriotic conscience, as the law requires, then we may want to reform our corporate governance standards to improve its patriotic comportment, if corporate patriotism is a virtue. This must become a part of the broader challenge of reforming corporate governance law to depart from shareholder primacy and take corporate social responsibility more seriously. The challenge is to develop ethically responsible reforms that invite patriotic conscience into the boardroom while keeping the door shut to bigotry and discrimination. This mix is hard enough to get right in the individual human heart. It will prove harder still to build into the design of our corporate governance law. Yet the

---

[45] *See* Scott C. Herlihy, et. al., *Director Tenure: A Solution in Search of a Problem*, Harvard Law School Forum on Corporate Governance and Financial Regulation (Jan 23, 2015), http://corpgov.law.harvard.edu/2015/01/23/director-tenure-a-solution-in-search-of-a-problem

[46] FRANK H. EASTERBROOK & DANIEL R. FISCHEL, THE ECONOMIC STRUCTURE OF CORPORATE LAW 91 (1991).

importance of the issue compels us to struggle for a proper solution, lest others work towards solutions we may deem improper.

In 2008, a U.S.-based shareholder-activist submitted a "shareholder proposal" to the Board of Directors of the Monsanto Corporation, a Delaware firm with global operations, which, if adopted, would have required Monsanto's directors to "solemnly swear (or affirm)" this oath:

> I will support and defend the Constitution of the United States against all enemies, foreign and domestic. I will bear true faith and allegiance to the Constitution of the United States. I take this obligation freely-recognizing that approval of my nomination and election as a Director of the Board of the Monsanto Corporation brings with it significant personal responsibility. I take this oath without any mental reservation or purpose of evasion; and that I will well and faithfully discharge the duties upon which I am about to enter.[47]

Monsanto petitioned the Securities Exchange Commission (SEC) for permission to exclude the proposal from the corporate proxy, pursuant to an SEC rule that allows firms to exclude shareholder proposals that would "cause the company to violate any state, federal, or foreign law to which it is subject."[48] Monsanto claimed the loyalty proposal conflicted with basic requirements of Delaware corporate law:

> [T]he Proposal ... would impermissibly restrict the directors' exercise of their fiduciary duties.... The directors could be forced, as a result of taking the oath, to vote against (or refrain from taking) a proposed action even if such action were permissible under applicable law and, as determined by the directors in the exercise of their fiduciary duties, would otherwise be in the best interests of the Company and its shareowners.[49]

This is an interesting confession of a major corporate board's view of the relationship between fiduciary obligation and national allegiance.

---

[47] Monsanto Corp., SEC No-Action Letter, 2008 WL 8785663 Fed. Sec. L. Rep. (CCH) (Nov 7, 2008). [hereinafter Monsanto].

[48] Shareholder Proposals, 17 C.F.R. § 240.14a–8(i)(2) (2015).

[49] Monsanto, *supra* note 47 at 3.

The abiding principle, according to Monsanto, is "the Company and its shareowners." Adhering to that charge can sometimes require directors to make decisions that may not comport with "true faith and allegiance to the Constitution of the United States." Delaware law, of course, requires directors to always follow "applicable law," but this "true faith and allegiance" verbiage suggests a responsibility for something more (at least it did to Monsanto's lawyers), and the only "more" directors can know under Delaware law is more for the shareholders. The SEC allowed Monsanto to exclude the proposal from the corporate proxy by returning a "no-action letter" that contained little analysis.[50]

The Monsanto shareholder's proposal would not have outright forbid foreign nationals from serving on their company's board, but it would certainly have made appointment of foreign directors more difficult. Regulation of the nationality of corporate directors is not unknown in other countries. Danish corporations, for example, must have Danish citizens comprise at least half of the board, and the chairperson of the board must be Danish. In the United States, general director nationality requirements would likely run afoul of federal law, not to mention American values, which prohibit "national origin" discrimination in hiring.[51]

Even if it avoids explicit nationality restrictions, the Monsanto shareholder proposal is an undesirable approach to improving the patriotic deportment of American firms. It neglects the global corporation's legitimate need for directors from many nations, and its purple "loyalty oath" approach would likely hinder – rather than advance – open, critical, discourse on patriotic concerns in the boardroom. A critical kind of patriotism can only take root in the boardroom if directors are licensed to speak freely about their honest assessment of what impact a proposed course of corporate conduct will have on

---

[50] *Id.*

[51] 42 U.S.C. § 2000e-2(a) (2013) ("It shall be an unlawful employment practice ... to fail or refuse to hire ... any individual because of such individual's ... national origin."). Title VII does permit national origin discrimination in hiring if it is "in the interest of the national security of the United States under any security program in effect pursuant to or administered under any statute of the United States or any Executive order of the President." 42 U.S.C. § 2000e-2(g). Again, I am concerned here with the general case.

national interests. Patriots do not need loyalty oaths, and good men and women will often refuse to take them. Nevertheless, the Monsanto shareholder proposal reflects an identification of, and an effort to grapple with, the problems of corporate patriotism with which this chapter has been concerned. The somewhat embarrassing loyalty oath proposal should motivate the development of reasonable alternative reforms, lest this kind of thing prevail.

★★★

The nation has not always been a central organizing institution in human society and it has not always been the principal font of human morality. Perhaps someday our species, our cultures, will evolve to the point where we can support moral development in terms of devotion to all humanity, or even all living things. Or even all things. Or maybe we will find breakthroughs in moral understanding and instruction that do not require the mechanics of relational affect at all. Maybe, too, we will develop universal political institutions that safeguard democracy and fundamental rights without need of national association. I love my country, but I can imagine and even hope that my progeny, some or many generations hence, will have no need for that kind of love. For now, it seems that we do need it. We do have it, anyway, and we must deal with it responsibly. Patriotism is a value to which we, now, would do well to subscribe with pride. We should insist that our institutions are designed in such a way that serve, rather than undermine, our national interest. Shareholder primacy not only excludes patriotic conscience from the boardroom, it insists that the national interest be ignored or run under if that will make bread. Shareholder primacy firms push their slavering maw not just into the marketplace, but also into government and foreign relations – spaces that might otherwise be realms of patriotic activity.

The problem of corporate patriotism, never fully silent, is becoming fully voiced in our time. The problem should be addressed through corporate governance reform. I will examine such reforms in the context of the general prescriptions that follow from this inquiry in Chapter 8.

6 CORPORATE LAW AND THE CONFUSIONS OF CONSUMER CULTURE

"Society is a joint-stock company, in which the members agree, for the better securing of his bread to each shareholder, to surrender the liberty and culture of the eater."

Ralph Waldo Emerson[1]

"To ignore it is to court nostalgia. To engage with it, however, is to risk ... mak[ing] the same point over and over: technological consumerism is an infernal machine, technological consumerism is an infernal machine."

Jonathan Franzen[2]

In this chapter, I want to deepen my critique of shareholder primacy by examining the connection between corporate law and consumer culture. In Chapter 2, I raised doubts about how well consumers are served under the prevailing corporate governance system by focusing on the ways in which firms can "mislead" consumers about product attributes, including especially health risks associated with a product, or by "locking in" consumers into consumption habits that can be harder to break than they anticipate. I then emphasized that firms work to capture government regulation, which, under the standard justification for shareholder primacy, is supposed to be available to restrict such corporate malfeasance. My emphasis on corporations exploiting consumers in that introductory critique was really just a salient entrée into a deeper kind of problem about the relationship between corporate law and consumerism that we must address.

---

[1] RALPH WALDO EMERSON, *Self Reliance*, in EMERSON'S ESSAYS (1841, 1926).
[2] Jonathan Franzen, *Perchance to Dream: In the Age of Images, a Reason to Write Novels*, HARPER'S MAGAZINE, Apr 1996, at 35, 43.

In its formative stages, the "spirit of capitalism" was one of comprehensive discipline, frugality, and savings.[3] Max Weber claimed these values, which served as handmaiden to the accumulation necessary for the development of large-scale industry, were eased into the economic system with the help of the Protestant religious outlook. But that was a long time ago. The principal systemic imperative in "late capitalism," or fully developed capitalism, is not accumulation but consumption. Contemporary policymakers, influenced by the legacy of the economist John Maynard Keynes, perennially insist that *consumption* must be encouraged in order to fuel development and ensure prosperity.[4] Whether this "Keynesian consensus" is good economics is beyond the present inquiry.[5] My point is rather to draw critical attention to the relentless emphasis that the consensus outlook places on spurring consumer demand. We must know what to make of such consumption, and what it is making of us. Understanding what consumerism "means" is essential to a mature assessment of the society we are making for ourselves, and the legacy we are leaving to the future. Consumer culture is a defining feature of modern life. And it is a

---

[3] *See* MAX WEBER, THE PROTESTANT ETHIC AND THE SPIRIT OF CAPITALISM (1905, 1958).

[4] *See* JOHN MAYNARD KEYNES, THE GENERAL THEORY OF EMPLOYMENT, INTEREST, AND MONEY 96 (First Harbinger ed., 1964). According to Keynes, consumers have a propensity to increase consumption when their income increases, but not by as much as their income is increased. Keynes called this "a fundamental psychological law." *Id.* Because consumers save an ever greater portion of their income, demand will ultimately be insufficient to justify productive investment of capital. This under-investment means under-employment. Workers seeking to provide for their own future consumption fail to supply the demand sufficient to justify the current investment that would employ them. Under such conditions, Keynesianism calls on policymakers to take steps to encourage consumption. Keynes formalized these ideas but they have a long lineage. In an essay from 1930, Adolf Berle wrote: "At this very moment we are having campaigns appealing to consumers to buy goods, not because they need them but as a matter of charity in order to keep men employed." Adolf A. Berle, Jr., Presentation at the Conference on Business Management as a Human Enterprise at the Bureau of Personnel Administration: The Equitable Distribution of Ownership (Dec 11, 1930) (unpublished essay on file with the Seattle University School of Law Adolf A. Berle, Jr. Center on Corporations, Law & Society).

[5] The familiar motto, "We are all Keynesians now," is quasi-apocryphally attributed to Milton Friedman, who was quoted to that effect in a *Time Magazine* cover story in 1965. *We Are All Keynesians Now*, TIME, Dec 31, 1965, at 74. Friedman, however, insisted that what he actually said was, "In one sense, we are all Keynesians now; in another, nobody is any longer a Keynesian." *See* Milton Friedman, *Letter to the Editor*, TIME, Feb 4, 1966, at 15. It is enough for present purposes to assert that this is a widespread view in both formal economics and ordinary politics.

cardinal normative concern. The principal work of this chapter is to grapple with what corporate law has to do with it.[6]

THE MEANING OF CONSUMER CULTURE

Groucho Marx said, "When I hear the word culture I reach for my wallet."[7] Corporate law scholars, too, seem to worry that cultural analysis will operate as the pretty ruse of a theoretical pickpocket, leaving us dazzled, perhaps, but poorer in understanding than when we started out. The conventional categories of legal analysis favor inquiries that are plainly tractable, even quantifiable. This is motivated by an estimable desire to get at the usable knowledge that objective, scientific approaches promise. It is also driven by a scrupulous commitment to avoiding methods that risk illiberally celebrating or condemning particular values or ways of life, which cultural analysis might seem to imply.[8]

Mainstream corporate law scholarship exemplifies this tendency. It has principally been concerned with analyzing the shareholder predicament in corporate affairs, construed in terms of financial risk and return. "Progressive" corporate law scholarship looks beyond the shareholder's stake but also has largely eschewed cultural assessment,

---

[6] This chapter is based on material that was first published as David G. Yosifon, *The Social Relations of Consumption: Corporate Law and the Meaning of Consumer Culture*, 2015 B.Y. U. L. REV. 1309 (2015).

[7] Peter Borsay & Callum Brown, *Review of Books*, 22 URBAN HISTORY 139 (1995) (quoting Groucho Marx). Groucho's quip was a variation on the line attributed to the Nazi leader Hermann H. Goering: "Whenever I hear the word culture, I reach for my revolver." The Goering quote is said to be apocryphal. *See* PAUL F. BOLLER, Jr. & JOHN GEORGE, THEY NEVER SAID IT: A BOOK OF FAKE QUOTES, MISQUOTES, AND MISLEADING ATTRIBUTION 36 (1989) ("This statement actually. . . comes from Hanns Johst's drama *Schlageter*, produced at the State Playhouse in Berlin in 1933."). It is conceivable that Goering was familiar with the Johst play and used the line himself.

[8] *See* Dan M. Kahan, *The Cognitively Illiberal State*, 60 STAN. L. REV. 115 (2007) (examining the psychological limits of liberalism). The exception is that corporate law scholars have given some attention to the culture of the corporate boardroom. *See, e.g.*, STEPHEN BAINBRIDGE, THE NEW CORPORATE GOVERNANCE IN THEORY AND PRACTICE 77–104 (2008) (exploring the utility of boardroom culture as a means of encouraging directors to work honestly and effectively). Examination of this culture, however, has been for the purpose of understanding how firms act or fail to act in the shareholder interest, without any study of the general cultural implications of that activity.

tethering its analysis instead to countable versions of "harm" such as environmental externalities, declining wages, or tobacco-related deaths. The insights supplied by all of this work is crucial, but it leaves out of the conversation an important part of what people want us to talk about when we talk about corporations. It lets pass, and thus gives a pass to, the cultural significance of corporate law. This chapter is concerned with developing a way of scrutinizing that significance.

There is persistent ambivalence in both theoretical discourse and common experience about the meaning of our consumer culture. Something about that ambivalence can be understood as stemming from disintegrity in the social relations of consumption in our society. These social relations involve, crucially, the relationship between producer and consumer that is dictated by our corporate governance law, and embodied in the decision-making dynamics of the directors who command corporate operations.

If our consumer culture is (in part) a function of the social relations of consumption, then perhaps we can improve the character of that culture by introducing greater integrity into those relations. This can be accomplished through the reform of corporate law. Legitimate concerns about consumer culture, I argue, contribute to a broader set of arguments for reforming corporate governance law to require corporate directors to attend to the interests of multiple stakeholders in corporate decision-making, and not just the interests of shareholders. Regardless of whether one embraces this prescription, the analysis developed here can enrich our understanding of what is at stake in our corporate law: what it is, what it does, and what it might do.

While mainstream corporate law scholars have generally not struggled with consumer culture, intellectuals in other disciplines have evaluated it with interest. A robust tradition in academic cultural history explains the emergence of consumerism in what we might broadly call "functionalist" terms. Mass consumerism emerged in the late nineteenth and early twentieth centuries as a reliable means of channeling a wide range of human desires in an efficient, predictable manner that was compatible with the formalized, sanitized way of life dictated by corporate capitalism. For the working class, the romance and erotics of consumerism was a compensatory salve for the ignominy of hyperrationalized industrial labor. For the wealthy, conspicuous consumption became a way of overcoming status anxiety in a world with unprecedented social mobility. For American culture as a whole, consumerism in the twentieth century became a central organizing principle of individual and associational identity, replacing the centrality of the worker and civic-minded ethic that had theretofore dominated the American scene.[9]

Commentators have been spooked by consumerism from the beginning. Consumer culture, many have said, sterilizes and homogenizes the otherwise messy but sublime human condition. It promises transcendence, but it does not deliver. Instead, it sets us back. This declensional tradition can be traced at least to William Wordsworth – "Getting and spending, we lay waste our powers . . . / We have given our hearts away, a sordid boon!"[10] – and has echoed in American letters from Thorstein Veblen to Bob Dylan, who warned that: "advertising signs they con / You into thinking you're the one / That can do what's never been done / That can win what's never been won / Meantime life outside goes on / All around you."[11] Consumer culture, on this reading, is manipulative and degrading.[12]

---

[9] *See, e.g.,* COLIN CAMPBELL, THE ROMANTIC ETHIC AND THE SPIRIT OF MODERN CONSUMERISM (1987); T. J. JACKSON LEARS, NO PLACE OF GRACE: ANTIMODERNISM AND THE TRANSFORMATION OF AMERICAN CULTURE 1880–1920 (1981); PETER N. STEARNS, AMERICAN COOL: CONSTRUCTING A TWENTIETH-CENTURY EMOTIONAL STYLE 209–14 (1994); *See* THORSTEIN VEBLEN, THE THEORY OF THE LEISURE CLASS (1899, 1994); Richard Wightman Fox & T. J. Jackson Lears, Eds., THE CULTURE OF CONSUMPTION: CRITICAL ESSAYS IN AMERICAN HISTORY, 1880–1890, (1983); STEPHEN NISSENBAUM, THE BATTLE FOR CHRISTMAS 139 (1996) (arguing that "[c]onsumer capitalism and civic virtue were not commonly associated with each other in early nineteenth-century America," but the emergence of the modern Christmas rituals "helped intensify and legitimize a commercial kind of consumerism").

[10] WILLIAM WORDSWORTH, *The World Is Too Much with Us, in* THE COLLECTED POEMS OF WILLIAM WORDSWORTH 307 (1807).

[11] Bob Dylan, *It's Alright, Ma (I'm Only Bleeding), on* BRINGING IT ALL BACK HOME (Columbia, 1965).

[12] Even as we can locate criticism of "consumerism" as a distinctly historical phenomena, we can also see it as a more or less universal feature of reflection on the human condition. Wordsworth wrote his lament about our "sordid boon" in 1807, before large corporations or modern consumer culture was widespread. We could probably give some biographical account about Wordsworth being at the vanguard of a bourgeoning cultural phenomenon, but we could also surely find expressions like this offered by sensitive thinkers since we first climbed down from the trees, or at least since we started planting the beer. The issue I am pursuing here is what our institutions do – in particular what corporate law does – to exacerbate, mitigate, enliven, subdue, or improve this eternal aspect of the human

The most strident critics of consumerism claim that the situation is worse than what Dylan described. It is not so much that consumer culture keeps you from the life that is going on around you – the fact is, according to the most mournful tally, there is no longer any real life going on anywhere other than the shadow, shallow life of consumerism. These people say things like: "All that once was directly lived has become mere representation."[13] Consumer culture empties out and replaces other forms of meaning from social life, in particular, meaning that previously was made in community, politics, and religion. One critical tranche laments the homogenization of consumerism, the "mass" and uniform nature of culture produced under corporate auspices. A contradictory line worries that consumer culture is splintering, with so many niches and subniches identified, or created, that there is no unifying culture that can give society or the nation any sense of itself as a cohesive whole. Both perspectives are agreed in their disgust and despair at the whole thing. Among the consequences of consumer culture's dominance is that people lose both the motivation and the ability to critique the economic system, even as the compulsion to consume authorizes a socially disruptive globalization of production.[14] If this is true, it poses an additional challenge to the canonical account of shareholder primacy theory, which presupposes a political dynamic sufficient to generate a regulatory regime that will constrain the externalizing tendencies of shareholder primacy operations.

Nineteenth- and early twentieth-century scolds warned that consumerism was feminizing the culture. Traditional outlooks associated men with production and women with consumption. The declining significance of production and the new authority of consumer culture threatened to collapse these distinctions, and feminize men.[15] A more contemporary appraisal has moved from worry that consumerism is

---

condition. As to Dylan, he of course was commoditizing the con of commoditization. This does not dispel but rather more deeply demonstrates the infinite jest of consumer culture on which the critics of consumerism hate.

[13] GUY DEBORD, THE SOCIETY OF THE SPECTACLE 12 (Donald Nicholson-Smith trans., 1999) (1967).

[14] FREDERIC JAMESON, POSTMODERNISM, OR, THE CULTURAL LOGIC OF LATE CAPITALISM 265–67 (1991); TYLER COWEN, IN PRAISE OF COMMERCIAL CULTURE 200–01 (1998).

[15] The critical theorist Rita Felski, examining the allegedly "castrating" effects of consumer culture, reports that: "*Seduction* is a recurring term used in the writing of male intellectuals

feminizing to now insisting that it is "infantilizing," encouraging a perpetual state of arrested development by consumers who always want and are never satisfied. Benjamin Barber, a critic who uses the term "infantile" to ridicule consumerism, actually seems to have in mind something worse, since infants at least enjoy the objects of their desire once they get their hands or mouths around them. For Barber, consumers waste their lives wanting and getting, but "[t]he ethos animating postmodern consumer capitalism is one of joyless compulsiveness."[16] Norman O. Brown famously showed the capitalist accumulator, the miser, as constipated, intent on avoiding the lurid spectacle of expelling his "filthy lucre."[17] The modern consumer, to Barber's mind, is no longer holding it in, but instead cannot stop holding it out: "[h]e is less the happy sensualist than the compulsive masturbator, a reluctant addict working at himself with little pleasure."[18]

Nevertheless, a different tradition of cultural assessment celebrates corporate consumerism as a vehicle of personal and social liberation. Consumer culture expands the possibilities of not just material pleasures, but also our inner life. It provides ordinary people with an accessible means of creative escape from the narrow terms of identity otherwise provided only by stultifying tradition or work. Changes to traditional gender roles wrought by consumer culture count as an *achievement* for apologists of consumerism – hardly a condemnation – as it improves the relative status of women and liberates men from overly rigid gender identities.[19] Consumerism may be a somewhat vapid or fleeting approach to self-discovery, but its superficiality replaces otherwise pernicious, oppressive, and, ultimately, *boring* discourses on identity that draw their authority from racism, sexism, classism, and heteronormativity. The acolytes of this tradition insist,

---

to describe the manipulation of the individual by marketing techniques, eloquently evoking the mixture of passivity, complicity, and pleasure seen to characterize the standpoint of the modern consumer." RITA FELSKI, THE GENDER OF MODERNITY 62 (1995).

[16] BENJAMIN BARBER, CONSUMED: HOW MARKETS CORRUPT CHILDREN, INFANTILIZE ADULTS, AND SWALLOW CITIZENS WHOLE 51 (2007).

[17] NORMAN O. BROWN, LIFE AGAINST DEATH: THE PSYCHOANALYTIC MEANING OF HISTORY 234–307 (1959).

[18] BARBER, *supra* note 16 at 51.   [19] *See* FELSKI, *supra* note 15 at 61–91.

contra Dylan, that far from being a con, advertising is testimony to our abundance. It is "the last utopian idiom."[20]

Consumer culture, scholars in this vein emphasize, has also been a crucial site of modern civil rights movements. Consumer goods helped create and carry the message of race and gender equality, quintessentially through music, but also through books, movies, and television. To give one kind of example, the reach of the "protest singers" of the 1960s was catalyzed, undoubtedly, by efficient corporate operations getting the message into the hands, ears, and minds of millions of people. To give another kind, corporate commercial speech played a key role in generating and circulating knowledge about the availability of birth control devices, which played a crucial part in women's liberation. The culture of consumerism has also promoted integration, diversity, and pluralism in racial and ethnic affairs through sartorial styles, food, furnishings, and entertainment. Consumer culture is thus inseparable from the liberating social, cultural, and political movements that transformed American society in the middle and late decades of the twentieth century, relatively peacefully. (More peacefully than could have been done without it, anyway.) At the end of the twentieth century, these impulses also gave shape to the "velvet revolution" in the Soviet bloc, where the desire for consumer culture helped force political change.[21]

In a sense, everything depends upon which of these distinct interpretations of consumer culture, the condemning or the celebratory, is right. What seems to be at stake, in the words of James Livingston, is "whether emotional frugality or expenditure is the proper structure of

---

[20] JAMES LIVINGSTON, AGAINST THRIFT: WHY CONSUMER CULTURE IS GOOD FOR THE ECONOMY, THE ENVIRONMENT, AND YOUR SOUL 115–16 (2011) [hereinafter LIVINGSTON, AGAINST THRIFT] ("Could advertising be the thesaurus of our real feelings, the indispensable, vernacular language we use to plot our positions on the emotional atlas that is everyday life?").

[21] See generally LIZABETH COHEN, A CONSUMERS' REPUBLIC: THE POLITICS OF MASS CONSUMPTION IN POSTWAR AMERICA (2003); DEIRDRE N. MCCLOSKEY, THE BOURGEOIS VIRTUES: ETHICS FOR AN AGE OF COMMERCE 25–26 (2006) (emphasizing the bleak and oppressive nature of cultural life for the vast majority of people in the premodern era); see also Elisa Glick, The Dialectics of Dandyism, 48 CULTURAL CRITIQUE 129–30 (2001) (emphasizing the role of consumer culture in both identity formation and political engagement in the gay rights movement).

[our] souls."[22] At stake, too, is the attitude that we should have, skeptical or celebratory, to recurring, mainstream macroeconomic and political claims about the importance of consumption activity, and the imperative of encouraging ever greater levels of consumption, in order to ensure economic development and political stability.

Yet, in another sense, I think the better way to understand these two interpretations is to see them as both being truthful and accurate aspects of what consumer culture *is*, in the experience of those who are immersed in it. The contradiction between the two interpretations is itself integral to characterizing our cultural predicament. Although artists and analysts typically focus on one or the other conceit, I regard the tension expressed by the divergent assessments of consumer culture as commonplace, explicitly or implicitly, in the lived experience of consumerism among ordinary men and women in our society. I think attention to the connection between corporate law and consumer culture can help explain why.

THE CONSUMER AGENCY PROBLEM

Grappling with the confusions of consumerism has not been a feature of traditional corporate law scholarship. The focus of the field has instead been on one important problem in the social relations of *production* under corporate capitalism: the agency problem that attends the separation of ownership and control in industry. To see corporate law's connection to consumer culture, we must begin close to this same starting place but facing a different direction. The corporate reorganization of the economy that separated ownership and control in production *also* disaggregated production and consumption. This disaggregation inaugurated new social relations of consumption and created a *consumer* agency problem. Before the mid-nineteenth century, most business activity was organized through familial relationships, and most of what was consumed was produced by relatives or neighbors.[23]

---

[22] LIVINGSTON, supra note 20.
[23] ALFRED D. CHANDLER, Jr., THE VISIBLE HAND: THE MANAGERIAL REVOLUTION IN AMERICAN BUSINESS 17 (1977) ("[T]he family remained the basic business unit" in the

Where consumers produce for themselves in family or kin networks, the interests of production and consumption are aligned.[24] The problem, of course, is that under such "primitive" organizing principles, little is produced *or* consumed. The disassembly of household economies and their reconstitution in specialized factories produced more, but required people who had once acquired food, clothing, and entertainment within household or community networks to navigate the purchase of such items instead in the marketplace.

When production and consumption are so separated, to repurpose the verbiage Adam Smith famously used to describe the corporate shareholder's predicament (which I quoted in Chapter 1), "it cannot be well expected," that corporate directors "will watch over [consumer interests] with the same anxious vigilance" with which consumers would watch over it themselves. We should anticipate that "negligence and profusion" regarding the "affairs" of consumers "must always prevail" in corporate operations.[25] Smith saw the *shareholder* agency problem, and readers of corporate law scholarship have been seeing it ever since. Yet the *consumer* agency problem convened by the same economic developments has rarely been identified, and has never been pursued with the academic doggedness that has served the shareholder agency problem.[26]

United States at least through the 1840s."). *See also* Christopher Clark, *Household Economy, Market Exchange and the Rise of Capitalism in the Connecticut Valley, 1800–1860*, 12 J. Soc. Hist. 169, 173 (1979) (finding that into the early nineteenth century, "[r]ather than relying on the market, rural families supplied their wants both by producing their own goods for consumption and by entering in complex networks of exchange relationships with their neighbors and relatives").

[24] Putatively aligned, for present analytic purposes, but actually disjointed in other ways: the machinations of patriarchy, the neuroses of family, and other miseries.

[25] ADAM SMITH, THE WEALTH OF NATIONS 849 (1776, 1904). I quoted this passage in full in Chapter 1.

[26] *See* Marleen O'Connor-Felman, *American Corporate Governance and Children: Investing in Our Future Human Capital During Turbulent Times*, 77 S. CAL. L. REV. 1255, 1281 (2003) ("[T]he factory detached work from the household, transforming the family from a self-sufficient production and consumption unit to a consumption division."); *see also* Gardiner C. Means, *Collective Capitalism and Economic Theory*, in THE CORPORATION TAKE-OVER 62, 67 (Andrew Hacker ed., 1964) (noting that in subsistence systems, "production policy and the instruments of production are controlled by units which combine the interests of consumer, worker, owner, and management.").

One early twentieth-century economist did come close to formulating the corporate consumer's predicament in the agency problem terms that I am urging. In his 1923 book, *The Control of Industry*, Dennis Robertson (a mentor to Ronald Coase) dedicated a chapter to examining "Industry and the Consumer."[27] Robertson cataloged "the grievances, real or imaginary," of consumers under the capitalist system. He includes familiar protests against advertisers who "[f]rom every hoarding and newspaper ... explain vociferously to the consumer what he wants," among other complaints.[28] Robertson reviews prevailing (then and now) solutions to these problems, most of which involve the palliatives of general welfare legislation. Hitting on the social relations formulation, Robertson writes that such remedies "all embody, in one form or another, the ambitious notion of undoing the great division of function which first took place when Eve picked the apple and Adam ate it, and reintegrating the consumer with the producer."[29]

There was promise in Robertson's image, but he did not quite grasp it. There may have been a division of labor between Adam and Eve, but there was no agency problem as such. As spouses, their well-being was inextricably intertwined.[30] There is no tension or division of interests between production and consumption where the functions are separated under such affective relations. Eve has no incentive to malinger or thieve since any harm that comes to Adam from bad fruit is suffered by her, too. Love aligns their interests better than any stock option plan could hope to. It is true that Eve faltered in her production responsibilities, and that Adam bears the burden of her lapse when he consumes.[31] They are both expelled from the Garden. But there is a difference between what it means to lose Paradise through

---

[27] Robertson's book furnished the line quoted and made famous by Coase, comparing corporations to "islands of conscious power in this ocean of unconscious co-operation, like lumps of butter coagulating in a pail of buttermilk." D. H. ROBERTSON, THE CONTROL OF INDUSTRY 84 (1923), *quoted in* R. H. Coase, *The Nature of the Firm*, 4 ECONOMICA 386, 388 (1937).

[28] *Id.* at 101.   [29] *Id.* at 103.

[30] "Therefore shall a man [or woman] ... cleave unto his [or her] wife [or husband]: and they shall be one flesh." KING JAMES BIBLE, Genesis 2:24.

[31] "God called unto Adam ... Hast thou eaten of the tree, whereof I commanded thee that thou shouldest not eat?" KING JAMES BIBLE, Genesis 3:9–11.

manipulation or indifference, and what it means to lose it through loving incompetence. She *meant* well.[32] The social relations attending the consumption are crucial to characterizing its meaning, and the world that the consumption is making. The cost of Adam and Eve's eating, calculated only by countable things like lost leisure time in the Garden, or hours later suffered tilling arid soil or engaged in painful childbirth, may be the same whether their expulsion was a result of being fooled or being foolish. But there is a subtler meaning to their consumer experience that resides in the nature of the relationship between producer and consumer.[33]

Showcasing the social relations of consumption adds a fulcrum to the analysis of consumer culture that otherwise puts more emphasis on corporate marketing than it can bear. We cannot understand the consumer culture of the Garden only by evaluating the words and manner used in saying, "try this luscious apple." The Devil may have used razzle-dazzle. Eve might have used sex appeal. The formal attributes of the speech can tell us something about what the apple "signified" beyond the crunch and sweetness of the fruit. But to more deeply understand the meaning of the consumption, to understand the soul it makes and the culture it creates, we must understand the motives and relationship of the producer in consort with the consumer. This factor has largely been missing from both condemning and celebratory analyses of consumer culture.

EXPLOITING MARX

Insisting that there is a "consumer agency problem" under corporate capitalism is meant to leverage the insights of a familiar schema with a long pedigree in conventional corporate theory. My use of the "social relations of consumption" invokes a more distant tradition. I find that a lot of Marxism goes nowhere, but a little can go a long way. Marx used the idea of the "social relations of *production* " to reference the set of

---

[32] "[W]hen the woman saw that the tree *was* good for food, and that is *was* pleasant to the eyes, and a tree to be desired to make *one* wise, she took of the fruit thereof, and did eat, and gave also unto her husband with her..." KING JAMES BIBLE, Genesis 3:6.

[33] "[T]he serpent was more subtil than any beast of the field..." KING JAMES BIBLE, Genesis 3:1.

relationships in which humans become enmeshed in order to sustain themselves and their families (or "reproduce" themselves, in Marx's tongue-in-cheek phrase). Different "modes" of production involve different kinds of social relations. For example, the social relations in which a feudal subsistence farmer is engrossed to get his daily bread are very different from the social relations to which a wage laborer in a mechanized factory submits in order to sustain herself. Marx stressed that the "social relations of production" are essential to the way human beings think about themselves and the world they live in. He famously wrote: "It is not the consciousness of men that determines their existence, but their social existence that determines their consciousness."[34] "Class" consciousness, for example, arises under the social relations of capitalism, as the conditions of production make clear to some men and women that they have common interests that are in tension with the common interests of other men and women. The obfuscations of ideology, including especially the viewpoint of dominant classes, are part of the "social existence" and can impede people from accurately perceiving the stakes (their stake) in the relations of production, leading to what Marx's collaborator Frederic Engels dubbed "false consciousness."[35] The "social relations of production" idea has proved useful, but, like mainstream corporate theory's focus on the shareholder agency problem, it gives short shrift to the social relations of *consumption* in shaping the predicament of men and women, and their culture, under corporate capitalism.[36]

---

[34] *See* KARL MARX, A CONTRIBUTION TO THE CRITIQUE OF POLITICAL ECONOMY 21 (Maurice Dobb ed., S. W. Ryazankay trans., 1970) (1904). This assertion, if not taken too rigidly, is consistent with the claims of contemporary social psychology, which emphasizes the often unseen influence of situation in shaping human cognition, preference formation, and decision-making. *See generally* Jon Hanson & David Yosifon, *The Situational Character: A Critical Realist Perspective on the Human Animal*, 93 GEO. L. REV. 1 (2004) [hereinafter Hanson & Yosifon, *The Situational Character*] (summarizing and assessing psychological research of this sort).

[35] Again this idea is given social scientific imprimatur by contemporary psychological research on "system justification theory." *See* Hanson & Yosifon, *The Situational Character, supra* note 34 at 101–106.

[36] Marx does not use the phrase "social relations of consumption." I find only one brief use of the phrase in the annals of legal scholarship. The contracts scholars Ian MacNeil wrote in 1983: "[t]he social relations of consumption have perhaps in the past ... [been] largely dependent on the social relations of production. They have now, however, become increasingly independent and, in the developed world at least, perhaps a good deal more important

Marx also stressed that under capitalist social relations of production, workers becomes "alienated" from the goods they create. Workers no longer identify with the products of their labor (as they do in precapitalist conditions), and the role and identity of labor is invisible to the consumer of what is produced. Instead of reflecting the labor that made them, commodities come to be conceived in terms of their "exchange value," that is, the amount of money for which they can be sold, or bought, in the market. To consumers, this "exchange value" seems to exist *sui generis* in the commodity, like the power presumed to be present in the amulets of reverential fetish in "the mist-enveloped regions of the religious world."[37] The critics of consumer culture see this "commodity fetishism" (whether they use the term or not) as perverse and perverting, reducing not only labor but consumption, too, into just factors in the creation of exchange value. All meaning that might seem to be in the consumption is really inauthentic, empty, just epiphenomenal to the generation of exchange value. The celebrants of consumer culture, on the other hand, view this commodity fetishism (by name or not) as opportunity. The alienation of labor from what it produces is precisely what liberates consumer culture, and consumers, to make their own meanings out of the things they buy and use.[38] It is the separation of production and consumption that liberates consumption from the culture of the family and other subordinating institutions ("with all memory and fate / driven deep beneath the wave.")[39]

EXTENDING COASE (WITH AN ASSIST FROM STEVE JOBS)

While the social relations between producer and consumer are changed by corporate capitalism, it is not accurate to construe the consumer,

than the material social relations of production." Ian R. MacNeil, *Values in Contract: Internal and External,* 78 Nw. U. L. Rev. 340, 387 n.151 (1983). MacNeil does not appear to have pursued this idea in these terms in his subsequent voluminous writings.

[37] Karl Marx, 1 Capital: A Critique of Political Economy 83 (Ben Fowkes trans., 1992) (1867) [hereinafter Marx, Capital] (explicating "[t]he fetishism of commodities and the secret thereof").

[38] *See* Livingston, Against Thrift, *supra* note 20, at xv.

[39] Bob Dylan, *Mr. Tambourine Man,* on Bringing It All Back Home (1965).

and consumption decisions, as becoming *isolated* from the producer. Corporate capitalism may catalyze the alienation of labor from the goods it produces, but corporate social relations nevertheless shape and contextualize the meaning of consumer acts. The picture that emerges from the standard account of shareholder primacy theory is that the consumer decides what will be consumed, and corporations supply it. But this is not really how it works, no more than individual family members decide what will be for dinner, and then have it provided by the Eve or Adam of the clan tasked with meal preparation. In the home, what is to be consumed is a function of complex collaboration, involving some communication and substantial deference, among members. The same is true of consumer culture under corporate auspices. The decision about what is to be consumed is a complex collaboration between firm and consumer. It is still a *relationship* of consumption.

Many commentators have pointed to, but never quite put their finger on, what Frederic Jameson had in mind when he wrote that market-based consumption "rarely has anything to do with choice or freedom, since those are all determined for us in advance"; we "select among" the things that have been produced, "but we can scarcely be said to have a say in actually choosing any of them."[40] Lest this be dismissed as a rambling of postmodernism, the economist Gardiner Means (of Berle and Means) noted the same thing when he wrote that the "allocation of resources through corporate enterprise is both a matter of efficiency in production and importantly a matter of what is produced. A consumer veto over wasteful use of resources after the use has been made is by no means the same as consumer control over the issue."[41] This is also what Steve Jobs had in mind when he said that it was *not* Apple's role to give consumers what they want because, as Jobs said: "It's not the consumers' job to know what they want."[42] Figuring out what the consumer wants, should want, or will want

---

[40] FREDERIC JAMESON, POSTMODERNISM, *supra* note 14 at 266.

[41] *See* Means, *Collective Capitalism and Economic Theory*, *supra* note 25 at 82.

[42] John Markoff, *Apple's Visionary Redefined Digital Age*, NEW YORK TIMES (Oct 5, 2011) (obituary of Steve Jobs), www.nytimes.com/2011/10/06/business/steve-jobs-of-apple-dies-at-56.html. Another version of this came from Henry Ford (possibly apocryphal): "If I had asked people what they wanted, they would have said faster horses."

under corporate capitalism, is in significant measure left to the corporation. The consumer may gain tremendously in some dimensions by turning this power over to the company, as the firm may be able to galvanize possibilities that are beyond the consumer's own imagination and beyond what could be thought up or put out by collaborative consumption decision-making in household or in kin networks. But it is not without its (agency) problems.

Ronald Coase himself got at this, or showed a glimpse of it anyway, in a neglected footnote in his famous 1937 article on *The Nature of the Firm*. In that article, Coase wondered why the economy in free societies exhibited both "planned" and "unplanned" modes of production. He saw firm-based production as "planning" (which he likened to Soviet-style centralized planning) because in firms all the factors of production are owned and coordinated "in house." He called production activity "unplanned" when it took place through "spot markets," with capital and labor coming together only transactionally, episodically. Coase saw that while production capacities maintained "in house" could be wasteful, it was nevertheless preferable where the transactions costs involved in serial market transactions were too high – learning prices, finding factors, coming to terms, etc. This is the genesis of the "transactions costs" theory of the firm. In the neglected footnote, Coase saw a hint of the implications of his model for thinking about consumption:

> There are certain marketing costs which could only be eliminated by the abolition of "consumers' choice" and these are the costs of retailing. It is conceivable that these costs might be so high that people would be willing to accept rations because the extra product obtained was worth the loss of their choice.[43]

This is not just conceivable, but is, in fact, widespread in the corporate organization of consumption. Had he pursued the insight, Coase would have seen that short of "rationing," the consumer already gives up substantial "choice" when consuming corporate goods as compared to when consuming goods produced through other arrangements. The issue is not really "rationing." Consumption is "rationed" everywhere – by the family in the home, by the consumer in the market, by the

---

[43] *See* Ronald Coase, *The Nature of the Firm*, 4 ECONOMICA 386, 394–95 (1937).

government in centralized planning. The question is *who* is doing the rationing, and what is their motivation or relationship to the consumer. The consumer gives up substantial choice, control, and interest when consuming corporate goods as compared to when consuming goods produced through other modes. This is the insight that Emerson identified in the quote at the start of this chapter. Freedom over consumer culture is relinquished in favor of the better securing of bread, or iPhones.

Jameson moved from his observation that the consumer "selects" rather than "chooses" among goods and services, to argue that the "homology" to this kind of consumer freedom in political freedom is "parliamentary democracy of our representative type."[44] This is getting there, but it is not quite right. As I described in earlier chapters, the obligation of the state (the "parliamentary democracy") is to govern in the public interest. But a very different obligation obtains in the firm, which is charged to pursue not a public purpose, but profits for shareholders. Where the shareholder interest is in tension with non-shareholders, the shareholder interest must always prevail. The ambivalent meaning of our consumer culture reflects the fact that under our law, firms are indifferent as to whether they serve shareholders by discerning and serving consumer desires, by suggesting amiable new desires, or by exploiting consumers and other stakeholders. It is not always possible – indeed, the point is that it is usually *impossible* – to disentangle these profit-seeking operations. Who can tell? Is smoking cool, or is it exploitative? Is junk food delicious or pernicious? One cannot say, in an ethically serious way, just by observing consumption of cigarettes or junk food. Nor, I think, can one say so from an evaluation of tobacco or fast food advertising alone. The meaning of consumption cannot be isolated from the nature of the firm's relationship to the consumer.

CORPORATE GOVERNANCE AS A SOCIAL RELATION OF CONSUMPTION

Corporate law's agnosticism as to the source of the firm's profits is obscured through the social relations of consumption that corporate

---

[44] *Id.*

law incarnates. It is obscured because corporate directors are not snakes, and they are not devils. They are human. Modern psychologists have confirmed what everyone has always known: people are highly motivated to view themselves in affirming ways and to be viewed affirmatively by others. This impulse is so powerful that, according to Mark Twain, it even affects the French.[45] Directors are motivated to see themselves as serving consumers, not mulcting them. They satisfy this motive by patronizing sanguine conceits about the nature of their work, including the idea that firms only profit, or profit the most, when they behave in a socially responsible manner. In Chapter 2, I referred to this as the "Pareto fallacy of corporate profitability," and it appears to be a crucial feature of the self-affirming, dissonance-avoiding psychology of corporate directors. The disintegrity in this is reflected in our consumer culture.

There is friction between the law of corporate governance and the way firms and corporate directors talk about what they do.[46] In 2016, to give one example, Apple Inc., a key arbiter of our contemporary consumer culture, attracted accolades from civil libertarians when it refused to comply with a judicial order requiring Apple to get its computer scientists to build a software program that would allow the federal government to unlock a user-locked iPhone. (The government wanted to examine the contents of a phone that belonged to one of the terrorists responsible for the 2015 San Bernardino massacre.) Some saw Apple's stance as evidence of corporate conscience, resisting a government bent on violating privacy rights. This is the way Apple "branded" its resistance to the judicial order.[47] Even if you think it was important to resist that draconian judicial order, as I do, Apple's resistance was not evidence that Apple has a social conscience. And

---

[45] *See* Mark Twain, *What Paul Bourget Thinks of Us,* 160 THE NORTH AMERICAN REVIEW 48, 55 (1895).

[46] *See* Lisa M. Fairfax, *Easier Said Than Done? A Corporate Law Theory for Actualizing Social Responsibility Rhetoric,* 59 FLA. L. REV. 771, 789–792 (2007) (finding that while 98 percent of the Fortune 100 companies deploy corporate social responsibility rhetoric in their corporate operations, just 19 percent made the top 100 Best Corporate Citizens List of the Domini 400 Social Index).

[47] *See* David G. Yosifon, *Apple's Tim Cook Voicing Corporate Interest, Not Social Conscience,* SAN JOSE MERCURY NEWS, Feb 25, 2016, www.mercurynews.com/opinion/ci_29561999/ david-yosifon-apples-tim-cook-voicing-corporate-interest

it does not suggest that corporate decision-making can be counted on to play a responsible role in confronting the hard policy questions of our day. No doubt Apple CEO Timothy Cook and his fellow directors sincerely believed they were doing the right thing in that case, but they could not and would not fight the order unless they believed it was in the best interests of their shareholders. And what they believe is in the best interests of their shareholders will not always be good for society. Witness reports of deplorable labor conditions in Apple's supply chain, and Apple's refusal to repatriate billions of taxable dollars to the United States to avoid paying those taxes.[48] Firms like Apple present themselves as principled when their conduct is well regarded, and plead that they are fiduciaries when their practices are criticized. They are right about the latter, but the former is never true. It is this kind of obscurantism that confuses our understanding of what corporations are, what they do, and what our consumer culture means.[49]

THE LOVE THAT DARE NOT SPEAK ITS NAME

Human nature dictates that directors believe and say they serve shareholders by serving consumers. Corporate law dictates that those beliefs be formed in ignorance, by prescribing and constraining the way that directors think and talk about corporate decision-making. Directors have an obligation to become informed about, and to deliberate on, the consequences of corporate policy for the shareholders. Directors' minds and voices are thus actively turned, by legal injunction, to contemplation of the shareholder interest. At the same time, corporate law forbids directors from giving supportive voice to policies that would aid non-shareholding stakeholders at the expense of shareholders. Square pegs of social responsibility that cannot fit the round hole

---

[48] *See* Anna Williams Shavers, *Human Trafficking, The Rule of Law, and Corporate Social Responsibility*, 9 S.C. J. INT'L L. & BUS. REV. 39, 86 (2012) (reviewing allegations about Apple's labor practices).

[49] *See also* David G. Yosifon, *The Dalai Lama and Corporate Law*, THE CORPORATE SOCIAL RESPONSIBILITY PODCAST (2014) (downloaded using iTunes) (critiquing a public dialogue between directors of Silicon Valley corporations and His Holiness the Dalai Lama on the relationship between corporate operations and compassion).

of shareholder primacy are left unplaced in the corporate conscience. While shareholder primacy reigns, corporate social responsibility in the boardroom is "the love that dare not speak its name."[50] And if it cannot speak, then it cannot fully flourish, and cannot be contrasted with or balanced against the one love that is normative for directors: the shareholder interest. The limitations imposed on directorial discourse by shareholder primacy necessarily influence the mind, conscience, and decisions of corporate directors. The combination of forced speaking on behalf of shareholders, and forbidden speaking about non-shareholders, gives shape to a particular kind of knowledge and practice and precludes others. It keeps directors thinking carefully about the shareholder interest and thinking only casually about non-shareholder interests. By limiting the form and content of directorial deliberation, corporate law ensures that the cognitive dissonance that might otherwise emerge in the simultaneous pursuit of profit and directorial self-affirmation finds instead easy, harmonious resolution in directors' minds, and in the corporate conscience.[51]

A study by the social psychologist Dan Ariely suggests the kind of boardroom shading that I have in mind. Ariely and his collaborators designed an experiment called the "Dots Test," which put subjects before a computer screen that flashed a series of images of squares with dots inside of them. Sometimes the dots were distributed with more to the left side of the square, and sometimes they were distributed with more to the right. For each image, subjects were told to determine which side of the square had more dots. The images flashed too quickly for subjects to actually count the dots, so they were forced to make uncertain judgments. Subjects were told they would receive one cent every time they hit the computer key indicating more dots on the left side, and five cents every time they hit the key indicating more dots on the right side. Subjects were also told that they would not be evaluated for the correctness of their answers. Ariely summarizes his scheme: "[b]y creating this skewed payment system, we gave the participants an

---

[50] LORD ALFRED DOUGLAS, *Two Loves*, in TWO LOVES & OTHER POEMS 25 (1894, 1990).

[51] On the importance of dissonance avoidance in human cognition and decision-making, *see* Hanson & Yosifon, *The Situational Character*, *supra* note 34 at 107–25 (summarizing social psychological studies).

incentive to see reality in a slightly different way ... [T]hey were faced with a conflict between producing an accurate answer and maximizing their profit."[52] Subjects then responded to 200 images flashed in rapid succession.

Subjects did not just repeatedly hit the key indicating more dots on the right. That would have made them more money, but it would have undermined their desire to also maintain a self-conception as being socially responsible, honest people. Instead, the experimenters found a widespread tendency towards a little bit of cheating but *no self-conscious recognition of cheating.*[53] That is, people were biased towards the higher-payout interpretation of what they were seeing, but they viewed themselves as making fair and objective assessments. Of perhaps particular relevance to the decision-making dynamics of the boards of our most powerful corporations, Ariely found that "creative" individuals were more prone to click on the right (higher-paying) key than were other types of people. The greatest divergence between creative types and the baseline population came in squares with a small difference in the number of dots on the left and right. The creative types were not more prone to engage in "bold" lies but rather were more prone to lie to themselves and the experimenters at the margins. Ariely concludes: "the link between creativity and dishonesty seems related to the ability to tell ourselves stories about how we are doing the right thing, even when we are not."[54] Governing under the substantive and procedural dictates of shareholder primacy, directors can privilege the shareholder interest and shortchange other shareholders, all the while subjectively believing that their decisions are not just profitable for shareholders but fair to everyone involved.

Of course, it would be naïve to think that directors always actually put their shareholders first, consciously or subconsciously. Sometimes

---

[52] *See* DAN ARIELY, THE (HONEST) TRUTH ABOUT DISHONESTY 126–30 (2012).

[53] *Id.* at 163–91. Ariely argues that there is a fundamental human tendency to be "morally flexible" in this way (it is "hardwired," if you must), but he emphasizes that "cultural context" can influence the "magnitude of the fudge factor that is considered acceptable for any particular domain." *Id.* at 242. Acceptable not just to observers, but to the liar in him or herself.

[54] *Id.* at 172. Interestingly, Ariely's team found no correlation between higher or lower "intelligence" as such and the tendency to cheat in a manner that deviated from the norm. *Id.* at 176.

it seems obvious that corporate directors are ignoring the law of corporate governance and are sacrificing corporate profits in favor of some other value. These exceptions further highlight the disintegrity brought on by the rule. Especially in such instances, the law of corporate governance, with its insistence on shareholder primacy, forces opacity and disingenuousness into the deliberative process in the boardroom, making it impossible to draw anything but muddied conclusions about the meaning and significance of corporate operations in our culture.

Consider, for example, this tale that comes out of the subprime mortgage crisis of 2008. In the fall of that year, Bank of America was poised to buy the investment bank Merrill Lynch, which was going down in a sea of bad consumer debt.[55] After a tentative merger agreement was in place, Merrill Lynch's financial position worsened (from an already dire situation). Bank of America's board considered abandoning the merger, which it may have had the right to do under the standard "material adverse change" clause of the merger agreement. Regulators within the federal government, however, believed that a collapse of the Bank of America–Merrill Lynch merger would devastate already staggering credit markets, threatening to destroy the economy. That is, regulators were concerned that a privately useful decision by Bank of America's board might be socially destructive. This the regulators communicated to the directors. Also, the regulators warned that if the board insisted on exercising its right to terminate the merger, the government might try to exercise its power under federal banking rules to remove the incumbent members of the Bank of America board, in the public interest.

Lo and behold, upon further deliberation, the Bank of America directors decided they would, after all, go ahead with the merger. In his engaging review of this episode, Professor Robert Rhee concludes that the directors were obviously influenced by the regulators' threat to replace the board, and it seems clear that the directors were

---

[55] *See* Robert J. Rhee, *Fiduciary Exemption for Public Necessity: Shareholder Profit, Public Good, and the Hobson's Choice During a National Crisis*, 17 GEO. MASON L. REV. 661 (2010).

also genuinely concerned about the pressing social interests at stake in their decision.[56] However, it is even clearer that the social responsibility implicated in their decision played no part in the explicit deliberation of the board. The minutes reflect that the board concluded the decision was in the shareholder interest. The statements of individual board members testifying before Congress reflect the same. Those minutes and that testimony were entirely predictable. They could have been written by anyone familiar with the board's decision but unfamiliar with the board's deliberation. That is because *any* other explanation of the decision would have been a confession that the directors had violated their fiduciary obligations to their shareholders. And yet the statements appear to be entirely unbelievable (except, perhaps, to the board members themselves). *At best*, our highest-level corporate discourse about this pressing social crisis was had through winks and nods, dumb and indecorous innuendo. In this way, our corporate law produces discourse on corporate social responsibility that is at once entirely predictable, totally unbelievable, and utterly useless.

A critical (realistic) observer of the Bank of America–Merrill Lynch transaction is forced into incredulity reading the directors' assertions that the decision to proceed with the merger was made because they decided it was in the shareholders' interest. Always our discourse on corporate social responsibility must be subsumed within this smoke-filled mindset. It is corporate law, through the shareholder primacy norm, which keeps our corporate directors from talking openly and honestly about what is at stake in their decisions and what should wisely be done about it.

The shareholder primacy norm creates the perverse situation in which serious assessment of corporate decision-making relating to socially pressing matters must *begin* by discounting the actual deliberations by directors making the decision. The boardroom is as Balzac said of Paris: "No one who knows Paris believes a word that is said there, and not a word is said of what really goes on there."[57] Our current corporate governance law breeds cynicism and confusion

---

[56] Rhee, *supra* note 55 at 684.
[57] Honoré de Balzac, Père Goriot 136 (A. J. Krailsheimer, Trans. 1842, 2009).

about corporate conduct, and these become core features of corporate capitalism's consumer culture.

★★★

Consumer culture is an important part of our culture. It operates alongside other important cultures and subcultures, but is indisputably a part of how meaning is now made, individually and socially. That is why it is nostalgic, per the Franzen quote at the start of this chapter, to ignore it. Artists, policymakers, and scholars concerned with critically assessing the human condition, and the American situation in particular, set themselves too small a project if they pass over a critical assessment of consumerism.

Where consumer culture is addressed, two interpretations echo, never far from each other, in the interpretive landscape. Consumerism is demeaning and exploitative. Consumerism is satisfying and liberating. Those who only condemn it lose us in their pretension, but those who only celebrate it seem naïve. This ambivalence suggests a confusion. This confusion can be traced to the social relations of consumption in the modern economy. Shareholder primacy in corporate governance law encourages firms to deal with consumers in an insincere way, and contributes to a consumer culture that lacks integrity.

The social relations of production under simple, kin and community relations cannot produce a consumerism that is transcendent. The separation of production and consumption creates the efficiencies and attenuation necessary to endow a liberating, pluralistic, experimental type of consumer culture. Corporate law critics must, therefore, pursue their progressive purpose in a manner other than that of the joyless scold who is always seeking to shut down advertising that deploys sex, humor, or whimsy in "misleading" ways.[58] Consumer culture, however, will always be haunted by the consumer agency

---

[58] *See, e.g.*, my own earlier proposal to address the obesity epidemic by prescribing a "tombstone" advertising regime for junk food products, which would limit advertising of such goods to black lettering on white background, describing in simple, precise terms the item offered, its ingredients, price, and place of provision, in David G. Yosifon, *Resisting Deep Capture: The Commercial Speech Doctrine and Junk-Food Advertising to Children*, 39 Loy. L.A. L. Rev. 507 (2006).

problem so long as production and consumption are orchestrated under the shareholder primacy norm. There will always be, must always be, a suspicion that consumerism is inauthentic, that it lacks integrity, that there is manipulation in it. This constrains its creative and liberating power.

The social relations of consumption are, of course, but one aspect of the meaning of consumer culture. They explain only a part of the mystery. Endowing these social relations with greater integrity, a possibility I will explore in the next two chapters, will not give us final answers about the value and meaning of consumerism. We will still be left with the deeper questions: is simplicity or complexity in consumption the better route to personal happiness and social justice? Does the quickness with which we become bored with a consumer delight and start looking for a new one reflect superficiality in us, or does it reflect well on our unquenchable curiosity, showing that the world is always short of us, that we are always grasping beyond it? Should we buy now or save for later? Can we develop, as has been sought from Aristotle to Norman O. Brown, "a science of human nature, able to distinguish real human needs from (neurotic) consumer demands"?[59] Reforming corporate governance law will not answer these questions for us. But it may help us finally get to these questions, free from the confusions attendant to disjointed social relations of consumption.

[59] BROWN, *supra* note 17, at 256.

7 FOREIGN MODELS OF CORPORATE GOVERNANCE

"Now I submit that you can not abandon emphasis on 'the view that business corporations exist for the sole purpose of making profits for their shareholders' until such time as you are prepared to offer a clear and reasonably enforceable scheme of responsibilities to someone else."[1]

— Adolf A. Berle

Unless an alternative is imagined, criticism is just "hand-wringing,"[2] a kind of neurotic self-regard less productive even than the onanism at which the phrase hints. Michael Jensen and William Meckling long ago noted that it is a mistake, upon locating a previously unappreciated kind of "agency cost," to automatically conclude that one had discovered that existing arrangements were "non-optimal."[3] A situation can only be called a problem if it admits of a solution. Yes, it would be better if coal were found above ground rather than below it. But as one's uncle says: if wishes were horses, we would all get taken for a ride. In this chapter and the next, I explore corporate governance reforms that I think are both desirable and plausible.

The absence of a coherent, salient alternative to our current corporate governance model in mainstream public policy discourse in the United States leads to complacency in the ordinary course and perversity in times of crisis. The subprime mortgage debacle of 2008 had many fathers (and surely some mothers), but among them was

---

[1] *See* Adolf A. Berle, Jr., *For Whom Corporate Managers Are Trustees: A Note*, 45 HARV. L. REV. 1365, 1367 (1932).

[2] FREDERIC JAMESON, POSTMODERNISM, OR, THE CULTURAL LOGIC OF LATE CAPITALISM 207 (1991).

[3] *See* Michael C. Jensen & William H. Meckling, *Theory of the Firm: Managerial Behavior, Agency Costs and Ownership Structure*, 3 J. FIN. ECON. 305, 328 & n. 28 (1976).

146

undoubtedly the regular operation of the shareholder primacy norm itself. Firms pushed as hard as possible to profit as much as possible, with scrupulous disregard for the collateral consequences of their success or failure, just as they are supposed to under shareholder primacy.[4] But the basic regulatory response undertaken in the rubble of that catastrophe, the Dodd-Frank reforms, were conceived as a way of getting our corporate governance to be *more* focused on shareholders the next time.[5] This is digging within the hole.

Nobody in the Bush or Obama administrations, in Congress, or among influential media figures seemed to consider the credit crisis to be a moment ripe for reconsideration of how corporate governance law was dealing with the rights and responsibilities of different stakeholders in corporate enterprise. In the 2016 presidential election, anticorporate populism took hold in both parties, as Donald Trump, on the right, and Bernie Sanders, on the left, pilloried a system both said was "rigged" for powerful interests. But neither showcased the mast, ropes, and tackle of corporate governance law, and the Trump administration neither promises nor will deliver any change to it. Many factors contribute to these political dynamics. But one factor has been a failure of imagination – a failure to conceive of

---

[4] Assessing the role of corporate governance in the subprime mortgage fiasco is Claire A. Hill & Brett H. McDonnell, *Reconsidering Board Oversight Duties After the Financial Crisis*, 2013 U. Ill. L. Rev. 859, 860 (2013) ("Corporate behavior in the crisis yielded enormous negative externalities for the greater society."); Christopher M. Bruner, *Corporate Governance Reform in a Time of Crisis*, 36 J. Corp. L. 309, 313 (2011) ("It is patently clear that excessive risk-taking to boost financial firm stock prices must figure prominently in any account of the financial and economic crisis emerging in 2007."); Nicholas Calcina Howson, *When "Good" Corporate Governance Makes "Bad" (Financial) Firms: The Global Crisis and the Limits of Private Law*, 108 Mich. L. Rev. First Impressions 44 (2009) ("In this case, however, more effective corporate governance may not be a serious part of the solution; instead, 'good' (or effectively functioning) corporate governance may have been one of the major factors that contributed to the global financial meltdown.").

[5] *See generally* Stephen Bainbridge, Corporate Governance After the Financial Crisis (Oxford University Press, 2012) (reviewing policy responses to the financial crises; Bainbridge is a critic of these responses, but his overview shows they were *meant* to improve shareholder primacy). Dodd-Frank also established the Consumer Financial Protection Bureau as a new federal agency charged with regulating consumer financial business. The CFBC does not alter corporate governance commands but endeavors to pursue external regulation of the retail financial sector. *See* Donald C. Lampe & Ryan J. Richardson, *The Consumer Protection Bureau at Five: A Survey of the Bureau's Activities*, 21 N.C. Banking Inst. 85 (2017).

responsible, plausible institutional alterations that could offer transformation without calamity.[6]

OTHER MODELS AVAILABLE AROUND THE WORLD

One way to break the spell of institutional fetishism in our thinking
about corporate reform possibilities is to showcase actually operating
alternatives. The American model of corporate governance is not the
only model in use in the world. Corporate governance systems in at
least some other wealthy democracies are decidedly less shareholder
centric than we see in the American design. Differences in history,
culture, and politics among nations preclude us from thinking of these
foreign systems as options that can simply be plucked off the global
shelf and installed in the United States.[7] But appreciating that alternatives to the shareholder primacy norm do actually function in other
societies can lend us some confidence that a change to the American
model would not necessarily be disastrous or completely insane, even if
turns out to be a bad idea.

Broadly speaking, countries whose political equilibrium evince col-
lectivist, liberal, social-democrat policies have corporate governance
standards that vindicate active regard for non-shareholding stakeholders. Among these are Germany, France, and Japan. Nations with more
conservative, free-market, limited-government political traditions, like
the United States and the United Kingdom, have greater shareholder
centrism in corporate governance.[8]

---

[6] *See* ROBERTO MANGABEIRA UNGER, WHAT SHOULD LEGAL ANALYSIS BECOME? (1996).

[7] *See* CHRISTOPHER BRUNER, CORPORATE GOVERNANCE IN THE COMMON-LAW WORLD 17
(2014). ("[H]istorical, cultural, and political context drive the formation of law and the life
of legal systems to such an extent that countries could not meaningfully converge on some
purported 'best' law even if they genuinely sought to do so.").

[8] *See generally* MARK ROE, POLITICAL DETERMINANTS OF CORPORATE GOVERNANCE 3 (2003).
Christopher Bruner argues that the United Kingdom is more shareholder centric than is the
United States, the latter of which he considers to be stakeholder-oriented in its corporate
governance. *See* Bruner, CORPORATE GOVERNANCE IN THE COMMON-LAW WORLD, *supra*
note 7. I criticized Bruner's description of American corporate law in Chapter 4. He is
surely correct to say that shareholders in the United Kingdom have greater *say* in corporate
governance decisions than in the United States, where the board has essentially all the
power. But Bruner is on much weaker ground for his claim that American directors are

Let us consider the German system in some detail, as it showcases elements used in a number of European and Asian countries. Like the United States, Germany is a wealthy, democratic, modern country. But its corporate governance system differs significantly from the American model. Most salient are structural differences. German law requires that large companies be controlled by a Supervisory Board, which is comprised of an equal number of shareholder *and* labor representatives.[9] Importantly, this "codetermination" system is not imposed on every German business corporation. Worker representation is not required for firms with less than 500 employees. Companies with more than 500 employees must have 1/3 of the board made up of worker representatives, and firms with more than 2000 employees must have half the board comprised of worker-appointed directors.[10]

licensed to pursue non-shareholder interests. Somewhat contradicting Roe's central thesis, Bruner claims that a nation is more capable of focusing on shareholder interests in corporate governance when it has developed a robust social safety net, such as national healthcare guarantees and long-term unemployment benefits. Countries that do not have expansive social welfare programs, he says, need to be more solicitous of non-shareholder interests within corporate governance. This argument does not hold if, like me, you consider the United States to have a relatively thin social safety net but believe that the United States nevertheless has a shareholder-focused corporate governance system. I will instead take Bruner's argument as additional justification for why genuine multi-stakeholder governance is needed in the United States, and why it may be politically palatable if the case for it can be made.

[9] A lower-level Board of Managers is responsible for day-to-day decision-making, but the Supervisory Board determines important policies and strategies and has ultimate monitoring obligations. *See generally* Thilo Kuntz, *German Corporate Law in the 20th Century* (Mar 10, 2017) in Harwell Wells (ed.), Research Handbook on the History of Corporate and Company Law, Edward Elgar, 2018 (Forthcoming), https://ssrn.com/abstract=2930974; *see also generally* Peter Muchlinski, *The Development of Germany Corporate Law Until 1990: An Historical Reappraisal,* 14 German L. J. 339 (2013); and David Charny, *The German Corporate Governance System,* 1998 Colum. Bus. L. Rev. 145 (1998).

[10] *See* Kuntz, *supra* note 9; *see also* Martin Gelter & Genevieve Helleringer, *Constituency Directors and Corporate Fiduciary Duties,* in The Philosophical Foundations of Fiduciary Law (Andrew S. Gold & Paul B. Miller, eds., 2014)(describing the German system). In the event of a deadlock among shareholder and labor representatives, the tie-breaking vote is cast by the Chair of the Supervisory Board, who is elected by the shareholders. *See* Mark J. Loewenstein, *Stakeholder Protection in Germany and Japan,* 76 Tul. L. Rev. 1673, 1677 (2002). To my formalist mind, this makes the term "codetermination" inapt. Nobody says that the United States Senate is "codetermined" by the two major political parties. Rather, we say that *one* party controls the Senate, and the other party is in the minority. It seems better to say that under the German system shareholders control the firm, and the workers have minority representation on the board. But this is not the way it is treated in the literature.

Diversity in organizational design is thus a defining feature of the German corporate governance ecology.[11] A number of other European countries, including Austria, Denmark, Sweden, Hungary, and, as of 2014, France, also have mandatory labor codetermination in their corporate law.

Of greater interest to me than *who* is serving on the board, is *what* the board is charged with doing. Board composition impacts whether the firm can achieve its mission, but that question is secondary to the determination of the mission itself. The academic literature does not speak with exacting clarity on the law of corporate purpose in Germany. This might be surprising to the uninitiated, who perhaps would like to think of law, especially on such an important matter, as something that can be "looked up." But it will be all too familiar to those who know the continuing debates in the American context as to what the law requires or allows directors to do with the firms they manage.[12] One of the reasons that it is difficult to decipher with precision what the law of corporate purpose is in Germany, and in other European and Asian nations, is that shareholder derivate litigation, which can help clarify such ambiguities, is a much less important component of corporate law systems in other parts of the world than it is in the United States.[13] Nevertheless, an instructive and reasonably reliable picture of a corporate governance system actively concerned with the interests of not just shareholders, but other stakeholders too, emerges from examination of the German scene.

In the late nineteenth and early twentieth centuries, German corporate law was strongly committed to shareholder primacy. But this shareholder focus was criticized by influential German intellectuals,

---

[11] Within this prescribed diversity, however, German corporate governance law allows less private ordering by chartering deviation than is allowed in the American system.

[12] *See* Chapter 4.

[13] Impediments to shareholder litigation in other legal systems include large minimum investment and holding thresholds to bring suits, and the fee-shifting rule, widespread in Europe, that requires a lawsuit's loser to pay the winner's legal fees. *See* Martin Gelter, *Why Do Shareholder Derivative Suits Remain Rare in Continental Europe?*, 37 Brook. J. Int'l L. 843 (2012). Recently the Delaware legislature overturned a Delaware Supreme Court ruling that fee-shifting could be imposed in shareholder derivative litigation by charter provision. After the legislative action, fee-shifting is forbidden in Delaware firms. *See generally* Stephen M. Bainbridge, *Fee-Shifting: Delaware's Self-Inflicted Wound*, 40 Del. J. Corp. L. 851 (2016).

including a prominent German businessman, scholar, and politician named Walter Rathenau, who penned a touchstone book in 1917 expressing the view that German corporate governance should *not* focus exclusively on shareholders but should instead be "steeped in the spirit of responsibility for the common good and public weal."[14] In one of the horrifying ironies of Nazism, the German National Socialist Party's corporate law policy was strongly influenced by the legacy of Rathenau, who was Jewish. When the Nazis took power, they changed Germany's corporate law to explicitly provide, under §70 of their 1937 corporate law reforms, that: "The managing board is, on its own responsibility, to manage the corporation as the good of the enterprise and its retinue and the common weal of folk and realm demand."[15] As the Harvard Law School scholar Detlev Vagts commented in a later review of the change, "[o]ne omission ... [was] noteworthy – nothing was said about the shareholders!"[16]

For those of us wondering what use the German example has for altering the American shareholder primacy norm in a more socially conscious direction, the fact that deviation from shareholder primacy in Germany was initially achieved by the Nazis gives ... pause. According to the contemporary German legal scholar Thilo Kuntz, "the main pillars of modern German corporate law remain firmly grounded in the 1937 reform."[17] Therefore, inevitably, "the question arises as to which extent the 1937 [law] represents a work of Nazi ideology."[18] Luckily, Kuntz's verdict is that the "§70" paradigm was not distinctly Nazist, but rather reflected a working out of longstanding economic and political trends, a settlement of the competing claims of German capital, labor, and society under corporate auspices, which had nothing in particular to do with Nazism. Fordham Law School's Martin Gelter corroborates this view when he writes that it was the Weimar era which was "the beginning of the emancipation of the corporation from its shareholders"[19] in Germany.

---

[14] *See* Kuntz, *supra* note 9 (quoting WALTHER RATHENAU, VOM AKTIENWESEN (1917)).

[15] Detlev F. Vagts, *Reforming the "Modern" Corporation: Perspectives from the German*, 80 HARV. L. REV. 23, 40 (1966).

[16] *Id.* at 40.   [17] *Id.* at at 15.   [18] *Id.*

[19] *See* Martin Gelter, *Taming or Protecting the Modern Corporation? Shareholder-Stakeholder Debates in a Comparative Light*, 7 N.Y.U. J. L. & BUS. 641, 680.

Relatedly, it is curious to note that the Nazi corporate law reforms also introduced into German law the view that it should be the board, and not nettlesome shareholders themselves, who have commanding decisional authority over corporate operations and policymaking. This viewpoint, which in the mainstream American context today we blithely call "director primacy," was at the time of its installation in German corporate law under the Nazis known as the *Führerprinzip*: the *Führer* principle.[20] German corporate policymakers, however, apparently drew their ideas about the *Führer* principle not directly from Nazi ideology, but from American corporate theorists and American practice.[21] So, let's just all agree that we might learn from the German corporate law experience without being interpolated into any Nazi association.

In his 1966 study of German corporate law, Vagts found that there was little for corporate scholars to make of the §70 injunction as a mode of corporate governance during the Nazi era because Hitler's government quickly came to *directly* interfere with German corporate operations, commandeering them to aid its war effort. Such direct influence, Vagts concluded, could not be disentangled from any independent operation of the §70 rule, and he found no court cases interpreting the provision.[22]

After the Nazi regime was destroyed in World War II, the continuing vitality of German corporations was central to the survival and recovery of the German nation. Codetermination in corporate governance became a part of the postwar political settlement, although scholars insist worker involvement in firm governance had a legacy in Germany that was "a hundred years old" before it became national law after World War II.[23] In fact, while the Nazis instituted the rule that firms had to be run for the good of the common weal, they had *abolished* nascent forms of worker participation in corporate governance that had been on the march before they took power. After the war, ordinary Germans and the occupying Allied command viewed German capitalists as having been complicit in the Nazi rise to power

---

[20] Kuntz, *supra* note 9 at 15.   [21] Gelter, *Taming or Protecting*, *supra* note 19 at 54.
[22] *See* Vagts, *Reforming the "Modern" Corporation*, supra note 15.
[23] Kuntz, *supra* note 9 at 17.

and the warmongering that followed. Codetermination was therefore viewed as a way of achieving the de-Nazification of German enterprise. There was also an anti-leftist aspect to codetermination, since it was viewed as a compromise that could ward off nationalization of industry, or full-blown communist insurrection.[24] Fascists to the right of them, Reds to the left, (West) Germany stuck in the middle with codetermination. Codetermination was not established in one single reform, but was incrementally adopted in a series of increasingly expansive legislative acts between 1952 and 1976, when the current regime was adopted.[25]

After World War II, efforts were made to scrub the 1937 corporate law's language, especially §70, of its National Socialist aura, while maintaining a public-regarding orientation in German corporate governance. In the end, according to Vagts, postwar reforms "eliminated the whole [§ 70] clause as unnecessary because self-evident."[26] That, it must be said, is not exactly an interpretive canon one would find in the index of an Anglo-American treatise on statutory construction. In any event, fifty years after Vagts' study, the literature reflects the same basic interpretation of what German corporate governance commands. Gelter concludes that German corporate law requires directors to focus on the "interest of the enterprise," and that "[w]hile no uniform interpretation of the term has emerged, postwar scholarship continued to understand the enterprise or the corporation to be distinct from shareholder interests."[27] Most commentators agree that the "interests of the company" concept, used not just in Germany but in the corporate law of many European countries, indicates that it is proper for the firm to serve interests beyond those of the shareholders. A 2015 European Commission Report on corporate governance standards in Europe expresses the view that under German law: "Directors are not obliged to act *only* in the interest of the shareholders, *as long as* they

---

[24] Kuntz, *supra* note 9 at 19–20.

[25] The German Supreme Court upheld the constitutionality of the 1976 expansion of the codetermination regime by noting that the rights of shareholders were bound by "social restrictions." Gelter, *Taming or Protecting, supra* note 19 at 696–97 (citing Bundesverfassungsgericht [BVerfG] [Federal Constitution Court] Mar. 1, 1979, Entscheidungen des Bundesverfassungsgerichts [BVerfGE] [Decisions of the Federal Constitutional Court] 50, 290, 315f.

[26] Vagts, *supra* note 15 at 40.   [27] Gelter, *Taming or Protecting, supra* note 19 at 58.

secure the company's profitability in the long run."[28] In his survey of differences in the law of corporate purpose among nations, Amir Licht concludes that "German corporate law directs managers' fiduciary duties to a diverse group of multiple constituencies, including shareholder[s], employees, and society as a whole."[29]

The "interests of the company" standard applies as the baseline corporate governance standard in Germany irrespective of whether a firm has a sufficient number of employees to be subject to the codetermination requirement or not. For companies that *are* subject to codetermination, the broad social orientation of the German standard means that labor representatives on the supervisory board are no more charged with narrowly representing the interests of labor than are shareholder-appointed directors charged with exclusively pursuing profits. Indeed, there is clear decisional law specifying that German directors are *not* to serve the constituency that put them on the board, but rather are to serve the interests of the company as a whole.[30] Nevertheless, some analysts claim that the distinct shareholder and labor election of director representatives in the German codetermination system results in collusion between those two groups against *other* corporate stakeholders who are not represented on the board. An example is seen in the Volkswagon Group's massive automobile emissions scandal of 2015, where the firm was found to have deployed massive, systematic fraud to evade strict regulations on pollution in their industry. This malfeasance was pulled off at the expense of consumers and the environment, at a time when Volkswagon was regarded as both highly profitable for its shareholders and very generous to its workers.[31]

---

[28] *Study on Directors' Duties and Liability, Prepared for the European Commission,* Annex 332–333 (2013) (Gerner, Carsten et. al.)(emphasis in original), ec.europa.eu/internal_market/company/docs/board/2013-study-analysis_en.pdf.

[29] Amir N. Licht, *The Maximands of Corporate Governance: A Theory of Values and Cognitive Style,* 29 Del. J. Corp. L. 649, 735 n. 336 (2004).

[30] *See* Martin Gelter & Genevieve Helleringer, *Constituency Directors and Corporate Fiduciary Duties, supra* note 10 at 12 & n. 62. Case law also makes clear, for example, that worker representatives on the board are not supposed to share confidential board-level information with union representatives or other workers.

[31] Martin Gelter, *Employee Participation in Corporate Governance and Corporate Social Responsibility,* in Handbook on the Economics of Social Responsibility:

The German model showcases elements that are in place in many other countries. Codetermination is widespread in northern and eastern Europe. But it is also clear from the experience of other European nations that codetermination is not *necessary* in order to achieve multistakeholder governance. Many European nations without codetermination adopt a standard that expects directors to balance the interests of "the company," including its workers and consumers, against the interests of shareholders.[32] Until recently, for example, France did not have any codetermination system, but its corporate law nevertheless has long held that French corporations should be governed to serve a broad set of social interests.[33] While it is again difficult to pin down precise black letter law, commentators agree that the French "corporate governance system is not primarily intended to serve shareholder interests, but also those of employees and other stakeholders, and the public interest in general."[34] Authorities refer to a concept of "intérêt

---

INDIVIDUALS, CORPORATIONS AND INSTITUTIONS (Lorenzo Sacconi and Giacomo Degli Antoni eds., 2018), https://papers.ssrn.com/sol3/papers.cfm?abstract_id=2798717. Such collusion is not unique to codetermination regimes. *See* Abram Chayes, *The Modern Corporation and the Rule of Law,* in THE CORPORATION IN MODERN SOCIETY 25, 43 (Edward S. Mason, ed., 1966). ("[T]he growth of strong unions has [not] been free of problems. It may be said that the bargain can too easily become an agreement to pursue joint ends at the expense of unrepresented parties"); David L. Ratner, *The Government of Business Corporations: Critical Reflections on the Rule of "One Share, One Vote,"* 56 CORNELL L. REV. 1, 35–36 (1970) ("Under current labor laws, there is a good deal of bona fide arm's-length bargaining between management and labor representatives over real questions of allocation of economic benefits and decision-making power within the corporate organization ... [I]t is quite possible, and indeed common, for the negotiations to result in an agreement that satisfies both employees and management at the expense of consumers or other unrepresented economic or social interest groups.").

[32] *See Study on Directors' Duties and Liability, supra* note 28 (the report indicates the contributions of "more than 60 local research assistants and renowned company law experts."). However, I think the report must be regarded with healthy skepticism. For example, it characterizes the UK as *not* shareholderist in orientation, while Christopher Bruner, a leading comparative corporate law scholar, credibly argues that the UK is probably the most shareholder centric system on the planet. *See* Bruner, CORPORATE GOVERNANCE IN THE COMMON-LAW WORLD, *supra* note 7.

[33] One set of commentators has it that "in France, worker representatives ... dislike [the] codetermination approach, evidenced by their reticence to have their anti-capitalist perspective co-opted into the corporate structure." Véronique Magnier & Darren Rosenblum, *Quotas and the Transatlantic Divergence of Corporate Governance,* 34 Nw. J. INT'L L. & BUS. 249, 289 (2014).

[34] Gelter, *Taming or Protecting, supra* note 19 at 704; *see also* Henry Hansmann & Reinier Kraakman, *The End of History for Corporate Law,* 89 GEO. L. J. 439, 446 (2001).

social" (the social interest) as being a core component of French corporate governance law.[35] Structurally, this principle has been pursued through heavy involvement of the French government in corporate operations, including significant direct state ownership of large firms, government control over access to credit, regulatory facilitation or obstruction of mergers, state designation or prohibition of monopoly formation, and the like.[36]

There is a hallowed, reverse *Dodge v. Ford* case from 1965 in France that is recognized as vindicating the "intérêt social" principle in French corporate law. The Fruehauf France corporation had a contract to produce sixty trucks on behalf of a private customer, who would ultimately deliver the trucks to China. The company had an American shareholder with a controlling interest in the firm who objected to the deal (on political grounds, not wanting to aid communist China) and caused the firm to cancel the contract. Minority shareholders (French shareholders) objected to the cancellation and sought judicial intervention. Rather than basing its holding on an assessment of disloyal motives by the controlling American shareholder, the French Court held that the decision to cancel the contract was contrary to the "intérêt social" principle of French corporate governance law, since it would have harmed the customer and resulted in the loss of 650 French jobs.[37] This is obviously not a crisp distillation of mechanical rules for multi-stakeholder governance, but it showcases a multi-stakeholder governance legacy which continues to hold interpretative power in assessments of the law of corporate purpose in France.[38]

---

[35] *See* James A. Fanto, *The Role of Corporate Law in French Corporate Governance*, 31 CORNELL INT'L L.J. 31, 47 (1998) ("The concept of the intérêt social, which permeates the French corporate code, permits directors to consider the interests of all constituencies in deciding upon corporate strategy.").

[36] Like other imperial powers, France imposed its corporate governance system in its colonies. Consequently, the corporate governance systems of many former French colonies in West Africa continue to reflect this legacy. Claire Moore Dickerson argues that where the national political system is unstable, the "intérêt social" principle in corporate governance can facilitate political corruption, making sound governance in both government and business more elusive. *See* Claire Moore Dickerson, *Sex and Capital: What They Tell Us About Ourselves*, 79 ST. JOHN'S L. REV. 1161, 1174 (2005) ("[T]he dominant perception in the [West Africa] region holds that the political system's catastrophic failure renders corporate governance meaningless.").

[37] *Id.*

[38] Gelter, *Taming or Protecting, supra* note 19 at 714–15. The case is Cour d'appel [CA] [regional court of appeal] Paris, May 22, 1965, JCP 1965 II, P 14274bis; D. 1968, Jur. p. 147.

Looking beyond Europe, we can find examples of corporate governance systems that emphasize stakeholder interests in important East Asian democracies with robust economies, such as Japan and Korea. Licht describes Asian corporate governance as being, of all the world's systems, the "least comprehensible to the Western observer."[39] This confusion may stem from the Western analyst's tendency to insist on legal formalism and to strongly separate law from other social institutions that shape behavior. I have adopted such a formalist approach in most of this book. But the formal approach, meant to highlight what is otherwise too easily obscured about corporate governance in the United States, apparently threatens to conceal more than reveal in the Asian situation. In the case of Japan, for example, numerous commentators note a clear divergence between de jure and de facto corporate governance norms, and insist that to really comprehend Japanese corporate governance we must be prepared to emphasize the latter.

In the late nineteenth century, formal Japanese corporate law was modeled on German corporate law. German law at that time was shareholder centric, but Japanese corporations of the era were in fact socially oriented enterprises, deeply influenced by and committed to serving the Japanese imperial government. Like German corporations, Japanese firms were decisively co-opted by the Japanese government before and during the Second World War. After Japan was defeated in 1945, the occupying American forces insisted on the reform of Japanese corporate law in favor of American-style shareholder primacy, with attendant securities market infrastructure and regulation. As with de-Nazification in Germany, these reforms in Japan were meant to impede the reconstitution of a corporate system that could support any renewed Japanese militarism. The Allied occupiers helped establish codetermination in Germany, but shareholder primacy in the traditional American style was imposed on Japanese corporate reconstruction.[40]

---

[39] Licht, *supra* note 29 at 736.

[40] *See* Michael Cody, *Hostile Takeover Bids in Japan? Understanding Convergence Using the Layered Approach*, 9 RICH. J. GLOBAL L. & BUS. 1 (2010) ("The occupation forces intended to set up a new competitive economic system with widely diffused share ownership (and power) so that the economic system would never again become an instrument for military designs.").

While the "black letter" corporate law in Japan has thus long stated that director obligations are owed solely to shareholders,[41] commentators unanimously insist that the deeper, more pressing and powerful norm of Japanese corporate governance has been an emphasis on serving stakeholder interests – most importantly, workers, suppliers, business partners, long-term stockholders (as compared to short-term investors), and Japanese society as a whole.[42] For example, the familiar idea that Japanese corporations provide lifetime employment to their workers is not a legal rule, but is a strongly held custom and widespread practice. Japanese corporations engage in extensive cross holding of each other's shares. These shares do not circulate on secondary markets, and thus the cross holding has traditionally impeded operation of the market for control. This hallowed (or dread) *keiretsu* structure has in turn provided sufficient (what we might call) "slack" to allow directors to manage in the interests of workers and others, rather than emphasizing returns to shareholders.[43]

Analysts suggest that this divergence between law and practice, or law and "law" (or "law" and law), should not be understood in terms

---

[41] Zenichi Shishido, *Japanese Corporate Governance: The Hidden Problems of Corporate Law and Their Solution*, 25 Del. J. Corp. L. 189, 199 (2000) ("The concept of fiduciary duty in Japan is also no less shareholder-oriented than its American counterpart . . . no case law exists that explicitly allows the balancing of interests of stakeholders.").

[42] *See* Licht, *supra* note 29 at 737 (the Japanese corporate governance system is "generally perceived as stakeholder-oriented"); Takashi Araki, *A Comparative Analysis: Corporate Governance and Labor and Employment Relations in Japan*, 22 Comp. Lab. L. & Pol´y 67, 68 (2000) ("Japanese corporate governance follows a stakeholder model . . . however, an important difference exists between the German and Japanese stakeholder models: namely, that the Japanese stakeholder model significantly relies on customary practices and thus shows a striking contrast with the institutionalized German stakeholder model"); Caslav Pejovic, *Japanese Corporate Governance: Behind Legal Norms*, 29 Penn St. Int´l L. Rev. 483, 486–87 (2011) ("One of the paradoxes of the Japanese model is that during the period when the model was presumably under the influence of American-style black letter corporate law, it actually diverged from the American model"); Sanford M. Jacoby, *Corporate Governance in Comparative Perspective: Prospects for Convergence*, 22 Comp. Lab. L. & Pol´y J. 5 (2000) ("Although not a social democracy, Japan's approach to corporate governance has strong similarities to the stakeholder system of continental Europe"). *See also generally* Bruce E. Aronson, *Japanese Corporate Governance Reform: A Comparative Perspective*, 11 Hastings Bus. L. J. 85 (2015). I am grateful to Professor Aronson for his helpful correspondence with me on these issues.

[43] *See* Cody, *supra* note 40 at 22–23. *But see* Yoshiro Miw & J. Mark Ramseyer, The Fable of the Keiretsu: Urban Legends of the Japanese Economy (2006) (doubting the significance of cross-holding as an impediment to shareholder primacy in Japan).

of sloppiness or breach of duty, but rather it should be seen as evincing the strong, abiding influence of Confucianism in Japanese culture.[44] Confucianism both emphasizes one's relational obligations to other people, which explains the emphasis on multiple stakeholders, *and* insists on the importance of locating the source of such obligations outside formal legal rules and compulsions of the state, which may explain the clear deviation from black letter principles originally imposed by foreign occupying powers.[45]

CORPORATE POLITICAL SPEECH IS LIMITED IN OTHER COUNTRIES

Business activity in general is subject to greater governmental regulation in many European nations than it is in the United States.[46] There are undoubtedly many explanations for this, but one piece of the story is that government, at least formally, is more insulated from corporate influence in Europe than it is in the United States. There is no *Citizens United* wrench in the works of corporate regulation in Europe.[47]

Again, the German example is illuminating. There, the law strictly limits how far in advance of an election political advertisements may be run by anyone, corporations and natural people alike. When election advertising is permitted, political parties are allocated television time based on their relative electoral standing. German law forbids speech that advocates hatred or discrimination along the lines of race, religion, gender, or culture, despite an ostensible guarantee of freedom of speech in the German federal

---

[44] *But see* Teemu Ruskola, *Legal Orientalism*, 101 MICH. L. REV. 179 (2002) (criticizing scholars for superficially treating the West as lawlike, and the East as lawless).

[45] *See* Amir N. Licht, *Legal Plug-Ins: Cultural Distance, Cross-Listing, and Corporate Governance Reform*, 22 BERKELEY J. INT'L L. 195 (2004)("in countries with a strong Confucian heritage, the cultural infrastructure calls on people to seek guidance for conducting their personal life and social interactions in sources other than the law.").

[46] *See generally* Leo E. Strine, Jr., *The Soviet Constitution Problem in Comparative Corporate Law: Testing the Proposition That European Corporate Law Is More Stockholder-Focused than U.S. Corporate Law*, 89 SOUTHERN CAL. L. REV. 1239, 1270 (2016).

[47] *See* Chapter 3.

constitution.[48] *Within* these comparatively strict political speech rules, German corporations are permitted to participate in campaign activities to the same extent as natural people or other organizations. Individual and corporate contributions to political parties is unlimited, as are independent campaign expenditures. However, the German system also provides for substantial public financing of political campaigns, making corporate money relatively less influential. Observers also note that, in general, campaigning in Germany is constrained by a political culture that is reserved, wary of Germany's calamitous history with fevered nationalism.[49] There are differences among European nations, but the general picture is that corporate political activity is more limited in Europe, both by law and by custom, than it is in the United States.[50]

Despite these institutional restraints, we need not naïvely conclude that European corporations wield no significant political power. As I emphasized in Chapter 3, the greatest relative strength of corporations in the regulatory arena comes not in high-salience, hot political times of grand political campaigns, but in the low-salience, cold days of ordinary governance, legislating, and rulemaking. When it comes to lobbying of this sort, Germany corporations, for example, appear to be active, and trending towards American patterns.[51] However, where firms are operating under a multi-stakeholder imperative, rather than strict shareholder primacy, there is, at least theoretically, less worry that such political activity will be socially destructive.

---

[48] *See generally* CAMPAIGN FINANCE: AN OVERVIEW OF AUSTRALIA FRANCE, GERMANY, ISRAEL AND THE UNITED KINGDOM, LIBRARY OF CONGRESS GLOBAL LEGAL RESEARCH CENTER (2009) [Hereinafter, "Campaign Finance: An Overview"]; *see also* Olga Khazan, *Why Germany's Politics Are Much Saner, Cheaper, and Nicer than Ours*, THE ATLANTIC (Sep 30, 2013).

[49] *Id.*

[50] Caroline Kaeb, *Putting the "Corporate" Back into Corporate Personhood*, 35 NW. J. INT'L L. & BUS. 591, 639 (2015) ("[C]ampaign financing by corporations plays only a limited role under the law and practice in Europe."). Japanese law permits most corporations to donate to the campaigns of individual candidates but not to political parties. *Political Finance Database*, INST. FOR DEMOCRACY & ELECTORAL ASSISTANCE, www.idea.int/data-tools/data/political-finance-database. There are no black letter prohibitions against independent corporate expenditures on political campaigns.

[51] *See Germany's Corporate Lobby: Turning American*, THE ECONOMIST (May 16, 2015).

BOARD DIVERSITY

An important recent development in the corporate law of many European nations is the adoption of mandatory gender quotas on corporate boards. Corporate boards all over the world have historically been dominated by men. In 2014, just 17 percent of board of directors positions in American corporations in the Fortune 500 were held by women. In that year, Germany had 14 percent and France 18 percent women directors in their large firms. In Japan and in the Middle East, less than 1 percent of corporate directors are women.[52] In 2003, Norway became the first country to adopt a gender quota as part of its corporate governance law, requiring that 40 percent of corporate board seats be held by women by 2008. This goal was achieved. In eight years, Norway went from less than 7 percent women on its boards to more than 40 percent, a remarkable transformation.[53] Other European nations, including Italy, the Netherlands, Belgium and France, have followed suit and adopted gender quotas. France has the most ambitious standard. It requires that the boards of all publicly traded firms, and large private firms, must have *equal numbers* of men and women on their boards. Germany, which has had gender balance rules in its political system for decades, considered but rejected proposals to adopt mandatory gender balance on corporate boards.[54] There does not seem to be any serious movement towards corporate board gender quotas in Japan.

There is an active debate in the academic literature as to whether gender quotas improve corporate productivity or not. But productivity aside, advocates of gender quotas consider the increased presence of women on the board as a factor that can help advance the stakeholder responsibilities that corporations have in the countries that have

---

[52] *See* Amanda K. Packel, *Book Review: Government Intervention into Board Composition: Gender Quotas in Norway and Diversity Disclosures in the United States* (Review of Aarron A. Dhir, Challenging Boardroom Homogeneity: Corporate Law, Governance, and Diversity (2015)), 21 STAN. J. L. BUS. & FIN. 192, 194 (2016).

[53] Douglas M. Branson, *Initiatives to Place Women on Corporate Boards of Directors – A Global Snapshot*, 37 J. CORP. L. 793 (2012); *see also* Anne L. Alstott, *Gender Quotas for Corporate Boards: Options for Legal Design in the United States*, 26 PACE INT'L L. REV. 38 (2014).

[54] *Id.*

adopted them. The idea is that feminist concepts of care and connection can enable attention to a wider array of constituents than can be achieved when men govern corporate enterprise without a critical presence of women.[55] As Véronique Magnier and Darren Rosenblum put it: "Some studies demonstrate that 'women' actually have distinct perspectives. If women board members hew to stereotypes (as some studies suggest), they would attend to vulnerable populations."[56] Gender diversity is one of the ways that European legal systems are seeking to operationalize multi-stakeholder corporate governance.

Gender quotas have not been forthcoming in the law of corporate governance in the United States, and it is doubtful they could be, constitutionally. There have been energetic movements calling for board diversification in the United States, especially along the gender dimension, and these have met with some success.[57] In the American context commentators also urge that more women on the board, or other modes of board diversification, will facilitate greater sensitivity or connectivity with the firm's various and distinct stakeholder groups. But where shareholder primacy reigns, the *reason* for the greater relatability and connection can only ever be corporate profitability. Shareholder primacy commoditizes diversity.

---

[55] See Kelly Y. Testy, *Capitalism and Freedom –For Whom?: Feminist Legal Theory and Progressive Corporate Law*, 67 LAW & CONTEMP. PROBS. 87, 95–99 (2004); *see also* Theresa A. Gabaldon, *Corporate Conscience and the White Man's Burden*, 70 GEO. WASH. L. REV. 944, 951–54 (2002); Ronnie Cohen, *Feminist Thought and Corporate Law: It's Time to Find Our Way Up from the Bottom (Line)*, 2 AM. U. J. GENDER SOC. POL'Y & L. 1, 24 (1994) ("Alienation and compartmentalization of different spheres of existence is one of the main themes criticized in feminist thought. Separation of the investor from the productive use of her assets is but one pernicious form of alienation.").

[56] Magnier & Rosenblum, *supra* note 33 at 293. *But see* Darren Rosenblum & Daria Roithmayr, *More Than a Woman: Insights Into Corporate Governance After the French Sex Quota*, 48 IND. L. REV. 889 (2015) (arguing that the gender quota affected the substance of corporate decision-making in France not so much because of the increased presence of women, but because of the increased presence of perspectives from different industries or countries that firms brought into the boardroom in the course of satisfying the gender quota).

[57] Marleen O'Connor-Felman, *American Corporate Governance and Children: Investing in Our Future Human Capital During Turbulent Times*, 77 S. CAL. L. REV. 1255, 1349 (2003)("[w]ork-family scholars report that one of the main problems preventing the successful implementation of work-family programs is that CEOs set the tone of the corporation's culture and most CEOs simply do not 'get it.'").

EFFICIENCY AND SATISFACTION

The literature admits of three opinions regarding the efficacy of the Anglo-American corporate governance system as compared to European and Japanese models. Some researchers claim that extant stakeholder regimes are less productive than shareholderist systems, other analysts insist that stakeholder systems are more productive than shareholderist system, and still others, drawing on the contrasting findings of the first two groups, conclude that the evidence is ambiguous and indeterminate.[58] Opinions on the relative merits of the two systems may be cyclical. For example, when the Japanese economy was booming in the 1980s, it was said in many quarters that American firms could not compete with Japanese companies unless they adopted Japanese governance forms. The reverse was heard as the American economy surged in the 1990s, and Japan's stalled.[59]

The productivity debate, however, may be somewhat beside the point, or at least too narrow a question, if we are concerned also with the distributional consequences of corporate governance and the social meaning of corporate law. The production of wealth is only part of the formula for increasing social welfare. If we do not have confidence that regulatory and tax-and-transfer functions of the government are well functioning (as shareholder primacy theory requires), then people may be better off in a less "productive" multi-stakeholder system than a

---

[58] *Compare* Gary Gorton & Frank A. Schmid, *Capital, Labor and the Firm: A Study of German Codetermination*, 2 J. Eur. Econ. Ass'n 863 (2004) (finding stocks of codetermined firms traded at a significant discount compared to similarly situated firms not subject to codetermination) *with* Felix FitzRoy & Kornelius Kraft, *Codetermination, Efficiency and Productivity*, 43 Brit. J. Indus. Rel. 233 (2005) (finding that the introduction of codetermination increased firm productivity). *Compare also* Hansmann and Kraakman, *supra* note 34, at 445 ("The growing view today is that meaningful direct worker voting participation in corporate affairs tends to produce inefficient decisions, paralysis, or weak boards, and that these costs are likely to exceed any potential benefits that worker participation might bring") with Brian B. Kim, *Stock Returns, Corporate Governance, and Long-Term Economic Growth*, 35 Ohio N.U. L. Rev. 685 (2009) ("the top five performing stock markets since World War II belong to stakeholder or mixed corporate governance structures. Overall, the average stock market returns of the shareholder economies equal the stakeholder average.").

[59] *See* Ronald J. Gilson, *Globalizing of Form or Function*, 49 Am. J. Comp. L. 329, 331–332 (2001).

more "productive" shareholder primacy one.[60] Yet even on this broader issue of social utility, Mark Roe, amazingly, concludes that we cannot clearly distinguish outcomes between the different systems. "[T]he effects on total social welfare," he writes, "are ambiguous."[61] And again: "[w]hether life is better for more people," under the Anglo-American or European system, "is hard to know."[62] This is a frustrating place to find agnosticism on the part of the world's foremost comparative corporate law scholar, but there it is. Roe appears roughly to think that different corporate governance systems represent different political and organizational paths to the same basic kinds of outcomes. The United States achieves its outcomes through greater ease of capital aggregation, economic dynamism, and job creation. The Europeans do it with less dynamism but stronger safeguards for workers and other groups. The stakes of corporate governance design, this suggests, may be marginal. Which is not to say that the margin is unimportant. A little happier (or then again, a little less happy) is a lot. Regardless, I think there are important differences in cultural meaning and social cohesion at stake in different corporate governance designs, even if measurable outcomes, like standards of living, are indeterminate.

PATH DEPENDENCE

As noted at the start of this chapter, national differences in corporate governance systems derive from and to some degree may depend upon the distinct political, economic, and cultural paths nations have taken in their own evolution. To the extent that corporate governance systems are "path dependent," it is not realistic to think we could just "plunk[] down"[63] one country's corporate governance system in another country that has been on a different path even if we wanted to.

---

[60] *See, e.g.*, Dieter Sadowski et al., *The German Model of Corporate Labor and Governance*, 22 COMP. LAB. L. & POL'Y J. 33 (2000) (collecting studies); Mark Roe, *German Securities Markets and German Codetermination*, 1998 COLUM. BUS. L. REV. 167 (arguing that codetermination weakens efficacy of German corporate boards).

[61] *See* Mark Roe, POLITICAL DETERMINANTS OF CORPORATE GOVERNANCE, *supra* note 8 at 3.

[62] *Id.* at 8.   [63] *Id.* at 7.

Scholars identify two related kinds of path dependencies in the corporate governance area. The first, more stark, relates to the capital structure of business enterprise. The second more subtly bears on national differences in culture and cognitive style.

Roe argues that where corporate governance is concerned with multiple stakeholders, stockholding tends to be highly concentrated in large financial institutions and wealthy families. This pattern is seen in Germany, France, and to some extent, Japan.[64] Conversely, where corporate governance is focused exclusively on shareholder interests, corporate ownership is more widely dispersed, as it is in the United States.[65] Roe argues that because multi-stakeholder corporate governance exacerbates equity's "agency problem," where such systems are in place shareholders must maintain relatively more control and influence over corporate operations, so they can reign in too much attention to other stakeholder interests in corporate decision-making. This precludes capital structures that have widespread public investors who cannot individually or collectively monitor and influence corporate governance. In contrast, a laser focus on shareholder primacy in corporate governance allows dispersed shareholders sufficient repose to invest at a distance, in small amounts, across many firms. The causality here, Roe smartly says, may go both ways. Some European countries have multi-stakeholder governance systems, and so they must have close ownership; or, countries have close ownership, and so they can have multi-stakeholder governance. The United States has widespread stockholding, so it must has shareholder primacy; or, it has shareholder primacy, so it can have widespread stockholding.[66] The implication is that multi-stakeholder governance may be less plausible where shareholding is widely dispersed, as it is in the United States.

Henry Hansmann and Reinier Kraakman, to the rescue, are skeptical of Roe's thesis, arguing that "the shareholder primacy model does not logically privilege any particular ownership structure."[67] They note that there are many American firms that are *not* widely dispersed

---

[64] *See generally,* Miw & Ramseyer, *supra* note 43.

[65] *See* Luca Enriques & Paolo Volpin, *Corporate Governance Reforms in Continental Europe,* 21 J. ECON. PERSP. 117, 118 (2007).

[66] *See* Roe, POLITICAL DETERMINANTS, *supra* note 8 at 7.

[67] Hansmann & Kraakman, *supra* note 34 at 443.

but operate under shareholder primacy, and, conversely, there are plenty of European firms that are widely held and operate under the codetermination and multi-stakeholder regimes.[68] So, perhaps multi-stakeholder governance is compatible with multiple ownership structures.

Comparative corporate law scholars also emphasize that corporate governance systems are contingent upon national history and psychology.[69] The German codetermination regime was not theorized first as a coherent system of corporate governance and then deployed as rational public policy. Rather, it represents a civic equilibrium, a "truce," among various political forces unfolding in a specific historical context. And now, regardless of that history, the path is well worn, and the codetermination system is deeply entrenched in Germany. It is "enormously important, symbolically and ideologically" in that country.[70] Whatever their economic or policy views of competing corporate governance systems, no German politician would "risk the massive public outrage"[71] that would attend an attempt to get rid of codetermination. The American system, too, was not built from blueprints filed in the law reviews, but emerged out of specific social conflicts and resolutions. The progressive political movement in the United States directed its ideology and energy at limiting the power of large financial institutions (that would otherwise support large block-holding of the German variety) rather than focusing on the law of corporate governance per se.[72] Shareholder primacy developed historically in the United States, and that history cannot be undone and redone as easily as theory can be critiqued and replaced.

---

[68] *Id.*; *see also* Clifford G. Holderness, *The Myth of Diffuse Ownership in the United States*, 22 REV. FIN. STUD. 1377 (2009) (arguing that American firms are no more widely held than are firms in other countries).

[69] *See also* Amir Licht, *The Mother of All Path Dependencies: Toward a Cross-Cultural Theory of Corporate Governance Systems*, 26 DEL. J. CORP. L. 147 (2001).

[70] JOHN W. CIOFFI, PUBLIC LAW AND PRIVATE POWER: CORPORATE GOVERNANCE REFORM IN THE AGE OF FINANCE CAPITALISM 70–71 (2010) (quoted in BRUNER, CORPORATE GOVERNANCE IN THE COMMON-LAW WORLD, *supra* note 7 at 226).

[71] Kuntz, *supra* note 9 at 27.

[72] *See* Mark J. Roe, *A Political Theory of American Corporate Finance*, 91 COLUM. L. REV. 10 (1991) ("American law and politics deliberately diminished the power of financial institutions to hold . . . large equity stakes . . . making the modern American corporation adapt to the political terrain.").

If it is true that stakeholder-oriented corporate governance in Japan is built upon Confucian traditions, then the workability of that system is not particularly relevant to considerations of reform in the United States, which does not have a longstanding or widespread Confucian culture. Similarly, it may be hard to impose strict shareholder primacy in deeply Confucian nations if it bucks against hallowed cultural values there. Licht argues that East Asian cultures inculcate a psychological outlook that makes people generally more sensitive to situational and relational dynamics, as compared to Anglo-American culture, which produces an outlook focused on individual rights and interests. The consequence, he claims, is that East Asian people may be more cognitively capable of multi-stakeholder governance, or less cognitively capable of shareholder primacy, than Western people, and vice versa. He calls this "the mother of all path dependencies," but he does not mean it in a biological sense, as he argues that the psychological tendencies he chronicles dissipate, especially intergenerationally, upon migration between societies.[73] Such material may also suggest justification for, or against, board diversification based on cultural background, depending on the goal set out for the corporate enterprise.[74]

CONVERGENCE

Largely contradicting the strong "path dependence" outlook in comparative corporate law, some authorities argue that there has been, over the last several decades, or will be over the next several decades, "convergence" among global systems towards the American shareholder primacy model. This was the core descriptive claim in an influential 2001 article by Hansmann and Kraakman, which was provocatively, even triumphantly, called, *The End of History for Corporate Law*.[75] Overlapping explanations are given for this purported convergence. Foreign firms in countries governed by less efficient, less

---

[73] *See generally* Licht, *The Mother of All Path Dependencies*, *supra* note 69.
[74] *See* Chapter 5.
[75] When Hansmann and Kraakman talk of convergence, they seem much more confident in describing ideological consensus and *de facto* corporate practices than *de jure* shifts to shareholder primacy: "convergence in the fine structure of corporate law proceeds more

effective corporate law, find it difficult to compete with the profit-making capacities of American companies and so are moving toward the Delaware model in order to survive. For example, in the 1990s, Japan's economy faltered after decades of strong growth. Many economists blamed the crisis on inadequacies in their corporate governance system.[76] There have, since then, been significant legal reforms in Japan endeavoring to impose greater emphasis on the firm's obligations to its shareholders. This is a continuing project, meeting with mixed results and social tolerance. Also, in developing nations, U.S.-influenced international institutions, such as the International Monetary Fund, force the reform of local corporate governance regimes to bring them into line with the canonical American model.[77]

Legal developments in the European Union may also herald convergence on shareholder primacy. In the United States, corporate promoters are free to incorporate in any state they wish, choosing the corporate governance law to which they will be subject regardless of where they do business. In contrast, other parts of the world have traditionally embraced a "real seat" doctrine, requiring firms to adhere to the corporate governance law in the country that hosts their principle place of business (this inevitably involves a multifactor inquiry). Commitment to this "real seat" doctrine was one of the early impediments to the European Union project. In 1973, one antagonist wrote: "the [European] community cannot tolerate the establishment of a Delaware in its territory."[78] These early worries may prove prescient. In a case known as *Centros Ltd.*, the European Court of Justice in 1999 ruled that member states in the European Union had to recognize and respect the governance rules of firms chartered in another member

---

slowly than convergence in governance practices." Hansmann & Kraakman, *supra* note 34 at 455.

[76] *See* Joe W. (Chip) Pitts III, *Corporate Social Responsibility: Current Status and Future Evolution*, 6 RUTGERS J. L. & PUB. POL'Y 334 (2009) ("The sidestepping of corporate governance controls by certain banks and companies in South Korea, and also in Japan, Indonesia, Thailand, and Malaysia – but not Hong Kong, Singapore, or Australia – seems to have made a significant difference in the unfolding of that crisis.").

[77] *See* Ronald J. Gilson, *Globalizing of Form or Function*, *supra* note 59 at 331 & n. 11.

[78] Clive M. Schmitthoff, *The Future of European Company Law Scene*, in THE HARMONIZATION OF EUROPEAN COMPANY LAW 3, 9 (1973).

state but doing business in their own country.[79] This ruling threatened to introduce the American "internal affairs" rule into the European context, with member states rushing to use U.K.-style company law, which is as shareholder centric as Delaware law.

The theoretical point to draw from these practical developments, from my point of view, is that corporate governance *can* change, despite the tug of path dependence. To the extent that there has been or will be global convergence on the American model, the problem with American corporate law will become a *global* problem. But if countries can move off of their paths towards greater shareholder primacy, then perhaps they can also move from shareholder primacy towards multi-stakeholder governance.

PERSISTENCE AND DIVERGENCE

Despite these economic and legal pressures towards convergence, there presently continues to be considerable diversity in corporate governance forms across different countries. In some ways there is clearly global *dispersion* rather than convergence. Gender quotas are becoming more widespread in Europe but are unlikely soon to be adopted in the United States or Japan.[80] France has recently moved *towards* codetermination, not away from it. The U.K., after voting in 2016 to depart from the European Union, is considering corporate governance changes that would allow workers and consumers a greater say in corporate policymaking.[81] Predictions and worry notwithstanding, the *Centros* decision did not result in a stampede towards

---

[79] Martin Gelter, *Centros, the Freedom of Establishment for Companies, and the Court's Accidental Vision for Corporate Law*, in EU LAW STORIES (Fernanda Nicola & Bill Davies, eds., 2015). The *Centros* cases seem only to allow choice of national form for new companies, not ones that already exist. This apparently cannot be evaded through formal machinations. *See* Centros Ltd. v. Erhvervs-og Selskabsstyrelsen [1999] E.C.R. Case C-212/97.

[80] *See* Magnier & Rosenblum, *supra* note 33 at 254.

[81] *See* Cydney S. Posner, *U.K. Enhancements to Corporate Governance: Will the New U.S. Administration Follow?*, HARVARD LAW SCHOOL FORUM ON CORPORATE GOVERNANCE AND FINANCIAL REGULATION, Dec 23, 2016, https://corpgov.law.harvard.edu/2016/12/23/u-k-proposed-enhancements-to-corporate-governance-will-the-new-u-s-administration-follow/#more-76602.

European chartering in shareholder-centric jurisdictions. Instead, as one analyst has it, European states have engaged in "defensive" regulatory competition, changing those features of their own laws that might cause promoters to instead use a foreign charter.[82] These changes, however, have been technical – for example, reducing capitalization requirements (big on the Continent but not in the U.K.) – rather than changes to the fundamental law of corporate purpose. There may be status quo bias here, with European firms considering it not such a big deal to stick with multi-stakeholder governance when that is what they have had all along. Or there may be some endowment effect in it, with non-shareholders indicating they will not tolerate an abandonment of multi-stakeholder governance prerogatives they have long enjoyed in the boardroom. A point for our purposes, anyway, is that once multi-stakeholder governance is in place, if you can get it in place, it is evidently not so horrifying that capital will flee from it the moment it can.

CONCLUSION

The examples of Germany, France, and Japan clearly show that multi-stakeholder corporate governance is feasible. But they do not provide precise, deductively applicable guidance, positive or negative, for use on the American scene. The civil law traditions in which these multi-stakeholder systems function do not yield really good cases, with hundred-page Delaware-style opinions, responding to eighty-page opinions from the court below, explaining what the corporation's directors did, what they should have done, and what it all means about the corporate system. The European Commission Report discussed earlier avers that under European corporate law, "[w]here the interests of the company are defined in a way that includes multiple constituencies, the managerial role necessarily involves the balancing of those interests."[83] That is the start of a conversation, but one searches the comparative literature in vain for a full script. Alive and kicking global

---

[82] *See* Gelter, *Centros, the Freedom of Establishment for Companies, supra* note 79.
[83] *Id.* at 74.

deviations from shareholder primacy in wealthy, free parts of the world should embolden the progressive ambition in the United States to develop a system of multi-stakeholder corporate governance here. The details about how to operationalize such a regime, we must work out for ourselves.

8 A SOCIALLY RESPONSIBLE CORPORATE GOVERNANCE STANDARD

"Not honesty alone, but the punctilio of an honor the most
sensitive, is then the standard of behavior."[1]
— *Meinhard v. Salmon* (Cardozo, J.)

"It is only the board that this, in the end, can come from."[2]
— Michael Jensen

The investigations chronicled in this book lead me to conclude that
we should alter our corporate governance law to require the directors
of our largest firms to actively attend to the interests of multiple
stakeholders, not just shareholders. This conclusion is out of step
both with prevailing law and the opinions of the most prominent
contemporary corporate theorists, both of which insist on exclusive
attention to the shareholders in firm governance. But would you be
surprised, as I was surprised, to find my basic thrust reflected in the
writings of two of the most influential free-market, pro-capitalist
thinkers this side of Adam Smith? I have here the words of F. A.
Hayek and Milton Friedman.

In a somewhat obscure essay from 1960, *The Corporation in a
Democratic Society*, Hayek wrote – no, Hayek *emphasized*:

> I should like ... to *emphasize* at once that when I contend that the
> only specific purpose which corporations ought to serve is to secure
> the highest long-term return on their capital, this does not mean

---

[1] Meinhard v. Salmon, 164 N.E. 545, 546 (N.Y. 1928) (Cardozo, J.) (describing the
standard of conduct required of a fiduciary).
[2] Michael C. Jensen, Professor of Bus. Admin., Harvard Bus. Sch., Presentation at the
Stanford Law School, *Beyond Agency Theory: The Hidden and Heretofore Inaccessible Power
of Integrity* (Feb 11, 2010).

that in the pursuit of this end they ought not to be restrained by general legal and moral rules.[3]

Did you catch that? Hayek, his double negative cashed out, thought corporations ought to be restrained not just by external governmental regulations, but also by *moral* rules. This is no small concession, not from the point of view of corporate governance law in the United States today. Hayek does not seem to think his ought about moral rules swallows his ought that firms should "secure the highest long-term return on their capital." But it does.

Ten years after Hayek let this slip, Milton Friedman did the same thing in his famous 1970 *New York Times Magazine* piece, "The Social Responsibility of Business Is to Increase Its Profits."[4] That essay is routinely held out in corporate law discourse, pridefully, by proponents of shareholder primacy, and disdainfully, by its opponents. Both sides seem to miss what Friedman wrote at the height of that essay:

> In a free-enterprise, private-property system, a corporate executive is an employee of the owners of the business. He has direct responsibility to his employers. That responsibility is to conduct the business in accordance with their desires, which generally will be to make as much money as possible while conforming to the basic rules of the society, both those embodied in law and those embodied in ethical custom.[5]

Ethical custom? There are many kinds of custom, but *ethical* custom typically tacks hard against "mak[ing] as much money as possible." Neither Hayak nor Friedman say more about how they think morality and ethical custom should operate in the boardroom. Maybe they did not really mean what they said in these passages, but said it to soften the blow of their core points. Yet these were not men prone to pulling intellectual punches.

---

[3] F. A. HAYAK, *The Corporation in a Democratic Society: In Whose Interests Ought It to and Will It Be Run?*, in MANAGEMENT AND CORPORATIONS 300–301 (1960, 1985) (emphasis in original).

[4] Milton Friedman, *The Social Responsibility of Business Is to Increase Its Profits*, THE NEW YORK TIMES MAGAZINE (Sep 13, 1970).

[5] *Id.*

I think what happened here is that both Hayek and Friedman, like Adam Smith before them and Richard Epstein after them, were keen to emphasize that their advocacy of legal designs that leave people free to pursue their individual self-interest did not mean that they wanted or expected to get a society in which money dominated all other values. These libertarian thinkers had a rich, complex idea of what humans desire, and they fully expected that a privately ordered society would prioritize many things others than profit. They wanted their readers to understand that their vision of a free enterprise system was not Dickensian parody, and they could not help but give a gloss of welfare maximization to arguments that were ostensibly about corporate profit maximization.

The self-interested activity of individual entrepreneurs and private adventurers undoubtedly involves the pursuit of profit subject to the restraints of morality and ethical custom. "It is not from the benevolence of the butcher, the brewer, or the baker that we expect our dinner, but from their regard to their own interest," Adam Smith wrote in *The Wealth of Nations*.[6] But what counts in the brewer's self-interest (I prefer the brewer) is not just how much cash is in the till at the end of the night, but how she is regarded by others and how she regards herself. "We address ourselves, not to their humanity but to their self-love."[7] Their self-love, not alone their bankbook. In his other great book, *The Theory of Moral Sentiments*, Smith wrote: "Man [and woman] naturally desires, not only to be loved, but to be lovely; or to be that thing which is the natural and proper object of love. He naturally dreads, not only to be hated, but to be hateful."[8] This is what Hayak and Friedman have in mind when they say that morality and ethical restraint should properly play a role in business.[9] But they are not thinking thoroughly here about how this conception should operate under corporate auspices. I think it is important that Hayak and Friedman's statements were written before the hostile takeover disruptions of the 1980s gave the "acid bath of economics" to obfuscations about

---

[6] ADAM SMITH, THE WEALTH OF NATIONS I.2.2 (1776, 1904).   [7] *Id.*
[8] ADAM SMITH, THE THEORY OF MORAL SENTIMENTS 166 (1969) (1759).
[9] *See* Einer Elhauge, *Sacrificing Corporate Profits in the Public Interest*, 80 N.Y.U. L. REV. 733 (2005) (exploring differences in the function of morality-based operational restraint in privately held companies, as compared to large public corporations).

what part morality and ethics play in the law of corporate govern-ance.[10] Once aggressive, profit-maximizing actors realized that cor-porate America was "wasting" shareholder wealth by paying workers more than necessary, exercising operational restraint in the interests of the environment, or the nation, or whatever, they forced the law to specify that this was not allowed under the shareholder primacy norm. These men would have written these passages differently after *Unocal*, *Revlon*, and Oliver Stone's *Wall Street*.[11]

The law does not prescribe for our corporations today the kind of governance that Hayek and Friedman advocated in these passages. My objective in this chapter is to explore how we might get our corporate governance law to look like something closer to what Hayek and Fried-man expressed. The ambition is to have a corporate governance law that embodies a meaningful temper on corporate profit maximization, and institutionalizes an obligation to fairness and social responsibility in corporate operations.

CONSCIENTIOUS ISLANDS IN AN ARCHIPELAGO OF CONSCIOUS POWER

I advocate a change to corporate governance law that would require the directors of large firms to actively attend to the interests of multiple stakeholders in corporate operations. The law presently requires dir-ectors to work "hard and honestly" on behalf of shareholders.[12] We should say instead: work hard and honestly on behalf of all corporate

---

[10] RICHARD A. POSNER, SEX AND REASON 437 (1992) ("Clear thinking ... is obstructed by layers of ignorance, ideology, superstition, and prejudice that the acid bath of economics can help us peel away.")

[11] *See* Chapter 4 (discussing Unocal and Revlon). Both Hayek and Friedman, in these essays and in other writings, were adamant that directors should not use their position in the firm to advance their own idiosyncratic concerns or pet charitable causes. Who could disagree? The real money, and the real institutional question, lies in whether directors should engage in operational restraint in service of non-shareholder interests, not the directors' own interests.

[12] FRANK H. EASTERBROOK & DANIEL R. FISCHEL, THE ECONOMIC STRUCTURE OF CORPOR-ATE LAW 91 (1991).

stakeholders. This would make our corporate law more theoretically coherent, and more ethically sound in practice.

Before I elaborate how a multi-stakeholder governance system might work, I want to first disarm criticism (or perhaps bring it on from some quarters) by emphasizing that I do not advocate imposing a multi-stakeholder system on all business activity in the country. It must be acknowledged: the desire to protect the vulnerable from exploitative business operations, and the desire to encourage investment and innovation in productive enterprise, are at some level in tension with each other. One way of balancing these goals is to prioritize one or the other in different contexts, and to try to select those contexts in a way that will maximize overall productivity and protection. What I have in mind is that only large corporations that operate at a national or international scale would be subject to the multi-stakeholder govern-ance charge. Many areas of law already impose substantially different rules for smaller and larger corporations. Examples include securities regulation, health care law, and antidiscrimination law. This is appro-priate. Size is a proxy for power, and power rightly should trigger a special concern about the social consequences of corporate behav-ior. Yet, by restricting the multi-stakeholder imperative to very big companies, the atmosphere of experimentation and entrepreneurial dynamism can run hot elsewhere in the economy.[13]

This roughly parallels what is done in Europe. Under the German system, for example, labor codetermination is triggered only upon crossing a threshold number of employees.[14] Smaller firms are run by and for capital investors. Labor force is an important signifier of firm influence, but it is not the best standard for determining a thresh-old for requiring multi-stakeholder governance. Especially in an era in which automation threatens extreme social disruption, we should not make number of employees the key factor triggering a social responsi-bility standard in corporate governance. Firm valuation is a better

---

[13] This book has focused on corporations, but the reformative program would have to apply to limited liability companies, limited liability partnerships, and other business forms that reach a size at which the multi-stakeholder standard would be triggered for corporations, otherwise the system would be easily evaded. Below the threshold, LLCs and the like can continue to structure their operations however they please.

[14] *See* Chapter 7.

proxy for size and power. This is the variable that is used, for example, in determining which firms are required to comply with certain aspects of Sarbanes-Oxley's corporate governance requirements, and which are exempt from them. I do not have a dogmatic view of exactly where the line should be. Sarbanes-Oxley uses a market capitalization threshold of $75 million to distinguish between firms that are subject to its strict audit committee prescriptions and those that are not. Something close to that, or perhaps a $100 million valuation, would be a reasonable starting place for thinking about where a demarcation for the multi-stakeholder system should be set.[15]

PROFITS, STILL

Under the multi-stakeholder governance standard that I imagine, corporate directors would still operate under a basic injunction to pursue profits for shareholders. Profits are not a sufficient indicator of the social utility of business, but they are a necessary component of it. Production without profit is consumption. To till the arid soil, to make it yield cool electronics, we must have the productive capacity of aggregated capital. Without a credible promise of profits, capital would be no more willing to join in corporate operations than would labor without wages. The pursuit of residual profits must therefore remain the basic orientation and measuring stick of corporate performance. But that pursuit should be circumscribed by an obligation to be actively, honestly, sincerely mindful of the interests of non-shareholding stakeholders as directors choose the means to this end. Extending a fiduciary responsibility to multiple stakeholders would

---

[15] *See* Regina F. Burch, *Financial Regulatory Reform Post-Financial Crisis: Unintended Consequences for Small Business*, 115 PENN ST. L. REV. 409 (2010) (discussing market capitalization thresholds in Sarbanes-Oxley). Some commentators argue that there should be more expansive exemptions for small- and mid-cap firms from the requirements imposed by Sarbanes-Oxley and Dodd-Frank. *See* Paul Rose & Steven Davidoff Solomon, *Where Have All the IPO's Gone? The Hard Life of the Small IPO*, 6 HARV. BUS. L. REV. 83, 89 n. 18 (2016) (explaining that under the Dodd-Frank reforms, the burdensome auditor attestation provisions of Sarbanes-Oxley no longer apply to firms with a market value of less than $75 million). This literature can inform a discussion about where the threshold for a multi-stakeholder system should be set.

mean directors would be forbidden from advancing shareholder interests by exploiting consumers, workers, or communities. It would mean a right to good faith and fair dealing for all corporate stakeholders. By departing from shareholder primacy and insisting that the legitimate interests of non-shareholder be considered in corporate operations, we remove the firm's motive to overreach in dealing with them. Or, at least, we remove the law's part in compelling that overreach.

The law should require the multi-stakeholder approach, and then give directors wide latitude in determining how it will shape corporate decisions. A multi-stakeholder system must be scrupulous in its demand for good faith, informed, and deliberate decision-making by corporate boards. And then it must offer sweeping deference to the substance of decisions that properly motivated boards make. This approach will encourage corporations to behave responsibly, even as it leaves substantive decisions about what counts as responsible open to discovery, experimentation, and difference. The law cannot micromanage the substance of corporate decision-making. That is "beyond the science of chancery."[16] But it can require that directors become informed about, think about, and earnestly talk about the consequences of corporate conduct for multiple stakeholders. Satisfying this obligation will take different forms in different circumstances but will usually take the familiar form of reading reports, hearing presentations, and engaging in discussion and debate.

Under prevailing law, courts do not impose liability for informed, un-conflicted, deliberate corporate decisions, even if the decisions are foolish or turn out disastrous for shareholders. We call this the "business judgment" rule. On the other hand, if directors are personally interested in a decision, or do not satisfy their process obligations in good faith, they lose business judgment rule protection and must demonstrate that their decisions were entirely fair to the corporation and its shareholders, or else face injunctive or monetary sanctions.[17] This framework could also be used in a multiple-stakeholder system.

---

[16] Meinhard v. Salmon, 164 N.E. at 546.

[17] Under 8 DEL. GEN. CORP. L. § 102(b)(7), the corporate charter can exculpate directors from having to pay money damages for violations of the duty of care, but courts may still provide aggrieved shareholders injunctive relief. I envision a similar system under a multi-stakeholder standard.

Informed, disinterested, good faith decisions could not be challenged by anyone. But directors who make corporate decisions without engaging their multi-stakeholder responsibilities in good faith would be exposed to sanctions. Shareholders, workers, consumers, or ordinary citizens affected by corporate operations could have standing to sue, derivatively (with the plaintiffs' bar standing at the ready to help, as always). A cause of action for non-shareholders to enforce the multi-stakeholder standard does not have to be easily or often deployed, but it must be there in some way, to make the system real.[18]

COUNTING STAKEHOLDERS

Socially responsible corporate governance is better conceived in terms of getting boards to think about recognizable categories of stakeholders, including workers, consumers, communities, and the nation, rather than using an idea of "the interests of the company" as a guiding standard. (The "interests of the company" is often used to describe the social responsibility standard in European systems, and is sometimes suggested as a formulation for use in the United States). To say directors should act in the best interests of the company is to beg the crucial question: what are the interests of the company? A synthetic legal entity has no interests apart from the human purposes the law intends for it to serve. I do not go as far as Margaret Thatcher, who said, "there is no such thing as society,"[19] but I do say there is no such thing as the interest of "the company," only the interests of human beings (or communities, or nations) standing in some relation to the

---

[18] The new public benefit corporation statutes provide no redress to non-shareholders for corporate governance failures. Delaware, not famous for lucidity in its statutory drafting, took pains to be clear on this point: "A director of a public benefit corporation shall not ... have *any* duty to *any* person on account of *any* interest of such person in the public benefit or public benefits identified in the certificate of incorporation ..." 8 DEL. GEN. CORP. L. §365(b) (emphasis added). The Model Public Benefit Corporation Statute provides that non-shareholders can be given standing to sue derivatively by specification in the charter. *See* MODEL BENEFIT CORP. LEGIS. § 305(c)(iv). My approach does not envision much opportunity for stakeholder enforcement of a multi-stakeholder standard corporate governance regime, but it envisions more than nothing.

[19] Margaret Thatcher, Interview for *Woman's Own* (Sep 23, 1987), www.margaretthatcher.org/document/106689.

company. We all have a stake in corporate operations. But it is the corporation that should serve our interests, not the other way around.

I have emphasized workers, consumers, communities, and the nation as corporate stakeholders in this book, but I have also used the term "stakeholder" loosely, and I mean it loosely. Some analysts are critical of the imprecision of the term. One famously pilloried it as seeming to include "terrorists and competitors, vegetation, nameless sea creatures, and generations yet unborn."[20] I say: yes, I mean to include most of those, to varying degrees, but also, it depends on the firm. Corporate governance should have reasonable regard for non-shareholder interests in corporate operations. If a corporation was running a for-profit prison that detained terrorists for the United States government, then it would be consistent with the system I imagine for the firm to run that prison in a way that respected the human, constitutional, and moral rights of the terrorists, even if doing was not profit-maximizing. Competitors, on the other hand, can usually look after themselves.

The multi-stakeholder approach only appears to suffer uniquely from the problem of loosely defining the interests that are supposed to be captured and addressed by its system. Shareholder primacy theory also recognizes a category of corporate "stakeholders" and fails to completely theorize it. Vegetation, sea creatures, the unborn – these already count among the things shareholder primacy theory purports to serve when it claims to be the most socially useful system of corporate governance. It is just that shareholder primacy puts the onus of identifying, limiting, and dealing with these stakeholders on other institutions, specifically, external governmental regulation. But how can vegetation petition for external government regulation to protect it from corporate overreach? Shareholder primacy theory does not say. How can generations yet unborn, or those already born but outside of the political community in which the firm operates, weigh in on pollution controls? Shareholder primacy is silent.

A multi-stakeholder standard should require corporate boards to actively address non-shareholder interests that are reasonably related

---

[20] Elaine Sternberg, *The Defects of Stakeholder Theory*, 5 CORPORATE GOVERNANCE: AN INTERNATIONAL REVIEW 3, 4 (1997).

to corporate operations. The firm is a nexus of production and consumption, and its attention should be devoted to the consequences of its operation for those who are in its nexus. A firm should pursue profit for *its* shareholders, with due regard for *its* workers, *its* consumers, the communities within which it operates, and the country whose law gives it existence. These are the stakeholders the firm can most directly affect, and they are the groups with which the firm will have a particular expertise or interest in engaging. Precisely how to specify the contours of inclusion in the corporate nexus must be left to individual boards operating in good faith.

The more attenuated from the corporate nexus some interest is, the less important or useful it will be for the firm to actively deal with it. For example, it would make more sense for the Starbucks Corporation to pay impoverished workers in its supply chain a decent living wage, or to responsibly steward the ecosystems from which it procures its coffee beans, than it would be for the firm to deploy corporate resources to stem the depletion of coral reefs in oceanic environments unrelated to its business.[21] In Chapter 4, I noted the curious dictum from the crucial *Unocal* case, in which the Delaware Supreme Court suggested that it would be appropriate, though not required, for a corporate board to privilege the interests of long-term shareholders as compared to short-term speculators if the interests of the two diverged in a particular context.[22] This is the sort of thing that would be appropriate for boards to do in a multi-stakeholder regime. For example, in considering "worker" interests, the board might reasonably privilege long-term workers over recent hires, it might put the interests of longstanding consumers over infrequent ones, or favor the local community over more distant places, and the like, although none of these distinctions would be compelled.

With respect to patriotism, we should have a corporate governance system that broadly states that the very largest firms chartered under United States law have a right and duty to consider the national interest

---

[21] *See* M. Todd Henderson & Anup Malani, *Corporate Philanthropy and the Market for Altruism*, 109 Colum. L. Rev. 571 (2009) (arguing that firms should engage in altruistic conduct, but only where they have a comparative advantage over other actors).

[22] *See* Unocal, 493 A.2d at 955–56; *see also* Chapter 4.

in the course of corporate operations. Having made that clear, we should then, in keeping with the expanded business judgment rule I have described, defer entirely to the substantive decisions boards make relating to this duty, so long as directors undertake their charge in good faith, in informed and deliberate fashion. Admitting patriotic conscience as an element of multi-stakeholder governance may make the corporate social responsibility reform project as a whole more plausible, theoretically and practically. Proponents of shareholder primacy have insisted that a charge that corporations should behave "responsibly" is too intractable, that it gives directors too little guidance about how to govern. Corporate patriotism may help with this a bit. For example, many people talk about corporations closing domestic factories and moving jobs overseas as a failure of corporate social responsibility. But such behavior is only clearly "irresponsible" if the interests of American workers are more important than those of foreign workers, who may be more desperate than their American counterparts.[23] Patriotism offers a sufficient level of abstraction, but one that is also not too abstract, to provide a framework through which corporate directors can approach the problem of social responsibility. Indeed, if patriotism's philosophers are to be believed, then it may be impossible for a corporation or a corporate board of directors to behave morally unless they form a morality through a devotion to a particular community – a particular nation.[24]

DIVERSE, UNPREDICTABLE OUTCOMES

Nothing, then, can be said with specificity about substantive changes in corporate behavior that would result from the multi-stakeholder standard I advocate. In his 1966 study of German corporate law that

---

[23] Of course there can be no orthodoxy in what constitutes a patriotic conscience in corporate behavior. An American firm that shuts down domestic production and opens a factory in China inserts an element of American influence in Chinese domestic affairs. Adolf Berle, who was a diplomat before he was a scholar, emphasized the ways in which American influence has spread around the world often more effectively through its corporations than its diplomatic corps. *See* ADOLF A. BERLE, JR., THE 20TH CENTURY CAPITALIST REVOLUTION 116–164 (1954).

[24] *See* Chapter 5.

required directors to run their firms in the interest of the "common weal," Professor Vagts opined that such a governance standard "is not the sort of concept that gradually acquires shape and substance through case-by-case adjudication."[25] Vagts speculated that outcomes in a multi-stakeholder system would "resemble less the 'reasonable and prudent man' conception of negligence law than the direction given regulatory commissions to lay down rules in the public interest."[26] This is an important insight but could be misleading as to the overall picture it suggests. Regulatory commissions charged with making rules in the public interest produce a single line of centralized, broadly applicable authority that cannot be easily evaded or altered. That is why too much authority vested in such agencies is suspicious from democratic, pluralism, and efficiency perspectives. Among the benefits of multi-stakeholder governance is that it decentralizes and localizes social interest protections that might otherwise have to be centralized in distant government bureaucracies. Under a multi-stakeholder corporate governance system, the decisions of any one firm might be as unpredictable or unguided as those promulgated by a regulatory commission. Yet across many firms the system will produce a broad array of conduct – a substantively diverse set of socially conscious decisions reflecting a pluralism of capacities and perspectives, rather than a single standard – as different firms pursue their social obligations in their own way, as the course of their business dictates.

NO SPECIAL COMPETENCE

Critics charge that corporate directors have no special competence for multi-stakeholder governance or for dealing with "social responsibility" generally. This is true. But it is true in the sense that *nobody* has any special competence for that. Legislators do not have special training for that. Donald Trump does not have special competence

---

[25] Detlev F. Vagts, *Reforming the "Modern" Corporation: Perspectives from the German*, 80 HARV. L. REV. 23, 47 (1966).

[26] *Id.*

for that. Bureaucrats do not. Yet shareholder primacy theory would hold government solely responsible for doing it, to the exclusion of corporations struggling to do it at all. I do not expect corporate directors to have a unique expertise in balancing social interests. We can expect and hope only for the exercise of ordinary human conscience in sober institutional operation. Directors' skill in this will reflect the general skill that men and women in our society in the educated and professional classes have, or can acquire. Then again, even today, people often *are* put on the boards of especially very large corporations because they do have, or are purported to have, some special expertise relating to the firm's labor force, consumer base, nation of operation, or other expertise. Board diversity – along gender, race, class, and other dimensions – would become genuinely important in a multi-stakeholder regime, as people from different backgrounds could be called upon to bring their unique experiences and vantages to the board to assist in the firm's responsibilities to differently situated stakeholders. And with a multi-stakeholder corporate governance system in place, ethical training could become a serious, coherent part of business school education and corporate job training.

Directors would not suddenly be transformed in their capacities or outlook by a reform of the corporate governance command. But it will change them. The requirement that decisions be informed and deliberate implies a responsibility to listen and to speak. The duty to actively deliberate in the presence of others about one's obligations triggers psychological and motivational dynamics that are self-reinforcing. Self-affirmation and dissonance-avoidance motives push us to conform our beliefs to our behavior, including our speech.[27] Requiring directors to express their responsibilities to multiple stakeholders to a group of witnesses – their fellow board members – can stoke within them an authentic commitment to that responsibility. The corporate soul is presently made in favor of shareholders through this kind of confessional discourse in the boardroom, and it can be remade for stakeholders that way. In the words of Michel Foucault:

---

[27] *See* Jon Hanson & David Yosifon, *The Situational Character: A Critical Realist Perspective on the Human Animal*, 93 Geo. L. J. 1, 107–116 (2004) (reviewing psychological studies on dissonance avoidance).

[T]he agency of domination does not reside in the one who speaks (for it is he who is constrained), but in the one who listens and says nothing ... And this discourse of truth finally takes effect, not in the one who receives it, but in the one from whom it is wrested.[28]

Or, if you will not have the Foucault, Lawrence Mitchell makes the same point with a lawyer's clarity: "[t]o understand the importance of being trusted is to understand the way in which the responsibility for trust reposed can affect character. It can create virtue where little had previously existed."[29]

DETERRING INVESTMENT, ENCOURAGING INVESTMENT

It may be true that the multi-stakeholder governance standard will, other things equal, diminish capital's eagerness to invest in business enterprise, as compared to the incentive the shareholder primacy norm gives to invest. A social responsibility corporate governance norm might cause greater concentration of ownership, and a diminished efficacy of broad capital markcts, as arguably happens under stakcholderist systems in Europe.[30] The cost of capital in corporate operations may thus be greater under a multi-stakeholder system than it is under shareholder primacy. But this can only be called a *problem* if the ease of capital aggregation seen under shareholder primacy is both efficient and fair. If shareholder primacy firms have a lower cost of capital than multi-stakeholder firms because the former can externalize costs to non-shareholders, or if their lower cost of capital comes at the expense of social, cultural, and political cohesion, then the higher cost of capital in multi-stakeholder firms is entirely appropriate. It is a solution not a problem.

---

[28] MICHEL FOUCAULT, 1 THE HISTORY OF SEXUALITY: AN INTRODUCTION 62 (1978, 1990).

[29] Lawrence E. Mitchell, *The Importance of Being Trusted,* 81 B.U. L . REV. 591, 599 (2001); *see also* LYNN STOUT, CULTIVATING CONSCIENCE: HOW GOOD LAWS MAKE GOOD PEOPLE (2011).

[30] *See* Chapter 7.

It is possible, on the other hand, that multiple-stakeholder govern-ance will lower the cost of *other* production factors, making investment more attractive for shareholders through the back door. For example, the hodgepodge of profit-constraining governmental regulation aimed at protecting non-shareholders, which shareholder primacy theory traditionally calls on to restrain corporate overreach, *also* reduces the incentive for investment in business enterprise. The disincentives of complex regulation may be mitigated by multi-stakeholder governance, as firms engage in operational restraint, requiring somewhat less exter-nal regulatory intervention. Further, many studies describe a wide-spread "distrust" of corporations among workers, consumers, and Americans generally, under the current system.[31] Altering the law in a way that makes firms more authentically trustworthy could induce greater trust among those groups. If workers were more willing to work, and consumers more willing to buy, and communities more willing to host, shareholders might make money more easily.[32] I tend to be skeptical of this kind of "it's actually more profitable" argument about multi-stakeholder governance, since I think corporations already know how to exploit profit-making opportunities, even where it involves behaving responsibly. But then again, perhaps lack of imagin-ation, cultural bias, and legal uncertainty do sometimes keep business-people from taking advantage of profitable opportunities until the legal system points the way to doing it.[33] Regardless, I am satisfied if the

---

[31] *See* Lisa M. Fairfax, *Easier Said than Done? A Corporate Law Theory for Actualizing Social Responsibility Rhetoric,* 59 FLA. L. REV. 771, 787. This attitude is prudent, given our current corporate governance law. Indeed, under the current system, corporations have an incentive to induce trust that is unwarranted, so stakeholders may trust firms too much. *See* Claire A. Hill & Erin Ann O'Hara, *A Cognitive Theory of Trust,* 84 WASH. U. L. REV. 1717, 1720 (2006).

[32] *See* Greenfield, THE FAILURE OF CORPORATE LAW 162 (2007) ("Employees' positive beliefs about the fairness of the firm provide appreciable benefits to the firm by decreasing the need to monitor employee behavior.").

[33] For example, I think it was legal for firms to specify in their charters that directors would not have to pay damages for violations of their duty of care long before Delaware amended its statute to specifically note exculpation was allowed. But almost no firms did so before the legislature explicitly invited it. After the menu option was put in the statute, nearly every large firm adopted exculpation. *See* David G. Yosifon, *Opting Out of Shareholder Primacy: Is the Public Benefit Corporation Trivial?,* 41 DEL. J. CORP. L. 461, 487–490 (2017).

multi-stakeholder system restrains exploitative conduct, even if it does not result in greater profitability.

A change from shareholder primacy to multi-stakeholder governance would impose on shareholders a system that differs from what they signed on for. It might cost them money. This is serious business, but not more ethically, constitutionally, or practically difficult than other kinds of regulatory disruptions to existing arrangements. Since the 1819 case of *Trustees of Dartmouth College v. Woodward*,[34] shareholders have "been on notice that states can change the law governing their corporations."[35] Indeed, government has routinely altered shareholder endowments, by weakening *ultra vires* protections, lowering vote requirements for the adoption of charter amendments, allowing charter provisions that sanction opting out of duty of care liability for directors, and most recently, introducing rules that allow for-profit firms to be transformed into profit-restrained public benefit corporations with less than a unanimous shareholder vote.[36]

MARKET FOR CONTROL

A serious multi-stakeholder governance system would have to allow consideration of non-shareholder interests both in the ordinary course and when directors are deciding whether or not to resist a takeover threat.[37] Actual takeovers can be wildly disruptive to workers and communities, as the untapped profits that motivate them are often found in liquidating the assets of a going concern, or maintaining corporate operations but slicing the incumbent workforce. The *threat*

---

[34] 17 U.S. 518 (1819).

[35] *See* David Millon, *Redefining Corporate Law*, 24 INDIANA L. REV. 223, 272 (1991).

[36] *See* Yosifon, *Opting Out of Shareholder Primacy, supra* note 33 at 501-504 (2017). *But see* Henry N. Butler & Larry E. Ribstein, *The Contract Clause and the Corporation*, 55 BROOK. L. REV. 767–68 (1989) (arguing that that Article 1, section 10 of the United States Constitution, which states that "[n]o State shall ... pass any ... Law impairing the Obligations of Contracts," forbids states from fundamentally altering the governance rules of existing firms).

[37] *Compare* Einer Elhague, *Sacrificing Corporate Profits in the Public Interest*, 80 N. Y. U. L. REV. 733, 848–852 (arguing that director discretion to consider non-shareholder interests should be more restricted in the takeover context than in the ordinary course).

of takeover can be just as disruptive. Michael Moore's 1989 documentary masterpiece, *Roger & Me*, chronicled what happens to a town (Flint, MI) not when the business that sustains it (General Motors Company) is taken over, but rather what happens when its directors, driven by the whipping threat of the takeover market, go all out for the shareholders, sending jobs out of the United States (to Mexico), leaving behind capital gains and social decay.[38]

Corporate takeovers are far less common in the European and Japanese economies characterized by multi-stakeholder corporate governance than they have been in the United States. Firms that do face hostile threats in those systems sometimes invoke multi-stakeholder responsibilities as part of a defensive entrenchment plan.[39] In the existing American system, the disciplining power of the market for control (it focuses the mind of incumbent management) is viewed as an important solution to the shareholder agency problem.[40] Allowing directors to rebuff hostile threats to protect non-shareholder interests will undoubtedly diminish its utility in this regard to some extent, allowing inefficiencies to fester in corporate operations. That is a regrettable thing, with a silver lining. There may be *net* gains from rigorous takeover markets. But, again, if there are insufficient mechanisms to ensure that those gains are distributed in a socially useful way then it is *better* not to net them.

Allowing attention to non-shareholders in the takeover context does not mean we will be entirely without the monitoring power of the market for control. Sacrifice of profits in favor of other interests should be subject to substantive judicial review for reasonableness in the takeover context, given the worry that resistance to takeover is motivated by directorial self-interest rather than legitimate corporate policy.

---

[38] ROGER & ME (Warner Brothers, Inc., 1989).

[39] *See, e.g.*, Leo E. Strine, Jr., *The Soviet Constitution Problem in Comparative Corporate Law: Testing the Proposition That European Corporate Law Is More Stockholder-Focused than U.S. Corporate Law*, 89 SOUTHERN CAL. L. REV. 1239, 1247 n. 11 (2016) (noting the Dutch pharmaceutical company Mylan's intention to reject an unsolicited bid in a part by asserting its responsibility, per Dutch law, to "act in the best interests of the company's shareholders, employees, patients, customers, communities and other stakeholders."). European governments also are not shy about interfering to stop corporate mergers or takeovers when they view them as adverse to the national interest. *Id.*

[40] *See* Chapter 1.

Indeed, anti-takeover defenses under the current shareholder primacy system are already a rare instance where substantive review for reasonableness is called for under Delaware law.[41] If directors are using non-shareholder interests as a pre-text for entrenching, then their defensive machinations can and should be enjoined.

FEDERALIZATION

To alter the shareholder primacy norm, we would have to change the way corporations are chartered in the United States. The federal government would have to preempt state chartering and set national incorporation standards. Delaware is never going to alter the shareholder primacy norm in its law. And if Delaware were somehow to stop offering shareholder primacy charters, another state would be happy to offer them and gain the franchise fees. States do not get into the corporate chartering game because they have a public policy interest in how corporations are run. They sell corporate charters as a revenue-generating device with which to fund other social policies in their state. The federal government, with access to a broader base of funding sources than any state government, could base chartering law on public policy concerns rather than simply a desire to maximize chartering fees. For corporations that operate at a national or international scale, and whose conduct can seriously impact many states and the whole nation, it is, in technical terms, ridiculous that the federal government does not take responsibility for corporate governance standards.[42]

---

[41] Delaware allows boards significant latitude to adopt defenses that can impede hostile threats if the board reasonably believes that doing so is in the best interests of their shareholders (even if legal theorists believe allowing such defenses harms the takeover market and shareholders in the aggregate). *See, e.g.,* Paramount Comm., Inc. v. Time Inc., 571 A.2d 1140, 1142 (Del. 1989). The junkyard dog of the takeover market is kept leashed while corporate law puts its faith in the fidelity of the board and the power of law and honor to keep directors working hard and honestly. The multi-stakeholder system would not see a significant mechanical or practical alteration in what boards would be entitled to do in the face of a hostile threat. We would, however, be altering the *reason* they are allowed to do it.

[42] Mark Roe argues that we should understand Delaware's dominance in corporate chartering as an expression the federal government's satisfaction with Delaware law. Delaware must supply law that complies with federal desires, lest the giant awake and assert its

Federal corporate chartering was given serious consideration in the early twentieth century, but the idea was finally abandoned by Theodore Roosevelt's administration in a political compromise that resulted instead in federal anti-trust regulation.[43] Yet, in practical terms, the federal government has become increasingly involved in the particulars of corporate governance since at least 1933, when the federal Securities Act was first adopted.[44] Conceivably, the federal securities laws or other federal law could impose multi-stakeholder governance standards on firms without actually requiring federal chartering. But to achieve the comprehensive reforms I am describing here, the most straightforward, transparent approach would be to adopt federal chartering outright. We could continue having state-based chartering for firms that are below the size threshold established for imposing multi-stakeholder governance. This will allow for competition and innovation to continue in the state laboratories, while requiring large, publicly traded firms with a national scope to be chartered federally.

Currently, American courts use the "internal affairs" rule to give effect not only to the chartering law of a firm's *state* of incorporation, but also the chartering law of a firm's *country* of incorporation. A California court will apply the corporate law of Singapore to a governance dispute bearing on a firm doing business in California, if the firm is chartered in Singapore. To achieve multi-stakeholder governance for large firms, the United States would need to adopt a version of the European "real seat" doctrine, which requires firms to comply with the corporate governance law of the jurisdiction where it has its real seat of power.[45] Otherwise, American firms would just

---

regulatory prerogative, costing Delaware its $500 million per year chartering business. *See* Mark J. Roe, *Delaware's Competition*, 117 HARV. L. REV. 588 (2003); *see also* Mark Roe, *Delaware's Politics*, 118 HARV. L. REV. 2491 (2005). That is a smart way to put it. My view is that Congress should no longer accept the corporate law Delaware has made.

[43] *See generally* Melvin I. Urofsky, *Proposed Federal Incorporation in the Progressive Era*, 26 AM. J. LEGAL HISTORY 160 (1982); MARTIN J. Sklar, THE CORPORATE RECONSTRUCTION OF AMERICAN CAPITALISM, 1890–1916: THE MARKET, THE LAW, AND POLITICS (1988).

[44] *See generally* Stephen Bainbridge, *The Creeping Federalization of Corporate Law*, 26 REG. 26 (2003); *see also* Camden Hutchinson, *Progressive Era Conceptions of the Corporation and the Failure of the Federal Chartering Movement*, __ COLUMBIA BUS. L. REV. __ (2018, forthcoming) (historical overview of movements for federal chartering).

[45] *See generally* Werner F. Ebke, *The "Real Seat" Doctrine in the Conflict of Laws*, 36 INT'L L. 1015 (2002).

reorganize in the Bahamas, or somewhere else, in order to avoid the American corporate social responsibility rule. As was shown in the last chapter, the "real seat" doctrine is how Germany can continue to enforce its codetermination regime on German companies, and it is how Japan can enforce its own standards on Japanese companies. The "real seat" doctrine is under attack in the European Union, but it nevertheless appears at present to maintain considerable vitality.[46] Foreclosing an international race to the bottom in corporate chartering would be a necessary component of a serious corporate governance reform.

LOOK LEFT: PROGRESSIVE CRITIQUE

At the heart of corporate power is corporate purpose. Change that purpose and you can change the corporate heart. The "orienting" approach to multi-stakeholder governance that I have outlined here is, I think, more plausible, theoreticallyand practically, than other more substantively insistent reforms that have been urged by other progressive corporate law scholars. Consider, in contrast to what I suggest, Professor Lawrence Mitchell's pioneering framework for enforcing "constituency statutes."[47] Mitchell proposed that boards operating in a multi-stakeholder regime be charged first and foremost with pursuing profits for shareholders, while also being required to consider the legitimate interests of other stakeholders along the way (I agree). However, under Mitchell's system, non-shareholder constituents would

---

[46] *See* Chapter 7.

[47] *See* Lawrence E. Mitchell, *A Theoretical and Practical Framework for Enforcing Corporate Constituency Statutes*, 70 TEXAS L. REV. 579 (1992). Mitchell developed his framework to aid the enforcement of "constituency statutes" that many states adopted in response to the takeover crisis of the 1980s. These statutes allowed (or required) boards to consider the interests of non-shareholders in corporate decision-making (either in the takeover context or in the ordinary course), but provided no guidance as to how that standard should be implemented. There was considerable scholarly interest in such statutes in the 1990s. I do not consider them to be important because Delaware did *not* adopt a constituency statute, and Delaware dominates American corporate law. Mitchell created a tool that has found little work. There are no cases interpreting the statutes. Nevertheless, Mitchell's framework is worth revisiting as a possible aid to implementing a federal multi-stakeholder corporate governance standard that I am exploring here.

have standing to challenge "corporate actions that they claim have injured them."[48] The complaining stakeholder would have the burden of proving the injury, and "the injury must have been to a legitimate interest."[49] To satisfy this burden, the "plaintiffs would need to resort to express or implied contracts with the corporation, legitimate expectations, and the like."[50] If the injury was established, the burden would then shift back to the board "to prove that its actions were undertaken in pursuit of a legitimate corporate purpose rather than the interests of the board itself."[51] Profits for shareholders would be considered a legitimate interest, but "the plaintiffs would be permitted to prove that the board's stated purpose could have been accomplished in a manner less injurious to their interests."[52]

This complicated framework is implausible for a simple reason. Everything in it depends upon whether or not the plaintiff's asserted "injury" is to count as an injury. Who can tell? Or rather, who will have the power to say? If the asserted harm was a breach of an "express" contract, then ordinary contract law, rather than corporate governance, is the more straightforward remedy. But if the injury relates to "implied" contracts (in the general sense), "legitimate expectations" (in the general sense), or what we might call moral and ethical questions, then for the plaintiffs to establish an injury and trigger the rest of the framework, a court must *decide* that the asserted interest was an actual, cognizable interest that was violated. The magnitude or relative weight of the interest, as compared to legitimate shareholder interests, would also need to be determined, in order to assess whether a "less injurious" corporate decision would have been possible. Judges have no independent way of making such a determination. To give such power to a judge would simply be to install the multi-stakeholder responsibility with the judge rather than the board. I would leave the discretion with the board.

The hypothetical that Mitchell uses to explicate his framework showcases this problem. He uses a variation of the *Revlon* situation.[53] Assume that a board accepted a high bid in an auction sale of their company. The bid would provide substantial gains to the shareholders

---

[48] *Id.* at 636.   [49] *Id.*   [50] *Id.*   [51] *Id.*   [52] *Id.*
[53] *Id.* at 636–37. *See* my discussion of Revlon in Chapter 4.

but would result in significant layoffs. A second bid would have given shareholders less but would have resulted in fewer layoffs. Can workers enjoin the sale? The only way to know would be to decide if the workers had a "legitimate interest" in not being fired for the purpose of providing higher returns to the shareholders. Do they? The question cannot be answered in law-like fashion by a judge. But it *can* be answered in the course of responsible governance by a corporate board. I would allow the board to accept the lower bid if, after sincere deliberation, they considered it to be profitable to the shareholders, while also being respectful of the reasonable interests of the firm's workforce. But I would not allow judges to second-guess the board's decision one way or the other.[54]

LOOK RIGHT: CONSERVATIVE CRITIQUE

Acolytes of shareholder primacy theory find multiple faults with the multiple stakeholder governance idea. First and foremost, of course, they regard it as *unnecessary*. They believe non-shareholders can look after their own interests in corporate affairs, or be protected by external regulation. Since boardroom attention to non-shareholders is not needed, directors should be compelled to manage only in favor of shareholders, who will then have the incentive to invest in corporate enterprise from which everyone will benefit. Most of this book has been dedicated to repudiating that view, making the case that shareholder primacy does not add up, and that multi-stakeholder

---

[54] Other progressive scholars have suggested less cumbersome but nevertheless substantively assertive standards for multi-stakeholder governance. For example, David Millon claimed that under a constituency regime, directors "should not" seek short-term profits, either in the takeover context or in the ordinary course, over "legitimate nonshareholder expectations." *See* Millon, *Redefining Corporate Law*, supra note 35 at 266. He would "invite[] courts to develop a new body of common law" to adjudicate these "necessarily loose normative guidelines." *Id.* at 268. In Millon's taxonomy, my approach affords "minimal protection" to non-shareholders in corporate decision-making. Millon claimed schemes such as mine "will have little if any beneficial effects for nonshareholders" because of continuing, unchecked pressures from the capital markets, management's investment in the stock, labor markets, and product markets. *Id.* at 266. I agree that these pressures will constrain – indeed, usefully constrain – the profit-sacrificing choices of multi-stakeholder firms. But I think genuine benefits to non-shareholders will nevertheless result.

governance is necessary to ensure that corporations operate in a socially responsible manner.

But besides thinking it is unnecessary, proponents of the canonical view also think that multi-stakeholder governance cannot be implemented effectively. Therefore, they say, we must stick with shareholder primacy even if does have some of the warts exposed in this book. The implausibility argument boils down to two related claims. The first is that corporate directors cannot serve "two masters," or multiple masters, since different stakeholders will inevitably have antagonistic interests. Asking directors to reconcile those contradictions charges them with a theoretically, cognitively, and practically impossible task. A stakeholder-oriented corporate governance regime may be the "dream" of corporate law reformers, wrote one critic, but "to most executives, the vision of a board of directors composed of advocates of competing objectives would be a nightmare."[55] The second, related core criticism is that directors will use the confusion regarding corporate priorities in a multi-stakeholder system as cover to seize more corporate wealth for themselves. For the unscrupulous director, the multi-stakeholder charge is not so much a nightmare as it is an opportunity. The most succinct statement of these objections is from Easterbrook and Fischel: "[A] manager told to serve two masters (a little for the equity holders, a little for the community) has been freed of both and is answerable to neither."[56]

These are legitimate concerns. But they are not as grave as shareholder primacists make them out to be. Part of the allure of the "two masters" critique stems from its familiarity (and maybe for some, its authority) as a biblical maxim. The scripture that yields the conceit, however, is ill-suited as support for shareholder primacy. In fact, the "two masters" source material might better support an idea of multi-stakeholder corporate governance. The mischievous line comes about halfway through the "staggering account of the Sermon on the

---

[55] Alfred F. Conrad, *Reflections on Public Interest Directors*, 75 MICH. L. REV. 941, 947, 950 (1977).

[56] *See* Easterbrook & Fischel, *supra* note 12, at 38. *See also* Henry Hansmann & Reinier Kraakman, *The End of History for Corporate Law*, 89 GEO. L. J. 439, 444 (2001) ("It is now the conventional wisdom that, when managers are given great discretion over corporate investment policies, they tend to serve disproportionately their own interests, however well-intentioned managers may be.").

Mount,"[57] which is a core piece of Jesus's teaching in the Christian gospels. It follows shortly after an instruction that, first of all, unambiguously repudiates capital accumulation: "Do not store up for yourselves treasure on earth, where moths and vermin destroy, and where thieves break in and steal. But store up for yourselves treasure in heaven . . . For where your treasure is, there your heart will be also."[58] Capital is a wasting asset, and property rights are fluid. Better to look to the hereafter, where dividends are posted without fail through eternity. After this setup comes the famous agency formulation: "No one can serve two masters. He will either hate one and love the other, or be devoted to one and despise the other. You cannot serve God and mammon."[59]

What is weird about shareholder primacy advocates using this instruction to justify their approach is that shareholder primacy urges exclusive devotion to *mammon*, rather than God or any other interest. It does exactly the opposite of what Jesus was urging. Shareholder primacists will say they only want to serve mammon in the boardroom and that the interests of God or other interests should be served in other domains. But that outlook *contradicts* rather than reflects the biblical teaching about two masters. It is shareholder primacists who would have directors serve mammon as one master, in the boardroom, and serve other interests elsewhere as another master – two masters, at least. Jesus said that you cannot do that.[60] If Jesus is right, and it is not possible to serve two masters, then surely the one master that should be served is the master of multi-stakeholder governance. After all, the Master that Jesus has in mind (God, not mammon) embraces a multi-stakeholder regime: honor your father, and your mother, *and* love your neighbor, among other things.[61]

---

[57] Leonard Cohen, *Democracy*, on THE FUTURE (1992, Columbia Records) ("The staggering account of the Sermon on the Mount / which I don't pretend to understand at all.").

[58] MATTHEW 6:21 (THE NEW AMERICAN BIBLE).

[59] MATTHEW 6:24 (THE NEW AMERICAN BIBLE).

[60] Lyman Johnson has emphasized that shareholder primacy forces otherwise ethical, socially sensitive agents of corporations to live their lives in a compartmentalized fashion that is psychologically and spiritually destructive. *See* Lyman Johnson, *Reflections on Three Decades of Corporate Law Scholarship*, 74 WASH. & LEE L. REV. 677, 689–690 (2017).

[61] In another famous line, Jesus seems to indicate that it *is* possible, and desirable, to serve two masters, when he instructs: "[R]ender to Caesar the things that are Caesar's, and to God the things that are God's." Luke 20:26 (The New American Bible).

It is also worth pointing out to those who would rely on the "two masters" trope as support for their corporate governance system that the biblical passage from which it comes tends eschatological. It serves as a step in an argument that *concludes*: "Therefore I tell you, do not worry about your life, what you will eat or drink . . . Look at the birds of the air; they do not sow or reap or store away in barns, yet your heavenly Father feeds them."[62] And finally: "Therefore do not worry about tomorrow, for tomorrow will worry about itself."[63] This may be good advice, or it may be bad advice, but it is hardly the stuff of long-term shareholder value.

Under the system I propose, directors' core obligation would be to pursue profits, but to do so with due regard for the reasonable interests of other stakeholders. No matter the wording, this principle will inevitably force directors to make hard choices between competing interests. In so doing, they will confront a commonplace human challenge. We know how to reasonably respect competing interests in our personal decision-making, and in our institutional roles, even if we cannot always articulate exactly how we do it. Many nonprofits are set up to serve multiple stakeholders with competing interests. Most law schools have a multifaceted mission that includes training students to be competent and ethical lawyers, supporting faculty who produce scholarship, and providing direct service to the communities in which they function through legal clinics. Undoubtedly these multiple goals involve tensions and introduce inefficiencies. But they do not result in paralysis nor provide cover through which administrators aggrandize themselves more nakedly than do corporate executives operating under the "single-master" shareholder primacy system.

As it is, corporate directors under shareholder primacy do not really serve just one master. Shareholders are no monolithic group. They have different risk and time horizon preferences. Those with a big portion of their wealth invested in a firm want it to be managed conservatively. Diversified shareholders want more risk-taking, they are unconcerned if any one firm fails and pine instead for the unlimited upside of a few wild successes. Older or infirm shareholders want

---

[62] MATTHEW 6:26 (THE NEW AMERICAN BIBLE).
[63] MATTHEW 6:34 (THE NEW AMERICAN BIBLE).

short-term profits. Younger, healthier shareholders want steady growth. The shareholder primacy norm does not provide a rule or any guidance for resolving these conflicting interests *among* shareholders. Yet, these kinds of tensions between differently situated shareholders generally do not result in debilitating conflict within corporate governance.[64] The reason is that the means of resolving those conflicts are clear: the board resolves them as best it can, in light of the exigencies of their particular business, and so long as they do so in good faith, nobody – neither shareholders nor courts – can interfere with the substance of their decisions.[65] Directorial authority is the solution to the "accountable to everyone" problem, and it can be deployed in service of multi-stakeholder governance just as it has served shareholder primacy. It turns out that a person, or a board, may serve more than one master, as long as the masters cannot second-guess or meddle in the servant's decision. Certainly giving this discretion to the board creates slack. This slack, under the current regime, is tightened by the law of fiduciary duty, attendant norms and culture, and the market for control. The same mechanisms will diminish the accountability problem in a multi-stakeholder system.

These retorts to the two-masters critique are lent some empirical backing by the fact that there are actually operating multi-stakeholder systems in other parts of the world that do not collapse under the confusions of the many-masters problem. Indeed, European-style multi-stakeholder governance systems not only attract European capital investment, they also attract substantial capital from *American* investors, including pension funds and other institutional investors.[66] "Such investors . . . happily place billions of dollars annually in entities that lack the governance mechanisms traditionally found in U.S. public

---

[64] *See* Daniel J. H. Greenwood, *Fictional Shareholders: For Whom Are Corporate Managers Trustees, Revisited*, 69 S. Cal. L. Rev. 1021 (1996).

[65] *See generally* Bainbridge, The New Corporate Governance in Theory and Practice 233 (2008) ("The chief economic virtue of the public corporation is not that it permits the aggregation of large capital pools, but rather that it provides a hierarchical decision-making structure well-suited to the problem of operating a large business enterprise with numerous employees, managers, shareholders, creditors, and other inputs.").

[66] Ronald J. Gilson, *Globalizing Corporate Governance: Convergence of Form or Function*, 49 Am. J. Comp. L. 329, 346 (2001).

corporations."[67] The top 40 companies on the Paris Stock Exchange have an average American and British ownership stake of 35 percent (domestically the British also adhere to shareholder primacy in corporate governance). There is also a great deal of investment flowing from the United States into Japanese corporations, which continue to operate under a stakeholderist paradigm.[68] To be sure, investors from the United States pressure European and Japanese firms to adopt American-style corporate governance. But the absence of the American style governance has not been sufficient to deter investment to begin with.

A final dose of reality with which to clear away the "two masters" myth is the fact that executive compensation in Europe, where multi-stakeholder norms are commonplace, is *lower* than it is under the shareholder primacy norm in the United States.[69] This is evidence against the assertion that the confusion-cloud of multi-stakeholder governance would give firm managers cover to take more for themselves. With responsibilities to a wider set of stakeholders, and with more stakeholder eyes on them, directors might be more encouraged, not less, to be faithful servants. Under a multi-stakeholder system, shareholders in particular may be more searching in their scrutiny of manager compensation, since there may be less skim to be split between owners and managers.

THE LIMITS OF SUBMISSION: STAKEHOLDER DEMOCRACY

The multi-stakeholder corporate governance system I propose for use in the United States does not have a codetermination component.

---

[67] *Id.* at 347. For up-to-date figures, *see* James K. Jackson, *U.S. Direct Investment Abroad: Trends and Current Issues*, Congressional Research Service (Mar 21, 2017), https://fas.org/sgp/crs/misc/RS21118.pdf.

[68] Janis Sarra, *Corporate Governance in Global Capital Markets, Canadian and International Developments*, 76 TUL. L. REV. 1691, 1743 (2002).

[69] William Arthur Williams & Thomas M. Fuhrmann, *An Inquiry into CEO Compensation Practices in the United States and Proposals for Federal Law Reform*, 43 NEW ENG. L. REV. 221, 237 (2009) ("The explosion of CEO pay is not a shared global phenomenon. In 2005, the latest year for which figures were available, "French CEOs made 56% of what American CEOs did ... German and British CEOs made 55%")(internal quotes and citations omitted).

Directors would still be elected by the shareholders. I also would not classify directors according to particular constituencies they are meant to serve – e.g., some directors for shareholders, others for workers, some for consumers, others for the public interest.[70] Such a classified system would make board deliberations cantankerous, with each director seeking to maximize return to her own charges at the expense of the other groups and the enterprise as a whole. Every director would have the obligation to make the firm profit while attending to the reasonable interests of non-shareholders. An unclassified multi-stakeholder board would provide directors the latitude to flexibly attend to different interests in the course of ongoing corporate decisions in dynamic environments.

Some analysts consider it naïve to think multi-stakeholder governance could be achieved without codetermination. Leo Strine, the Chief Justice of the Delaware Supreme Court, has stressed (off the bench) that whatever other basis is given for shareholder primacy under Delaware law, the reality is that shareholder primacy *necessarily* flows from the power structure of the corporation.[71] The fact that only the equity shareholders vote for directors, he argues, means that directors will serve only their interests. This would suggest that genuine multi-stakeholder governance would be impossible without some kind of role for non-shareholders in corporate democracy.

I do not think that necessarily follows. Investors in certain classes of Facebook, Inc. and Snap, Inc. had better hope it does not, as shares in those companies went public without voting rights.[72] (The nonvoting situation at such firms will undoubtedly bring the law of corporate purpose into an even more prominent role in corporate law jurisprudence, since the law of fiduciary duty is the only thing such disenfranchised shareholders have left to protect them.) The robust market for securities without voting rights suggests that fiduciary duties *can* be

---

[70] *Compare* RALPH NADER, ET. AL., TAMING THE CORPORATE GIANT (1976) (advocating that certain "public interest" directors on large corporate boards should be charged with uniquely looking after non-shareholder interests).

[71] Leo E. Strine, *Corporate Power Is Corporate Purpose I: Evidence from My Hometown*, 33 OXFORD REV. OF ECON. POLICY 176 (2017).

[72] *See generally* Lucian A. Bebchuk & Kobi Kastiel, *The Untenable Case for Perpetual Dual-Class Stock*, 103 VA. L. REV. 585 (2017) (describing and critiquing this trend).

sufficient to compel sound corporate performance. The same may be true in a multi-stakeholder regime. Non-shareholders would not necessarily need access to the corporate ballot; they could enjoy the benefits of corporate governance by the law commanding it, directors committing to it, and lawyers threatening lawsuits where directors fail to take it seriously. In many institutions we expect that those elected to a position of power will serve an interest that is broader than, and sometimes even in tension with, the interests of those who elected them. This is true in our representative political structures as well as in, for example, the election of university trustees by an alumni electorate rather than by current or future students, or by the community the university pledges to serve.

Nevertheless, there is a sting of realism in Strine's argument. If we want multi-stakeholder governance to have some bite, we might consider giving a wider set of constituents some bark in corporate democracy. I do not think this step is necessary to accomplish the fundamental reform in the purpose of corporate governance that I have been describing. But an expansion of corporate democracy is worth exploring, perhaps for the very largest firms (perhaps firms with a market capitalization of more than $1 billion).

Multi-stakeholder voting could be structured to allow each major stakeholder group to elect at least one director to the board. Once on the board, each director would have responsibilities to the whole corporate enterprise, not just the group that elected her. This is the way European labor codetermination systems operate (at least theoretically), with directors charged to serve the company and all its stakeholders, regardless of the constituency that voted for them.[73] In proportioning the firm's electorate for such a system, it would still be prudent to give the shareholders a commanding number of votes, followed by some say for workers, consumers, and perhaps other affected constituencies. Shareholders should have controlling votes because their interest is exclusively residual, even if they are not the only group with a residual interest.

Labor suffrage in European corporations now has a long history. We therefore know that such a system is workable, even though there

---

[73] *See* Chapter 7.

are conceptual and practical problems in deciding who gets to vote and when. In a large corporation (the kind of corporation that would be subject to codetermination) the workforce is not monolithic – different job categories have different interests, some workers are more transient than others, etc. It is beyond the scope of this inquiry to work out such particulars, but within its scope to confirm that these kinds of problems have been addressed in the course of decades of legislation and policy-making in other wealthy countries.

Consumer suffrage would be more innovative than labor codetermination. Scholars have approached the idea of consumers voting in corporate governance from time to time, only to abandon it as "absurd ... because it is unworkable."[74] But the idea is less absurd and more workable today due to new technologies. Many corporations already have in place technology that could facilitate consumer suffrage. Firms maintain "loyalty programs" that track how much consumers purchase and how consumers can be contacted. Through such mechanisms, with each purchase, consumers could accumulate votes or fractions of votes to be exercised on the occasion of the next corporate election. These technologies are especially feasible for the largest companies, which are the firms that would be subject to this kind of governance reform. Consumers uninterested in corporate democracy could opt out of such tracking programs or just ignore their accumulated votes. Details can be worked out over time through evolving policymaking and tinkering within a commitment to a broadened form of corporate democracy.

Eugene Rostow once lampooned proponents of an expanded corporate franchise who "would apparently hope to cure the present shortcomings of corporate democracy ... by adding new groups of apathetic and disinterested voters to the masses of stockholders who now fail to exercise their franchise intelligently."[75] The humor hides serious truths. Shareholders are rationally ignorant and usually give no attention to corporate elections. A neglected reason that such

---

[74] David L. Ratner, *The Government of Business Corporations: Critical Reflections on the Rule of "One Share, One Vote,"* 56 Cornell L. Rev. 1, 33 (1970).

[75] Eugene Rostow, *To Whom and for What Ends Is Corporate Management Responsible,* in The Corporation in Modern Society 46, 55–56 (Edward S. Mason ed., 1966).

ignorance is rational, however, is that corporate boards generally manage reasonably well in the shareholder interest, or try to. Boards do so, in part, to *keep* the slumbering shareholders in their rationally ignorant snooze. It is not just the exercise of the franchise, but the *possibility* of its exercise that makes voting a potent mechanism. Low voting rates might mean things are functioning well. Only when the bums really get up to no good do the people put down their idles and perversions to bother throwing them out.[76] If wider groups were given the franchise, they too could enjoy not using it, with the threat of its use keeping directors working in their favor. The efficacy of unexercised power was well put in *The Karate Kid*, when the great teacher Mr. Miyagi asks his student, Daniel, why he studies karate, and the correct answer comes: "So I don't have to fight."[77] The franchise is effective even in its nonuse. This is to say that corporate management need not fear harassment from an expanded corporate electorate that included workers and consumers or localities. Likely, they can expect apathy except where directors persist in misconduct.

Another innovation that could add to, or perhaps initiate, multi-stakeholder engagement in corporate governance, would be expanded use of "proposal" mechanisms.[78] The federal securities laws presently give shareholders the right to use the corporate proxy (the machinery of corporate elections) to put "proposals" relating to firm operations before their fellow shareholders for a vote. Profit-oriented investors use the proposal mechanism to promote corporate governance reforms they hope will make directors more accountable to shareholders.[79] However, as the SEC interprets the provision, proposals are not limited to bottom line issues. They can also address social and ethical matters related to corporate operations, including labor, consumer welfare, and political issues. Shareholder activists used the proposal mechanism to

---

[76] BAINBRIDGE, THE NEW CORPORATE GOVERNANCE, *supra* note 65 at 235 (shareholder voting is "not an integral aspect of the corporate decision-making structure, but rather an accountability device of last resort to be used sparingly, at best.").

[77] THE KARATE KID (Columbia Pictures, 1984).

[78] The ideas here are based on material first published in David G. Yosifon, *The Consumer Interest in Corporate Law*, 43 U.C. DAVIS L. REV. 253 (2009).

[79] STEPHEN M. BAINBRIDGE, CORPORATION LAW AND ECONOMICS 496 (2002) ("proposals in recent years have included such topics as repealing takeover defenses, confidential proxy voting, regulating executive compensation, and the like.").

urge firms to divest from South Africa in the 1980s, demand firms adopt same-sex partner benefits for employees in the 1990s, and encourage environmental sensitivity in the 2000s. The SEC's social issue proposal mechanism has always been inconsistent with shareholder primacy theory and doctrine, but the contradiction has been more or less ignorable because social issue proposals rarely garner much support from shareholder voters. But the mechanism would make more sense, and could become more potent, under a multi-stakeholder system. A way to buttress (or begin) a multi-stakeholder governance regime would be to allow non-shareholders to vote on shareholder proposals that relate directly to their interests. A bigger step would be to allow consumers, workers, or other stakeholders to initiate proposals themselves.

Workers and consumers certainly have as much interest in the subject matter of social issue proposals as do shareholders, and sometimes more. Consider the touchstone case of *Lovenheim v. Iroquois Brands, Ltd.*[80] A shareholder sought to include a proposal in Iroquois's proxy materials asking the board to review how the company treated geese in the production of its pâté de fois gras. According to the proposal:

> On some farms where feeding is mechanized, the bird's body and wings are placed in a metal brace and its neck is stretched. Through a funnel inserted 10–12 inches down the throat of the goose, a machine pumps up to 400 grams of corn-based mash into its stomach. An elastic band around the goose's throat prevents regurgitation. When feeding is manual, a handler uses a funnel and stick to force the mash down.[81]

Who cares? Shareholders might care because such practices could harm the reputation of the firm and reduce its value. (Although shareholders probably know less than directors about the bottom-line consequences of the practice.) Shareholders might also be sincerely concerned about being invested in such morally dubious practices. Workers also have both concerns, but they are the ones ordered by the firm to actually do these things to the birds. Consumers put the

---

[80] Lovenheim v. Iroquois Brands, Ltd., 618 F. Supp. 554, 556 (D.C. 1985).   [81] *Id.*

resulting product into their own bodies. For workers and consumers, the ethical involvement in the firm's activity is, in a sense, more intimate, more direct, than it is for shareholders. The proposal mechanism could help surface production issues that concern workers but are opaque to other stakeholders. It could give consumers a way of not just "selecting" from what is produced, but also having a say in what will be produced and how.[82] Communities with access to the proposal mechanism could express views about corporate activity in a more focused context than that afforded by ordinary politics.

Under the proposal mechanism as it presently exists, proposals that are approved by shareholders function, in most cases, only as "requests" to the board, rather than as binding initiatives. The SEC requires proposals to comply with the law of the state of incorporation, and because Delaware says that boards – not shareholders – manage firms, the proposal mechanism can only be used to make requests – not demands – of Delaware boards. For the reasons that I support director primacy in the multi-stakeholder regime,[83] this precatory requirement should remain in place for any expanded stakeholder proposal mechanism. The proposal mechanism so conceived is a glorified suggestion box, but glory can be powerful. It would be an effective means of at least informing directors (who, under a multi-stakeholder regime would be legitimately disposed to listen) of the concerns and opinions of corporate stakeholders.

These expansions of corporate democracy are at the far end of a spectrum of possible alternatives to shareholder primacy. The basic reform I have in mind and advocate is one in which shareholders, as the residual claimants, elect a board that is responsible not only to shareholders, but to other corporate stakeholders as well.

★★★

Corporations have generated enormous wealth and contributed to substantial social progress in the United States. We must have the efficient, creative production of goods and services that the corporate form enables. Nobody wants to return to the "penurious self-sufficiency

---

[82] *See* Chapter 6.   [83] *See supra*, text accompanying notes 16–18.

of the household system,"[84] much less the dreary, limited cultural life it contained. The depravities of abundance are preferable to the banality of deprivation.

But the shareholder primacy norm in corporate governance spurs exploitation. It encourages firms to overreach any other constituency, any other value, in the search for shareholder profits. It tears roughly at our cultural and political fabric. Its defenders claim that the system is socially useful, but corporations destroy the palliative regulatory system that proponents of shareholder primacy call on to cure the social ills even they expect it to cause.

We can root out what is rotten in our corporate operations without crippling the corporate form. The multi-stakeholder corporate governance system I have adumbrated here would require the directors of our largest firms to sincerely consider the impact of corporate decision-making on all corporate stakeholders, not just shareholders. In doing so, it orients powerful corporations to undertake business activity in a socially responsible way, even where doing so is not the *most* profitable path. It does this not by dictating what corporations must do, or say, or not say, but by requiring directors to be open and honest with themselves, each other, and the public about the consequence of corporate conduct for different stakeholders, and allowing such deliberation to influence their decisions. In this way the multi-stakeholder reform can bring greater integrity to our consumer culture, and our politics. It insists upon sincerity, clarity, and honesty at the core of corporate operations, so that we can with confidence enjoy the creative exploration of looser speech at the periphery, in consumer markets, and in the political domain. The destructive friction that results from shareholder primacy in corporate operations can be transformed into productive energy, by making social responsibility an integral part of our corporate governance law.

---

[84] See D. H. Robertson, The Control of Industry 104(1923).

CONCLUSION
It Can Happen Here

Imagine a candidate for national political office saying on the stump:

> And we *should* require the boards of directors of our largest corporations to give reasonable attention to workers and consumers and the environment, *and our country*, in corporate decision-making. Not just when it serves the bottom line for their shareholders, but *all* the time. Because *our* bottom line is that we all have a stake in corporate operations, and social responsibility should be part of the bargain when we grant a corporate charter.

Does this seem so far-fetched?

My reformative program may seem to be subject to a public-choice hoisting on its own petard. Throughout this book, I have emphasized that corporations and their shareholders enjoy a collective action advantage over other corporate stakeholders in the competition for regulatory favor. We therefore cannot expect government regulation to curb the externalizing tendencies of shareholder primacy firms. These same dynamics, one might argue, would also preclude the adoption of the multi-stakeholder governance solution that I propose. Shareholders benefit from the status quo corporate governance regime, and shareholder primacy corporations will work to maintain it.

But I do not despair of the political plausibility of my reform program. Ordinary public choice dynamics are upended in hot political moments. When a social issue becomes highly salient, otherwise dispersed groups with diverse interests can for a moment come together and overcome the collective action advantages that smaller, more focused groups typically enjoy in the political realm. The corporate governance reforms I have explored here could be implemented in such a time. Struggling to explain why the federal government has never rested corporate chartering standards from Delaware's stranglehold, Mark Roe speculated that the "serendipitous alignment of interests, policymakers, and scandals has never been right for full nationalization of corporate law."[1] The moment may be right now, or soon. Hot political moments also present opportunities to pass improved "external" regulation of corporate behavior through new labor law, environmental regulation, and the like. The problem is that once there is a return to ordinary, cool political times, the collective action advantages of shareholder primacy firms reemerge, and corporations begin to undermine the regulatory changes made in the hot moment.[2] That pernicious pattern can be broken if the reforms sought in the hot moment are directed at changing the structure of corporate governance rather than the regulatory fencing meant to constrain shareholder primacy.

Law is a provisional truce. Part of my motivation in writing this book is my belief, my understanding, that what is politically possible, for good or ill, can change quickly. When change is ripening, sound theory can guide it in a useful way, as surely as bad theory can shepherd it to ruin. As John Maynard Keynes wrote, "soon or late, it is ideas, not vested interests, which are dangerous for good or evil."[3] Public opinion on both the right and the left seems to be fed up with corporations, and appears to be galled in particular by the selfish, myopic nature of corporate political activity. Behind this animosity is an unarticulated dissatisfaction with the narrow, shareholder-focused agenda of the prevailing corporate governance system. In the last chapter, I described a range of reforms that could help crystallize and

---

[1] Mark Roe, *Delaware's Politics*, 118 HARV. L. REV. 2491, 2535 (2005). *See also* Sung Hui Kim, *The Failure of Federal Incorporation Law: A Public Choice Perspective*, in CAN DELAWARE BE DETHRONED? EVALUATING DELAWARE'S DOMINANCE OF CORPORATE LAW (eds. Iman Anabtawi, Stephen Bainbridge, Sung Hui Kim, James Park) (2018).

[2] *See, e.g.*, James J. Park, *The Competing Paradigms of Securities Regulation*, 57 DUKE L.J. 625, 675 (2007) ("During boom times, industry has more influence, there is less public demand for regulation, regulators tend to be more cautious, and less new regulation is produced. Busts tend to reveal scandals that cause public outrage, reducing industry influence, emboldening regulators, and leading to the passage of more restrictive laws") (citing, inter alia, Joseph A. Grundfest, *Punctuated Equilibria in the Evolution of United States Securities Regulation*, 8 STAN. J.L. BUS. & FIN. 1, 1 (2002)).

[3] JOHN MAYNARD KEYNES, THE GENERAL THEORY OF EMPLOYMENT, INTEREST AND MONEY 384 (1936).

respond to the scattered anti-corporate attitudes evident today across the American political spectrum, from socialist-leaning anti-corporate Bernie Sanders supporters, to nationalist-leaning anti-corporate Donald Trump supporters. I believe the prescriptions described here could prove satisfactory enough to keep these disgruntled groups from seeking more destructive alteration of the status quo. We must safeguard the corporate instrument against its own worst tendencies, which might otherwise spur radical political action that will destroy it, and maybe destroy much more. Corporate governance reforms that get directors talking about and working for not just shareholders but workers, consumers, and other stakeholders might contribute significantly to the long-term sustainability of the corporation as a mode of organizing production and consumption in our society.

The contradictions in our present system contain the elements of its reform. Greenwashing firms have primed the American people to think of corporate social responsibility as a core principle of corporate operations, making a proposal to legally require that standard not so dramatic a suggestion. Widespread social responsibility rhetoric in elite business culture suggests that the professional classes could embrace the idea of a de jure corporate social responsibility standard as normal. Ordinary people, workers, and consumers would likely welcome the change. What I am proposing here is little more than bringing the law into harmony with that cultural attitude. Many large firms already have all the tools they need to undertake multi-stakeholder governance. They have diversity officers and social responsibility officers. They make reports and host stakeholder summits. They have developed a rich language for talking about corporate social responsibility. All that is missing is the authority, the obligation, for corporations to act in a socially responsible way, authentically and lawfully, even where it costs shareholders money.

Before 2004, "realistic" baseball fans had to accept that if their team was down 3–0 in a best-of-seven series, the season was over. No team had ever overcome a 3–0 deficit. But in Game 4 of the 2004 American League Championship Series, with the Boston Red Sox down one run in the bottom of the ninth, with two outs, the Sox's Dave Roberts stole second base off of legendary Yankee closer, Mariano Rivera, then came around to tie the game on a base hit. The Sox won that game and the next three, forever altering our calibration of the possible. Similarly (well, not at all similarly, but also), as recently as the first decade of the twenty-first century, it would have seemed the height of political naiveté to think that the right to same-sex marriage would soon be recognized as a fundamental constitutional right in the United States. Now, in the second decade of the twenty-first century, marriage equality is the law of the land, and there is no significant political movement to roll back that transformation.[4] The election of Donald Trump as president of the United States shows not only that we can but also that we *must* expand our imagination of what is politically possible. For good or ill, nothing is politically impossible, certainly not the emergence of a widespread political will to alter the shareholder primacy norm in American corporate governance.

The reforms explored in this book are anchored in an abiding confidence in the corporation as an economic, social, and cultural institution. They reflect a commitment to the idea that solutions to business-related problems can come from within our firms, rather than always being imposed from the outside by external regulators. We must have integrity in our corporate operations, and, in the words of Michael Jensen, "it is only the board that this in the end can come from."[5] It would, therefore, be incongruous to assert with any specificity what policies or innovations should or would emerge from the multi-stakeholder corporate governance I propose. Perhaps corporate boards charged with the obligation to speak openly, honestly, and sincerely about the interests of multiple stakeholders would stop short of engineering an increase in the levels of addictive nicotine in the tobacco they grow for cigarettes. Or they might better alert consumers of junk food to the adverse health consequences associated with substantial weight gain. They perhaps would be quicker to include state-of-the-art environmental safeguards when drilling for oil in fragile ecosystems. They might delay moving a factory overseas and give workers advance warning of plans to do so. They might make worker

---

[4] *See* Obergefell v. Hodges, 135 S. Ct. 2584 (2015) (unconstitutional to exclude same-sex couples from marriage).

[5] Michael C. Jensen, Professor of Bus. Admin., Harvard Bus. Sch., Presentation at the Stanford Law School, *Beyond Agency Theory: The Hidden and Heretofore Inaccessible Power of Integrity* (Feb 11, 2010).

retraining a responsible component of an automation project. They might not do a deal that supported a foreign government hostile to the United States or its values. They might debate the ethics of ratcheting up the habituating features in their social media platforms and allow the ethical inquiry to shape the business decisions they make. What more to be said can only be said by specific corporate boards, managing particular firms, in a socially responsible manner.

INDEX